1972

CIVIL WARS IN THE TWENTIETH CENTURY

Robin Higham, Editor

CIVIL WARS IN THE TWENTIETH CENTURY

The University Press of Kentucky

Lexington, 1972

The National Security Program of New York University in cooperation with the National Strategy Information Center of New York has, since 1969, become the sponsor of a series of projects designed to extend and improve teaching about national security at the university level. Professor Frank N. Trager is Director of the Program. Its activities are supported through grants from private foundations.

These projects have included conferences, seminars, and the series of publications on national security of which *Civil Wars in the Twentieth Century*, edited by Professor Robin Higham, is a part.

ISBN: 0–8131–1261–3

Library of Congress Catalog Card Number: 78–160044

Copyright © 1972 by The University Press of Kentucky

A statewide cooperative scholarly publishing agency serving Berea College, Centre College of Kentucky, Eastern Kentucky University, Kentucky State College, Morehead State University, Murray State University, University of Kentucky, University of Louisville, and Western Kentucky University.

Editorial and Sales Offices: Lexington, Kentucky 40506

Contents

Preface

THIS BOOK GREW out of *Bayonets in the Streets* (1969), which for its part came out of a session of the Organization of American Historians held at Cincinnati some years ago. The original idea was to provide capsule histories of the various civil wars of this century, but a more promising approach seemed to be to have each author discuss a facet of the subject from the special vantage point of his own expert knowledge of a particular case. Each author was asked to keep his discussion brief, to provide a short bibliography, and to suggest some ideas for further research. In a number of cases the latter are implicit rather than explicit.

The product of these efforts, we hope, will stimulate students and scholars to consider other aspects of comparative history and political science and thus break out of the traditional isolationism of academic areas.

We are pleased to have had the cooperation of the University Press of Kentucky in our aim to produce the book quickly. We appear also unwittingly to have had the help of a number of states and their peoples and governments in keeping the subject very much alive.

Robin Higham

Nations Experiencing Civil Wars, 1900-1970

Colombia, 1899–1900
Mexico, 1911–17
Nicaragua, 1912, 1925–27, 1828
China, 1912–49
Ireland, 1916–22
Russia, 1917–20
Spain, 1936–39
Yugoslavia, 1942–46
Greece, 1944–49
Vietnam, 1945—
India, 1945–64
Colombia, 1948–53
Burma, 1948–54
Korea, 1950–53
Algeria, 1954–62
Cuba, 1957–58
The Congo, 1960–64
Laos, 1960–62
Yemen, 1962–64
Kenya, 1963–67
The Sudan, 1964—
The Dominican Republic, 1965
Iraq, 1966–70
Nigeria, 1967–70
Jordan, 1970

NOTE: *Not all of the authors agree on this list as to either places or dates.*

Editor's Introduction

COMPARED WITH the more cyclic units of human time-keeping, the term "century" is obviously contrived and arbitrary. The continuity of human history can hardly be denied, nor can history be so neatly packaged. To the historian, nevertheless, the term offers a convenience of reference and a yardstick to terminable discussion.

When a history of the twentieth century can finally be written, it may well record that this period had distinguishable subunits, that at about midcentury an Age of Privacy ended and an Age of Communications began. Alternatively, it may be seen that the first atomic explosions blew the century apart, so that its latter period began an Age of Anxiety. Certainly, at no other time of earth's history have its inhabitants been so immediately and persistently aware of contemporary violence and its potentialities. Such an awareness has obviously not led to world peace, yet it has compelled a sharper examination of the nature of war and a finer definition of its types.

Civil war differs from all other revolutionary activity in being essentially, though not invariably, the work of right-wing reactionaries or conservatives seeking to keep arbitrary freedoms they enjoy or think they are entitled to exercise. In some cases they anticipate revolution, using an inside rather than an outside enemy as their reason for armed conflict. Civil war is most apt to develop after colonialism or after the disposition of a long-standing dynasty, though not necessarily immediately afterwards. A civil war may also arise when a puritanical coup fails to be immediately decisive, as in Russia in 1917–18 or in Jordan in 1970.

The problem of the rightists is that they do not command the loyalty of more than a small proportion of the people, nor of more than part of the armed forces (primarily the army), nor do they command the economy, though they believe that they can after victory create a self-sufficient state capable of winning diplomatic recognition. Just as revolutionaries tend to be idealistic dreamers, so reactionary leaders of civil wars tend to gloss over serious difficulties and to underestimate the loyalty to the establish-

1

ment of the silent majority. In other words, where revolutionaries seek
the millennium, the leaders of the antirevolutionary civil war want the
good old days. Revolutionaries tend to be antiestablishment, uncivil guerrillas; reactionaries tend to be antidisestablishmentarian civil warriors.

Civil war is hard to define. It may be, as in Ireland, Russia, Algeria,
Indochina, or China, only a small part of a much larger upheaval; or it
may be, as in England and Nigeria, a sharp, clearly definable historical
event.

Some of the features of a civil war are: 1) that it is an overt internal
conflict with international overtones; 2) that it is organized by a socially
cohesive class seeking to protect arbitrary freedoms, which makes the conflict an essentially negative response; 3) that an extralegal government is
created which possesses, or believes it possesses, not only economic self-
sufficiency but also the loyalty of a sufficient part of the regular armed
forces to defy the rest of the country; 4) that this government possesses a
contiguous territory; and 5) that this government's actions will be a mixture of professional governance, aristocratic or gentlemanly standards, and
cruelty mixed with great humanity.

Outside interference in a civil war is usually thought of in terms of men;
the question is much subtler when only equipment is involved. But surely
it can be argued that the hands-off policy is best. If the outsider is going to
intervene, he has two viable alternatives: to restrict his help to material or
to engage in "coup de main deterrence." If he adds advisers to arms, the
natural tendency is "empire-building escalation"; if his interference is not
of effective riot-control proportions, he only escalates the conflict. At the
start of a civil war, as in the case of many other disturbances, the vast majority of the people are uninformed and uncommitted. They will be affected by the sheep factor—they will either follow their leader or be "run"
by fear snapping at their heels. The people only see and understand simple
objectives, even though their leaders may be playing a complex game,
which may include outsiders.

Foreign aid usually only prolongs a war. A study of the Biafran conflict
would, no doubt, reveal a reasonable case for the proposition that the relief sent to the rebels actually extended the conflict by relieving pressure
on the Biafran leadership, forcing postponement of Nigerian victory, and
therefore increasing the number of deaths from starvation. A similar and
much stronger case could be worked out for Vietnam, though both there
and in the Congo intervention may seem justifiable. The little known Ye-

meni conflict (1962–64) is an interesting example of a war which proved so unprofitable to the outsider that Nasser withdrew his forces from the quicksand. Intervention is usually undesirable, unwanted, and unrewarded.

The scale and decisiveness of foreign intervention in civil wars are regulated by a wide variety of factors, such as logistic convenience and geographic propinquity. Particularly if the intervening power is a democracy, it will be affected by emotional instability, the cleverness of psychological warfare, and the surges of internal politics.

In the case of our Civil War, the major world powers sensibly abstained or had their own worries to restrain them. They did not even grant the South diplomatic recognition, that accolade of respectability of immense psychological, political, diplomatic, military, economic, and ideological importance because it means that in the judgment of outsiders the rebellious state has a chance of success.

In Vietnam, the United States has come to view a long civil war between established governments fighting for the same people as a stand against aggression. But in 1970 that conflict began to be seen differently, as internal political necessities changed. In this connection, it seems not unduly cynical to observe that when a government has supplied arms in order to keep a "friendly" country in its sphere of influence or orbit, a sudden decision that it is immoral to do so serves no purpose but its rival's.

It is interesting to note that neither "civil wars" nor "internal wars" have been given any place in works such as Alistair Buchan's *War in Modern Society*, Theodore Ropp's *War in the Modern World*, or Morton Halperin's *Modern Military Strategy*, for instance, though some literature is building up on "internal war." One suspects that the real reason the Spanish Civil War was early named as such is that its arena was close to the heartland of the world of the day, and thus drew an enormous amount of attention. Moreover, it had its romantic, Hemingway side. The Nigerian-Biafran conflict is probably the nearest recent equivalent, with the press, Madison Avenue, liberals, and churches in the United States and Britain mistakenly backing Biafra—and losing. Korea, too, was a civil war, but with two peculiarities. The challenge to the authority of the United Nations came in an area so close to the one in which the League of Nations was thought to have failed in 1931 that President Truman felt compelled to act to save the U.N., probably a correct decision. Secondly, Korea was, like Spain, an isolatable peninsula, so that it was possible to limit the conflict. And the Korean struggle, like that in Vietnam, was a conflict between two arbitrarily established governments of one nationality. In the seventeenth century the Civil War in England was an insular one, helped by the fact that the Thirty Years' War (a civil war in many respects) was not only engaging the continent but exhausting it. In all these cases it can be argued that the real agrarian conservatives were the ones who created the war.

In Nigeria, for another example, Ojukwu represented the nineteenth-century Oxonian tradition of liberal, literary resistance to technology, while Gowon may be said to stand for the twentieth-century Sandhurst[1] view, or military acceptance of technology and its requisite managerial needs.

A civil war must always be seen as a state of change, or, more correctly, as resistance to change. The peculiar local patterns prevalent in any country, such as the perpetual Catholic-Protestant friction in Ireland, warlordism in China, and the French colonists in Algeria, must also be taken into account in viewing the phenomenon. In some cases civil wars have been associated with anticolonialism, as in America in 1776, or Algeria in the 1950s and early 1960s, or Indochina and Malaya; in other cases, they are part of the struggle against an outsider, as in Malaya and China after World War II. Such struggles may also develop in reaction to independence, as in the cases of Ireland and China. Or, as in the case of Nigeria, a civil war may be regional or tribal in origin.

In any postcolonial civil war, the conflict, a flickering interplay of constraints, tensions, history, loyalties, and miscommunication, may develop out of the long ideological struggle between the ideas of the French and Industrial revolutions inherited from the former colonial power. Or it may flow from the local hatred and arrogance which has severed all ties with a colonial past and broken down administration, leaving no authority but the army. Thus ideas as well as economics may move men to fight. The role of lawyers and journalists in creating this sort of chaos and prejudice has yet to be well considered.

Even in noncolonial states it must not be forgotten that civil wars may arise, as in nineteenth-century America, because of animosities generated like contempt by familiarities, communality of language (though not nec-

---

[1] I use the term here loosely in contrast to "Oxford," except that Sandhurst is only eighteen months of not very rigorous intellectual training, unlike West Point with its four-year curriculum, and that much of the real influence upon an officer's thinking in the British and colonial-legacy forces comes from the regiment.

essarily of meaning), exasperation, brutality, and fear. Distrust and refusal to admit failure may also play their part. The parallels with religious wars in the breaking up of the medieval Romano-Christian empire of the Papacy are worth considering. Dynamic states based on growing national characteristics and hatreds emerged to shatter the Church's polity. How effective these breakaway states were depended upon a variety of factors, but especially upon personality, geography, and the people who mattered and where their loyalties lay. The masses were willing enough to regard all outsiders as strangers and therefore probably enemies.

The social and economic after-effects of civil war, and indeed of interventionary war, are in themselves interesting fields of study. At what point, for instance, do wars cease to be stimulating to a nation and its economy and become instead debilitating? Can an argument be made, for instance, that Spanish intervention in sixteenth-century France was one of the sores which sapped the strength of Spain and left it invalid instead of a major power? Did two world wars kill Britain's chances of world leadership? The answer may lie not in the dollars-and-cents cost but in the subtler alienation of ambitious talent. The "lost generation" of Britain after World War I was not composed solely of its military casualty lists. More particularly, it was a generation of disillusioned and alienated survivors, disgusted not so much by the stupidities of the generals as by the selfishness and dishonesty of politicians. It will be fascinating to see what happens in Nigeria. Are the Ibos different? Will they be able to recover their positions in the state, or have others now filled the rebels' shoes? Will the road up be denied "former traitors" or will Gowon's promise be honored because the country cannot afford such prejudices?

Civil wars tend to make poor areas poorer and weaker, as illustrated by the extremely slow economic recovery of the American South after the Civil War. The liberation of slaves had, of course, seriously damaged its agricultural economy, yet the postwar South long remained hostile to the influx of industry which might have ameliorated its plight. One suspects that myths play a role in this phenomenon. Why did the so-called New South create the mint-julep plantation myth of the antebellum world? Or did the South also represent the Oxonian tradition? And did its lost generation shun not only politics but also business? In fact, they not only shunned it but were actually hostile to it in the tradition of the eighteenth-century French aristocracy.

The events in Jordan in September 1970 suggest that outside intervention may succeed when it is a moral force and when a civil war may appear to open the gates to unwanted foreign intervention. The 20,000 casualties reported may have been cheap compared to a full-scale intervention by the United States in addition to Syria and perhaps Israel.

The making of peace at the end of a civil war presents special problems. The losers know that they will be governed by the victors. They also know that they will be regarded openly or covertly as traitors. In such conditions, especially in a Vietnam, for instance, the question is exacerbated when neither side is in a clear position militarily; all the animosities may be reawakened by a political campaign in which rhetoric and terrorism are likely to run rampant, possibly leading to open sores festering again into war. Peace between sovereign states is less complicated if "unconditional surrender" is not a factor.

After colonialism, revolution, or civil war, it is essential for the new government to recreate an efficient administration and a robust economy. It is perhaps even more important to evolve a new national goal and a psychological attitude oriented to building rather than destroying. What can be done may be seen in Algeria, for instance, where, despite perhaps a million dead by 1962, the country has moved forward on a constructive path, deemphasizing the military past, yet interestingly, reverting to being very French.

After civil wars in the recent decades of the twentieth century there is considerable reason to be optimistic, despite their frequently heavy casualties. The new nations are capable of making enormous strides assuming that their ideological development or nationalistic myth permits the necessary foreign investment and technological aid. For instance, their food problem, regarded with such pessimism less than a decade ago, is now yielding in some areas, such as the Indian sub-continent, to a "green revolution." Indeed our chronic worriers are already warning of the problems of abundance! Civil wars may be jarring and scarring experiences, but they may also be the tempering some states need to succeed.

Because they destroy all authority but the army, revolutionary situations are more than likely to bring to the fore strong authoritarian military characters, such as Oliver Cromwell. These men leave a legacy of controversy as to their roles. A Tory parliamentary dictator such as Winston Churchill may describe them as tyrants and regicides, while a Whig historian such as G. M. Trevelyan may regard them as saviors of their people. The American press and its liberal allies in publishing will hate them because they are authoritarian, regardless of what they do. But

Richelieu was right when, in a similarly chaotic state to that found in many of the new post-1945 states, in a France with its Huguenot legacy of the religious civil wars, he put "raison d'état" first, as had Machiavelli in *The Prince*, a work Richelieu well understood. It is hard for liberals and radicals, who denounce politics while themselves engaging in it, to understand that the military may as a caste really abhor politics. Contrast, for example, men such as General George S. Patton, Jr., or General William T. Sherman ("If nominated, I will not run; if elected I will not serve") with a political general such as Juan Peron of Argentina.

In civil wars, more than in other conflicts, the military find themselves against their brother officers with whom they have trained and served. Whether this is good, bad, or overemphasized deserves further study. Could it be that because they have known each other better than enemies usually do, the war is more humane? Or does this communality of experience lengthen or shorten the war, or even have any measurable effect upon it?

In studying civil war it is necessary to inquire further into the agricultural climatic cycles as well as into business levels. From the English Civil War of the seventeenth century it can be argued, as Brinton has in his *Anatomy of Revolution*, that trouble of this sort comes in periods of prosperity rather than in those of depression. The right wing apparently feels its wealth is threatened and is willing to use money to preserve its nation and status. Conversely, the mass of the people may see a war, civil or not, as an adventurous escape from economic drudgery, thus giving the right its necessary support.

The role of diet, rather than hunger, in all this is largely an unknown, as are the role and place of women in regard to domestic chores, the preparation of food, and more active political roles. The role of women in civil wars is undoubtedly great and may well deserve a comparative study. To what extent are women the *eminence rouge* instigators of such wars, and what of their role as propagandists? Are ladies of the right dangerously unemployed because of their wealth? What is the aftermath of civil wars with respect to marital relationships?

All civil wars raise delicate distinctions and difficult questions, such as: 1) When does a civil war, as opposed to a rebellion, exist? 2) Should the government in power ruthlessly use force to suppress the affair as quickly as possible? Does it have the force needed? If it does use it, will this irrevocably cause it to lose national and international support? Is such sympathy important? Or should the government be humanitarian? Which side should the individual support, or should he merely withhold his loyalty from all factions? 3) When is a rebellious section of a country, nation, or state an independent entity? What are the implications of independence? Can it be supported? Will the people have done anything more than revert to the control of their former masters? 4) Is it wise for outsiders to intervene in civil wars? Under what circumstances is overwhelming intervention advisable? 5) Who should supply arms and under what circumstances and conditions? 6) Should anyone be allowed to supply relief? 7) For outsiders, how desirable is it to weaken the existing state and what will be the long-range consequences of such a policy? 8) Will the withdrawal of the pacifying power lead to another, even a double, civil war both within and between the sections of the liberated state? 9) Have Anglo-Saxon officials overconfidently assumed that internal wars and struggles are something that happens abroad but that their own states are invulnerable to such conflicts? If so, is this in part because the Anglo-Saxon ethic, especially the Protestant-liberal ethic, has stressed the mission abroad, assuming that right will invariably prevail at home? Or does this very ethic concentrate too much on proselytizing abroad because no man likes to look for the mote in his own eye? 10) Have the Latins and others been unfairly accused of constant revolution when in fact they, like the Russians, have experienced not revolutions but merely *coups d'etat* and have in fact avoided civil wars? 11) Is civil war something which only minorities such as the Irish, the Quebec separatists, or the Afrikaners undertake? And are not they, in actuality, the backward peoples in each situation, the negativists? 12) Are not, then, civil wars accidental affairs which need only the same minor military tactics to control them as Callwell prescribed for colonial operations in his *Small Wars?*

These and other such questions have much relevance to the state of the world in the 1970s. Civil wars are likely to continue. They are most likely to occur in underdeveloped countries where the military play a parasitic role and where the population is, perhaps because of a lack of effective media, uninformed, apathetic, and at a subsistence level. Real revolutions more commonly occur in wealthy countries, when the middle class becomes dissatisfied with its share of power. Revolutions are not successful if the army with its artillery and other weapons remains loyal. More often what occurs is a *coup d'etat* perpetrated by a group which can control enough of the armed forces to succeed, and whose success does not, in fact, have much effect upon even the bulk of the middle class. Thus it seems unlikely that a civil war can now occur in the United States. A hundred years ago this was a sparsely populated country with small scattered armed forces torn, when the moment came, by sectional loyalties. It is not the same today, when for all concerned the lure of success acts as a moral dampener to rebellious courses, despite an overpublicized phase of campus violence.

Currently the underdeveloped countries are fascinating to watch. Concurrently, medieval studies are on the decline because they lack easily identifiable relevance to modern social problems. Yet in fact, the underdeveloped countries are in many cases nations struggling to make the transition from the medieval to the early modern world while adjusting to twentieth-century symbols of change. The civil wars which beset the petty dynastic states of Europe in the late medieval–early Renaissance period are remarkably similar to the tribal clashes in present-day Africa. The political instability of the underdeveloped countries is not without historical parallel, and one can predict that there will be many more civil wars among them. In one generation Africa, for example, is trying to accomplish changes that required centuries in western Europe.

As is evident from the variety of questions already raised, the range of discussion in this book is a wide one. The viewpoints expressed are also wide-ranging. Consensus is sometimes approached but only occasionally achieved. Instead, the reader will more frequently encounter refreshing divergencies of viewpoint and opinion, and these have been most welcome.

I

CIVIL WAR, INTERNAL WAR, AND INTRASOCIETAL CONFLICT
A Taxonomy and Typology

MARTIN EDMONDS

M AN HAS ALWAYS endeavored to limit conflict and violence. Numerous experiments have been tried, but the record has not been impressive. In consequence, many have been forced to the conclusion that conflict is as enduring as man's existence.[1] Today there is added incentive to seek ways to manage conflict, for failure to control or limit it may well result in total or unacceptable levels of destruction.

One current method for trying to limit conflict is the construction of elaborate, sophisticated, and detailed typologies.[2] Such schemes focus not only upon different types of conflict, but also upon the possible and likely consequences if such conflicts break out. The object of these exercises is to distinguish between levels of interstate struggles ranging from those which do not warrant more than a limited effort to total war.[3] The line between limited and total war is seen to lie close to that point at which gains appear to be slightly greater than penalties.[4] The hope is that by sticking to limited rather than total wars, the level of destruction can be kept acceptable.

Such classifications of conflict and war are at present immediately relevant only to conflicts between states. Furthermore, they have only been done by and for those states which have the military capacity to intensify war up to and beyond the nuclear level and which have available a wide variety of military options. Lesser states, nevertheless, need to be familiar with these options because the consequences of miscalcu-

11

lation are likely to affect all states. Major states have always taken an interest in the internal affairs of lesser states. The success of typology-making, an essentially semantic form of war limitation, depends largely upon the rigor with which taxonomies are formulated and typologies constructed, their clarity, and the interpretations placed upon them by both allies and enemies.[5]

So far only the two most powerful states, Russia and the United States, have been constructing typologies because they are the only ones with the nuclear option. The success of the semantic exercise depends upon them; thus the greater the clarity they can achieve, the less the chance of a misunderstanding leading to a nuclear confrontation.[6] It appears that thus far they have limited interstate conflict, but not conflict *per se*. Perhaps they have only shifted the emphasis from nuclear to more limited forms of struggle.

It may be argued that by limiting war at the higher level, the super-powers have opened up new dimensions at the lower level where they can still become antagonists. It has been the declared policy of both major states to become involved under certain conditions in the internal and interstate conflicts of less powerful states.[7] A major feature of this intervention has been assistance to parties in intrastate conflicts and to one side in interstate conflicts. The general impression is that the ideological confrontation between East and West has, through a recognition of risks, assumed a new form at a new level.

However, this is not a new phenomenon. Interstate conflicts have

---

[1] For example, see Kenneth M. Waltz, "The First Image: International Conflict and Human Nature," in *Man, State and War* (New York: Columbia University Press, 1965), 16–41.

[2] Taxonomy: taken here to be the science of classification, establishing the principles underlying the interpretation of types, or a typology. R. Aron, *On War* (London: Secker and Warburg, 1958), 104–05; R. Osgood and R. Tucker, *Force, Order and Justice* (Baltimore: Johns Hopkins Press, 1967).

[3] Morton Halperin, *Limited War in the Nuclear Age* (New York: John Wiley, 1963), 15–16. The situation, however, is not simple; see Herman A. Kahn, *On Escalation* (London: Pall Mall, 1965), Introduction, 3–25.

[4] For example, see M. Shubik, *Game Theory and Related Approaches to Social Behavior* (New York: John Wiley, 1964), 15–19. See also J. Von Neumann and O. Morgenstern, *Theory of Games and Economic Behavior* (Princeton: Princeton University Press, 1953).

[5] T. Schelling, *Arms and Influence* (London: Yale University Press, 1966), 283–86.

[6] R. Aron, *Century of Total War* (Boston: Beacon Press, 1963), 171.

[7] H. Hovey, *United States Military Assistance* (New York: Praeger, 1965), 15; T. Wolfe, *Soviet Strategy at the Crossroads* (Cambridge, Mass.: Harvard University Press, 1964), 126.

spread into internal struggles in the past, just as major powers have intervened in minor wars before. The Spanish Civil War is a classic case of the former. But what was exceptional and on a large scale in 1936, and done overtly and directly, has today (1970) all the indications of becoming commonplace, covert, and indirect. In this development lies the paradox of man's current endeavors to limit violence. While one method tries to limit antagonism between the superpowers to a lower level, the present institutional arrangements for collective security under the United Nations seem incapable of dealing with this new feature of international politics.[8]

The paradox becomes doubly ironical when it is also considered that the only states powerful enough to provide substantial military and financial support to the U.N. so that it can intervene are the USSR and the USA. These are not only the two states with a permanent veto in the Security Council, but also the very ones increasingly involved unilaterally in the affairs of other states.

The complexion of the superpower military confrontation has changed. After two decades of concern with semantics, technology, and doctrines of nuclear strategic debate,[9] another dimension has been added.[10] When either the United States or the USSR now interferes, it does so in the belief that it is extending its interests, both in a nonzero-sum and in a zero-sum sense, at the expense of the other.

But such shifts in policy orientation have their backlash and side effects. Involvements require careful handling. The range of choices is extensive. Poor judgment can bring wrong and unanticipated results. For example, in Vietnam the United States misjudged not only the nature of the war but also the suitable form and amount of its own contribution; in consequence it has found its commitment to be much greater than originally anticipated. It has been argued that the Soviet Union's experience in Cuba, Egypt, and Indonesia was more than that nation had bargained for.[11] The backlash can also come from the reaction of one superpower to the other's involvement in a third-party conflict. This is a

[8] P. Calvocoressi, *World Order and New States* (London: Chatto and Windus, 1962), 88–98. See also I. Claude, *Swords into Ploughshares* (London: London University Press, 1965), 242, 257; United Nations Charter, Article 2 (7), 419–20.

[9] John J. Erickson, *The Military-Technical Revolution* (London: Pall Mall, 1966), 16.

[10] Osgood and Tucker, *Force, Order and Justice*, 159–60.

[11] Wynfred Joshua and Stephen P. Gilbert, *Arms for the Third World* (Baltimore: Johns Hopkins Press, 1969), 4; U. Ra'anan, *The USSR Arms the Third World* (Cambridge, Mass.: M.I.T. Press, 1969), 158, 244–45.

reminder that involvement in even the smallest incidents can escalate to major-crisis proportions.[12] Aware of this, both superpowers have been cautious, especially in each other's spheres of influence, as in Hungary and Czechoslovakia or the Dominican Republic.

Among the side effects emanating from this policy reorientation has been the lead that it has given other states who possess a relatively limited but nonetheless substantial military capability. Many of the weapons-producing states have now become involved. The number of secondary and potential weapons suppliers is considerable.[13] There are many reasons for this increased involvement in third-party conflicts by nonsuperpowers. Among other things, it is a convenient means by which a state's armaments industry can defray the enormous costs of military equipment development; it is also the way a client of a superpower can pursue an independent policy.[14] (Both reasons have been used to justify and explain French actions.) The policy has the added attraction of generally avoiding direct involvement in a war; it can be reversed without incurring disproportionate penalties; it can be a source of prestige; and it is an effective way to equal the political influence of the superpowers.

Leaving aside wars between states, it must be assumed that internal conflict within underdeveloped, "Third World," or emergent states is an area in which outsiders can find opportunity to further their influence and interests. This trend will increase. The number of states who can thus meddle is limitless. Only the form and degree of involvement will be limited by military capability, location, economic circumstances, and policy objectives. Furthermore, the nature of the internal conflict is a crucial qualification, for upon it depends the form and degree of external involvement.

With this last qualification the argument comes full circle. As it was significant to construct a typology of interstate wars, especially where the superpowers were directly implicated, so it is important to have a clear idea of the types and character of internal conflicts in which almost any state may be involved. If conflict is still considered something which should be limited, then a clear picture must be drawn of the extent to

---

12 Wolfe, *Soviet Strategy at the Crossroads*, 127, 158, 244–45.

13 For details of the production and types of weapons suppliers see L. A. Frank, *The Arms Trade in International Relations* (New York: Praeger, 1969), 50–151.

14 The total of French arms sales is now approximately 25 percent that of the United States. Its export returns have been noted as having substantial results. See ibid., 57–58.

which outside involvement can exacerbate the situation, precipitate further conflicts, or endanger internal stability in the long run.[15]

Two points have been made above: first, that constructing typologies has had some beneficial effects at the superpower level; second, that the focus will increasingly be upon wars between and within lesser states. Leaving aside the whole problem of wars between small states, the problem becomes what is meant by conflicts within states. The problem is not as simple as it might at first appear. "Internal war" is a term these days which covers a whole range of markedly different types of conflict. They differ according to such variables as internal and external involvement, motives, ideology, scale, duration, techniques, and numbers of participants. It is misleading to assume that all internal wars are fundamentally the same and to categorize them under a single heading, such as "local war," "internal conflict," "internal war," or, most commonly, "civil war." Because of its frequency and its misuse, this latter terms must be analyzed. By taking "civil war" as the focus of attention, it can be demonstrated both that the term in the final analysis denotes a very specific and exceptional form of "internal conflict," and that there are, in fact, many forms of "internal conflict," each with its distinctive characteristics. Isolating "civil war" reveals the characteristics of the rest and these characteristics have an important bearing on both the increasing degree of external involvement in internal conflicts and the objective of limiting conflict and furthering international peace.

Civil Wars

"Civil war," as a concept, falls within a taxonomy of intrasocietal conflict. It is a form of internecine conflict within a society. At one level, all wars and all conflicts are intrasocietal. Given the wide interpretation of "society," from the whole human race at one end of the spectrum to small communities at the other, the notion of intrasocietal conflict serves little more than to denote conflicts between human beings living within an identifiable, structured group. This would, of course, apply also to wars between states. To devise a more readily operational taxonomy, the parameters of "society" must be defined. This would meet the criticism of overgeneralization levelled at the notion of intra-societal conflict. The

---

[15] Osgood and Tucker, *Force, Order and Justice*, 159–69.

simplest and most readily available operational concept is the nation-state boundary. As indicated above in the discussion of the by-products of typology construction with regard to interstate wars, not only are nation-state boundaries easily identifiable by scholar and layman alike, but also the "reality" of the modern world demonstrates that these boundaries are both artificial and concrete, in the sense that they are artificially established and maintained. Within these boundaries, differing patterns of behavior are identifiable and enforced. Ethnic groups, nations, religions, languages, cultures, and customs overlap nation-state boundaries, but the nation-state remains the most significant demarcation between one group of people and another. Accepting the limitations inherent in the concept, the nation-state is taken here as the boundary of society. Civil war is one of many forms of intrasocietal conflict, but is one which happens to take place also within the boundaries of the nation-state. To denote this somewhat crude refinement, civil war is categorized as coming within the general taxonomy of "internal conflict." ("Internal conflict" is chosen in preference to "internal wars" because of the more specific use of the latter in recent literature.) This is done despite the fact that it may suggest nonviolent forms of internal conflict which are outside the parameters of this analysis.

The endeavor here, then, is to contribute toward distinguishing from among the whole gamut of internal conflicts what might reasonably be considered to be a "civil war," while *en passant* in part constructing a typology of internal conflicts. The purpose is to isolate from the plethora of academic studies by social scientists, historians, and philosophers what is a "civil war" and what are its principal characteristics in contradistinction to all other forms of internal conflict.

The taxonomy of internal conflict—those conflicts that occur within the boundaries of the nation-state—is preferable to the taxonomy related to intrasocietal conflict. But what must a taxonomy of internal conflict incorporate, in addition to the single parameter mentioned above of wars within state boundaries? First, it must make the assumption that violence is used, though it is not a prerequisite that such violence be organized or that it take a particular form. Second, because of the legal connotations of the nation state, it is assumed that any type of internal conflict is outside the law of the particular state. Third, it makes the assumption that there is no limit on the number of parties to the conflict—some can be from external states—but that the principal antagonists are citizens of the state. No assumptions are made about either the means or the ends; it is these two variables that essentially distinguish, within the taxonomy, the different types of internal conflict that can be identified. Perhaps most significantly, the taxonomy must make an assumption about the participants: that both principal parties to the conflict have the capacity to terminate the conflict, either by surrender or by victory. If this were not the case, in certain instances it would be impossible to distinguish between internal war and interstate war. This assumption is hard to keep consistent because of the extent to which external parties tend to become ideologically and materially involved in internal conflicts. But it is this very phenomenon that the construction of the taxonomy is designed to help isolate.

"Civil war" thus denotes a certain type of internal and intrasocietal conflict. Because of the persistent use of the term it is limited as a manageable concept and as a means of identifying any precise form of internal conflict. Considerable refinement is therefore required.[16] By way of illustration, compare the use of the term in the context of the Greek civil war (1946–49), the Lebanese (1959–62), the Chinese (1945–49), the Laotian (1959–62), and the Burmese civil war (1948–54). Alternatively, consider it in the context of the classic examples, the American, English, Spanish, and Mexican civil wars. It is hard to determine what conceptually these examples have in common. More often than not they are closer to the type of internal conflicts that are not generally categorized as being "civil," such as the Laotian war and the war in Vietnam, or the Philippine Hukbalahap war and the Malayan insurgency. The term "civil war" is loosely used to denote a whole range of internal conflicts, which in the first instance can serve only to distinguish them from wars between states.

As compared with the use of the term "civil war" by historians, journalists, and commentators, the analysis of internal wars and civil wars by social scientists[17] reveals a more consistent interpretation of the term.

---

[16] Such a refinement did not concern L. Bloomfield and A. Leiss, who categorized all internal conflicts as "local," distinguishing types according to the degree of external involvement. See U. S. Arms Control and Disarmament Agency, *The Control of Local Conflict* (ACDA/WEC-98) (Washington, D.C.: Government Printing Office, 1967), 7–8.

[17] Among over forty separate pieces of work, the following were included: C. Tilly and J. Rule, *Measuring Political Upheaval* (Princeton: Princeton University Press, 1965), 55; H. Eckstein, ed., *Internal War: Problems and Approaches* (Glencoe, Ill.: Free Press, 1964); J. Zawodny, "Internal Warfare: Civil War," in *International Encyclopedia of Social Sciences*, ed. D. Sills (New York: Macmillan, 1968), 7:499–502; L. P. Edwards, "Civil War," in ibid., 3:523; P. A. Calvert, "Revolution: The Politics of Violence," *Political Studies*, no. 15 (February 1967):

On the basis of a content analysis of their work, there is some agreement on three broad characteristics. Civil wars are types of internal conflict in which civilians are involved, in which violence is used, and in which the opposing forces are politically organized. There are, however, few conflicts in which civilians are not involved, either directly or indirectly, and violence is an everyday feature of the internal affairs of all states. That civil wars involve politically organized groups is important because it distinguishes them from forms of internal conflict that are *ad hoc*, disorganized, and spontaneous. For this reason, it would be fair to exclude from the category of "civil war" all minor outbursts of violence within a society. Civil war must imply a minimum scale of conflict, expressed as a proportion of the total adult population who are involved in the hostilities.

That wars are extralegal[18] is a valuable point here, for it introduces the implication that a civil war is not only illegal as a means of forcing a change in the type or system of government, but is also outside the law while it is in progress. In other words, during a civil war, the rule of law within the society as a whole can be considered to have broken down or to have no foundation. This raises two important considerations. The first is that the government, as sovereign authority, legally enjoys the monopoly of coercion within any state, and any challenge to that authority which employs violent means is, by definition, illegal unless a state of anarchy is considered to exist while the war is being fought. The bounds of legality, however, are hard to determine, especially between one state and another. Examples abound in which there has been abuse of authority by governments, especially in military dictatorships or one-party states, and it is a moot point whether violent opposition in such instances is illegal or not. In consequence of this phenomenon, violence is increasingly coming to be accepted in many states as a legitimate political weapon.[19] The second consideration is that where governments possess a monopoly of coercion within the state, civil wars must be comparatively rare events, at least on the minimum scale required, given the

---

5; H. Eckstein, "On the Etiology of Internal Wars," *History and Theory* 4, no. 2 (1965):163; C. W. Bain, "Civil War," in *Dictionary of Political Science*, ed. J. Dunner (London: Vision Press, 1966), 99; W. White, "Civil War," in *White's Political Dictionary* (New York: World Publishing Co., 1947), 324.

18 Zawodny, "Internal Warfare," 499.

19 Samuel P. Huntington, *Changing Pattern of Military Politics* (New York: Free Press of Glencoe, 1966), 39.

difficulty of organizing, planning, and equipping military opposition. This may well account for the fact that major civil wars generally involve an almost equal division within the government military forces.[20]

A further distinction between a civil war and other instances of internal conflict is that in the former the government is one of the parties immediately and directly involved in the conflict,[21] though it may be unclear who the government is. This distinction is designed to separate civil wars from the many incidents of civil violence in which the government is involved to maintain law and order. Although such disorders may be antigovernment, and may be well planned, organized, and on a large scale, as for example general strikes, they need not be directed at challenging the government's ultimate authority. More often than not they are antigovernment only in that they are intended to change policy or are designed to discredit either the current government or specific individuals within it. They are not intended as a challenge to the government's jurisdiction within the political system. Distinguishing between threats to the government's policy and those to its jurisdiction, civil wars are taken here to represent the latter. A civil war is thus defined as a direct challenge to the authority of the government and its place within the political system of the state.[22]

"Internal war" has been categorized as "any conflict within an autonomous political system which involves illegitimate violence aiming at a change in that order."[23] Within this definition, civil wars and other forms of internal war are hardly distinguishable. The definition does, however, stress the context within which violence takes place, refers to the autonomy of the political system, and conveys a legal connotation regarding the authority of the government and its monopoly of violence. In relation to civil wars, which are on a large scale relative to the size of the state, the government cannot possess at the outbreak of a civil war either a monopoly of violence or political control. The notion of autonomy becomes highly questionable where external support is available for antigovernment forces. It may well be that civil wars break out only because of the infiltration of arms from outside or the promise of such support once

---

[20] Edward Luttwak, *Coup d'Etat* (London: Allen Lane, Penguin Press, 1968), 22.
[21] See Bain, "Civil War," p. 99, and Edwards, "Civil War," p. 523.
[22] Bain, "Civil War," 99.
[23] H. Eckstein, "Internal Wars: A Taxonomy" (Mimeographed, Center for International Studies, Princeton University, 1960); Tilly and Rule, *Measuring Political Upheaval*, 99; Edwards, "Civil War," 523.

civil war has begun. If this be the case, the notion of political autonomy is undermined and the influence of arms-supplying states can prove to be extensive. While it would be reasonable to assume that antigovernment forces are more dependent upon outside support than government forces, the converse has, more often than not, been the case. This is mainly a reflection of the level of military capability existing within those states where civil war has broken out, and the tactical advantages enjoyed in the early stages of the conflict by the antigovernment forces.

The question naturally arises as to whether guerrilla war and variations of unconventional and insurgency war fall within the category of "civil war" or whether they are conceptually different. Within the general body of literature on guerrilla warfare,[24] a distinction is made between the guerrilla stages of the conflict and the final stage in which the war takes on a conventional character. Guerrilla exponents consider that the final overthrow of the government must be by the methods used by the government forces themselves; without this the victory will not be manifest. The classic case of this overt, conventional military confrontation after years of covert guerrilla war is the battle at Dien Bien Phu, in which the elite French forces were defeated in conventional combat by the Vietnamese guerrillas. Civil war involves the use by both sides in the conflict of conventional military techniques; guerrilla war does not,[25] except in the final stages. The distinction is important, for guerrilla warfare is not merely a technique of war but a politico-military form of protracted conflict which can carry on for a long time and begin from the lowest levels. I have said above that civil war must be on a minimum scale to distinguish it from minor instances of internal violence. Civil war is, moreover, of an essentially military nature, as distinct from the related political objectives. One interesting conceptual point, however, which arises out of these distinctions, is the moment at which guerrilla war verges upon civil war. Given the hit-and-hide tactics employed by guerrilla forces, compared

[24] Mao Tse Tung, *Selected Works* (Peking: Foreign Languages Press, 1965), 2:176–77; also [Ernesto] Che Guevara, *Guerrilla Warfare* (New York: Monthly Review Press, 1961), 75; N. V. Giap, *People's War, People's Army* (Peking: Foreign Languages Publishing House, 1961).

[25] J. K. Zawodny, "Internal Warfare: Guerrilla Warfare" in *International Encyclopedia of Social Sciences*, 7:503. ". . . all non-regular militarylike combat that has *accompanied partisan activities* in civil wars, revolutionary wars, and popular resistance to foreign invasion and occupation." (My italics.) For this reason the Greek "civil war," of 1944–49 is not considered here to be a civil war. See C. Tsoucalas, *The Greek Tragedy* (London: Penguin, 1969), 102–13.

with conventional forces, the answer might well lie in a combination of the relative numbers of antigovernment forces and the military equipment at their disposal. This latter capability may well depend in turn upon the extent to which outside support has been given.

If civil wars can be distinguished from guerrilla and insurgency wars, at least up to a certain point in time, can they likewise be distinguished from revolutions? "Revolution" is a broad, complex concept that in turn embraces a range of intrasocietal as well as internal conflict situations. Among a range of definitions of "revolution," most agree that it involves a rapid or accelerated change of legal or political power within a state through the use of violence.[26] A feature of revolution is that its objective is to instrument fundamental social change; for this reason, some consider that it must have popular support.[27] Like civil wars, revolutions are directed against the government, but unlike civil wars, they need not be on a large scale of conventional war, for the objective of bringing about fundamental political and social change can be achieved by alternative means. Many revolutions, for example, can and do take place within the confines of government circles and involve relatively few individuals. The techniques of these so-called revolutionary groups, even when they are reactionary, as they have been in many cases, have been categorized elsewhere.[28] They include, for example, the coup d'etat, the *golpe de estado*, the *cuartelazo*, and the palace revolution. More often than not, the revolutionary groups involve senior officers of the armed forces, hence their often reactionary character. Where a revolution emerges from below in the form of mass action to change social and political structures as well as the political leadership, and organizes itself along conventional military lines, it can be considered to be similar to a civil war. The main distinction

[26] Twenty-six works were referred to, among which were: C. Johnson, *Revolution and the Social System* (Stanford, Cal.: Hoover Institution, 1964), 10; P. Amann, "Revolution: A Redefinition," *Political Science Quarterly* 77 (March 1962): 36–53; D. Yoder, "Current Definitions of Revolution," *American Journal of Sociology* 32 (1926):441; W. Laqueur, "Revolution," in *International Encyclopedia of Social Sciences*, 13:501–07; Carl J. Freidrich, ed., *Revolution* (New York: Atherton Press, 1966), 5; S. Neumann, "The International Civil War," *World Politics* (1948), 33; R. Pelloux, "Remarques sur le mot et l'idée de Revolution," *Revue Française de Science Politique* 2 (Jan.–Mar. 1952):43; L. Stone, "Theories of Revolution," *World Politics* 18 (1965):159; C. Leiden and K. Schnitt, eds., *The Politics of Violence: Revolution in the Modern World* (Englewood Cliffs, N.J.: Prentice-Hall, 1968); J. Davies, "Toward a Theory of Revolution," *American Sociological Review* 27 (Feb. 1962):6.

[27] For example, Luttwak, *Coup d'Etat*, 21–22.

[28] S. E. Finer, *The Man on Horseback* (London: Pall Mall, 1962), 140–63.

between the two terms, however, is a negative one. Civil wars are not necessarily designed to alter the political and social structures within society. They are only aimed at challenging the government or the extent of its jurisdiction, even though subsequently such challenges may well have wider and even "revolutionary" repercussions.

Two features of civil war remain. The first is the situation in which there is "actual warfare between elements of the national armed forces leading to a displacement of government."[29] Instances of this form of civil war are rare, for it requires a divided loyalty on the part of the state's armed forces. The cause of this division is a vital factor. Usually it occurs after a coup d'etat which leaves the armed forces split between the incumbent government and the displaced one. This was the case in Yemen, where the division was not only between two governments, but also between two forms of government, monarchical and republican. Although a split in the armed forces is usually caused by revolutionary coups, it can also be caused by political, national, and ethnic divisions.

Finally, there is the situation in which a war is fought between the government and the forces of an area, group, tribe, or race which is seeking either autonomy within the state or separation from it. On occasions, these wars have been categorized as wars of national liberation, although the more common use of this term is in relation to wars against foreign occupation.[30] In civil wars of secession, all the requirements of civil war are met. Civilians are involved and violence is a dominant feature. The war is illegal and it represents a direct challenge to the authority of the government, not only within the political unit but also within the breakaway region. The techniques of war are conventional in that the breakaway forces are operating as a newly created national army, and the war is fought between two roughly matched sides. Although the secondary effects may well bring about changes in government, and may alter, at least in the newly created political entity, the political and social structure of the society, such a secessionary war cannot be considered to be, in the first instance, revolutionary. Although guerrilla tactics may well be employed, it cannot be considered to be entirely an insurgent war, and conventional methods have at some time to be used. And although the opposing forces are not necessarily drawn from the previously existing armed forces of the state, the fact that the opposing sides are roughly

[29] Luttwak, *Coup d'Etat*, 22.
[30] Ibid., 23; Osgood and Tucker, *Force, Order and Justice*, 161–64.

matched and are organized to conduct a conventional type of war indicates that such a war is a civil war.

Thus civil war is an internal conflict that, over and above an undefinable minimum scale of involvement, has the above characteristics; it can, however, adopt one of two principal forms. The first is a civil war between the government forces and a secessionist group seeking either political autonomy within the state, or a separate state. The second is a war between two elements of the armed forces, with civilian involvement, over the composition and form of the government.

In relation to external involvement, intervention, and interest, the characteristics outlined above are significant. External support in an internal war varies according to the nature of the conflict, the parties involved, and the objectives of the antagonists. Guerrilla warfare and revolutionary movements have ideological overtones, and external support tends to come from ideologically sympathetic states. As a generalization, the West tends to support incumbent governments, while the East aids the revolutionary and guerrilla groups. The support does not always have to be material, as in the case, for example, of long Communist use of the Ho Chi Minh trail through Laos and Cambodia. The demand for support from outside in the form of military materiel is high from both sides, though the government tends to procure qualitatively more advanced weapons than the opposition. This is a function not only of expense, but also of the demands of the particular tactical form the war takes.

In civil wars involving separation from the state, ideological considerations are secondary and external support is generally a crucial factor. Furthermore, the source of support is secondary; it is the equipment itself that counts. External states may discriminate between the two sides, though the decision to support one or the other side may depend in the final analysis on a range of considerations, from purely mercenary motives to positive feelings of sympathy for one or the other cause. Ideological reasons cannot be totally excluded.

There have been many cases of internal conflicts since World War II.[31]

---

[31] U.S. ACDA . . . . , *Control of Local Conflict*, 7. Bloomfield and Leiss isolated fifty-two cases of local conflict, of which thirty-seven were principally internal. The Stockholm International Peace Research Institute (SIPRI), *Yearbook of World Armaments and Disarmament*, 1968–69 (London: Duckworth, 1970), 366–71, identifies sixty-four cases of internal conflict, thirty-four of which were civil, with the remainder civil with international involvement.

Such analysis as has been done has been of the specific case-study type, in which typologies of war have not figured. Studies have been made of guerrilla wars, insurgencies, or revolutions; others have been made of anticolonial struggles, wars of national liberation, and coups. From among the many instances of internal war that conform to the two types of civil war defined above, only the following cases emerge:[32] First, there are civil wars of secession, such as the Burmese civil war (1948–54), in which the Karen and Shan tribesmen fought the Burmese government to establish an independent Karen state. Some 7,000 Karen soldiers were involved, though the war was complicated by the fact that the "White Flag" Communists were also involved in the fighting with support from Communist China.[33] Another example is the civil war between the Nagas and the Indian government between 1945 and 1964. This conflict is generally referred to as a "revolt" because it was unsuccessful; it is questionable whether it was on a scale large enough to warrant being considered a civil war. It was, however, a continuing source of concern for the Indian government. A third example is the war between the Iraqi government and the Kurds. This started in 1960 and ended early in 1970. The Somali war against the Kenya government between 1963 and 1967 is complicated to a certain degree by the fact that it was also associated with a border dispute between Kenya, Somalia, and Ethiopia. Other examples are the conflict between the Province of Katanga and the Congo from 1960 until 1964, in which the United Nations became involved, and the Biafran-Nigerian civil war between 1967 and early 1970.

The second group of civil wars, those between two elements of the armed forces of a state, includes the following cases: the Laotian civil war of royalists versus republicans between 1960 and 1962, and the Yemeni civil war, again of royalists and republicans, between 1962 and 1964. The former case is somewhat complicated, for although dates are attributed to it, the war represents only a short period in a history of

---

[32] The likelihood of there being more cases will not diminish in the future. ". . . the next decade or so may well experience a growing number of interstate wars in the Third World. Most of these . . . will resemble guerrilla war more than the well organized encounters of disciplined armies." Osgood and Tucker, *Force, Order and Justice*, 165. The same is probably true for internal wars.

[33] There is some disparity in the numbers. *Keesing's Contemporary Archives* 1–8 (March 1952):12062–65, lists 2,000 Karen troops; Lucien Pye, "The Army in Burmese Politics" in John J. Johnson, ed., *The Role of the Military in Underdeveloped Countries* (Princeton: Princeton University Press, 1962), 235, puts the figure at 10,000. See also Hugh Tinker, *The Union of Burma* (London: Oxford University Press, 1961), 47. Frank N. Trager, *Burma* (London: Pall Mall, 1966), 107, puts the figure at 7,000 Karens.

internal conflict involving a wide range of competing governments, revolutionary movements, and guerrilla warfare. The most unusual case of civil war, however, is that of the Sudan, which has elements of both these forms. The war, which began when the Sudan became independent, has been fought between the Arab Muslim provinces in the north, which dominated the government, and the Christian and pagan provinces in the south. The southern provinces, led by the Sudan African National Union, were fighting to gain greater representation within the Sudanese parliament. But simultaneously, many southerners were fighting either for autonomy within the Sudan or for the creation of the new state of Azania. The war is still in progress (as of 1971), and ties up approximately three-quarters of the Sudanese government troops.

It is interesting to note that the many incidents of internal conflict in Latin America do not figure within either list. For the most part Latin American internal conflicts have fallen into the category of either the coup d'etat, or the revolution. In Colombia and Cuba, guerrilla war must be included. There have not been significant secessionist movements, nor have the military been divided over issues of types of government, mainly because so many military regimes exist within the subcontinent. The nearest case was the collapse of the Jimenez regime in Venezuela.[34] On this occasion the military were divided, but not on the scale nor involving the degree of violence characteristic of the civil wars listed above. "The fundamental revolutions, except for the unique upheavals in Mexico, Bolivia, and Cuba, were no bloodier than palace revolutions, for the masses of the population, though they exerted pressure, did not generally participate in the actual fighting."[35]

Intrasocietal conflict and internal conflict have assumed many forms. Civil war is one of those forms, and should by now be distinguished from the rest. It is open to question whether the definition proposed here should be the one adopted. However, the justification of this exercise, if not the definition, may help towards clarifying what is meant by "civil war," and may isolate it from other internal conflict situations which are likely to be open to external exploration and intervention. International peace and stability is a laudable objective; threats to such stability are as likely, if not more likely, to come from internal conflicts as from interstate conflicts. We should begin to be clear as to what internal conflicts we are talking about.

[34] E. Lieuwen, "Militarism and Politics," in Johnson, *Role of the Military*, 144.
[35] Ibid.

Suggestions for Further Research

The study of internal conflict and civil war is rapidly expanding. Much attention in the past has been devoted to specific forms of internal war, especially guerrilla warfare. Relatively little has been done on issues surrounding the use of violence as a political technique in advanced industrial societies and in the emergent nations. Even less attention has been given to the political ends and objectives of minority groups in society for which violence is considered to be an appropriate means. Correlations need to be drawn between political systems and the characteristics of internal conflict. Surprisingly little is known, for example, of the incidence and nature of violence on the micro level at which civil wars occur. For the intellectually rigorous, the semantics of violence, revolution, and internal conflict still need to be sorted out.

II

CIVIL WARFARE
An American Legacy

JIM DAN HILL

THE TERM civil warfare is an invitation to conflicting ideas. In our history, "the Civil War" means a specific struggle, 1861–65. The long-range results of that struggle were revolutionary. There was enough civil warfare to justify the name. Even so, its territorial and nationalistic character, North versus South and a Confederacy versus the Union, also gave it all of the characteristics of a war between two independent and sovereign powers.

In the histories of other nations, civil warfare is more or less synonymous with riots, insurrection, rebellion, guerrilla warfare, and revolution. The last word in this series necessarily includes the overthrow of an existing government. Abortive revolution is the phrase for failure. All of these terms, however, are now among the most abused and misused words in the English language, particularly by our sensational news media. Indeed, exaggerative usage and misapplied adjectives have so bent and twisted "revolution" that it can mean almost anything, anywhere. Many magazines, books, broadcasters, and editors are now proclaiming the Sex Revolution. Than sex, nothing has changed less since Adam and Eve were expelled from the Garden. Not even in their primordial experience was it a "revolution." It was merely a "revelation."

The Department of Defense, though fond of neologisms, always approaches military terminology with caution. "Guerrilla warfare" was toyed with as the correct term for all organized, armed blood-letting intended to cure a sick society. But the Pentagon semanticists frowned upon the word guerrilla. "Unconventional warfare" met with less opposition, and is now the official and accepted phrase. Conversely, "conventional warfare" is any armed conflict between well-defined governments, each sovereign within its own well-recognized territorial limits.

"Legacy," the other dominant word in the title of this brief essay on a far-flung subject, is not so bothersome. The fathers of American independence were thoroughly aware of their own two-fold heritage. One came from their freedoms as colonists in a New World. Those freedoms stemmed from distance, mother country neglect, and the grim necessity for initiative, resourcefulness, and improvisation in order to survive within a primitive and hostile environment. The other heritage came automatically from the mother country: they were Englishmen, subjects of a proud kingdom and entitled to all the benefits of the Magna Carta and all subsequent historic documents and concepts, including the evolution of representative government, and rights under English common law. Being normal human beings, the Founding Fathers naturally claimed all of the advantages of each legacy. With equal rationality they often chose to be unaware of some burdensome responsibilities inherent in either the one heritage or the other.

As Englishmen, the colonial citizens had a historic right to resist monarchial absolutism. In each colony, the historic precedents of civil warfare against tyranny by a king or one of his governors were well known to every vociferous country lawyer, such as Patrick Henry. These precedents were the Magna Carta, 1215; the triumph of the Lords Ordainers and the secret execution of the unworthy Edward II, 1327; the deposition of Richard II by Parliament, 1399; and the killing of the unpopular Richard III on Bosworth Field, 1485. Thus the king's subjects in the forests of North America were never under any delusions as to the Divine Right and sanctity of kings. Indeed, that silly idea was unknown in England until James I became king in 1603. He had written this self-serving philosophy into a little book for the education and guidance of his courtiers and ministers. His son, Charles I, was stupid enough not only to believe it but to act upon it. Thus, that little book was a factor in the Great Rebellion, the rise of Cromwell, and the trial and beheading of Charles I, 1649. By that time the Crown Colony of Virginia was forty-three years old. Lord Calvert's Maryland was hardly out of its swaddling clothes, but the theocratic founders of Massachusetts, Rhode Island, and Connecticut were making their dreams come true.

Accordingly, within the young colonies there were tremors from the earth-shaking Great Rebellion. In New England some of the Regicides found safety. In Virginia, Nathaniel Bacon belatedly followed the path of Cromwell, overthrowing the tyrannical royal governor, Sir William Berkeley, shortly after the Stuart Restoration of 1660. The second Charles had seen the signs of the time. Divine Right notwithstanding, he did not send Berkeley back to Virginia. Thus the colonial Englishmen had a precedent of their very own. From this event, Thomas Jefferson may have derived his mistaken idea that a government can exist only with the consent of the governed.

England's Glorious Revolution of 1689 had its impact upon the colonial Englishmen. In Boston, Royal Governor Edmund Andros was overthrown, imprisoned, and sent "for trial" to England, where the charges were dismissed. The crown's lieutenant governor for New York and New Jersey, Sir Francis Nicholson, avoided a similar imprisonment by beating his angry accusers to the waterfront and safety aboard a homeward-bound ship. Neither colony experienced serious retribution; neither governor was returned.

A galaxy of philosophers, such as Richard Hooker, John Calvin, Edward Coke, James Harrington, John Locke, and others influenced the founding fathers. These intellectuals predicated many of their theories of resistence to tyranny largely upon the above-mentioned events in history, well known to the colonial Englishmen. The writings of Sir Edward Coke were usually at Thomas Jefferson's elbow. John Locke was a favorite among lawyers, teachers, and clergymen. The most important contribution of these philosophers was to provide the rationale and the rhetoric. In the concept of their dual rights as colonists and Englishmen, the American lawyers, merchants, and clergymen rationalized themselves into a tight, logical, and rather conservative pattern of thinking. Distance, mother country neglect, and improvisations for survival joined hands with England's evolutions toward popular government and the views of philosophers to make the colonials the most free of all free Englishmen. They intended to keep it that way. Royal governors learned to adjust. But in distant London, the Parliament, the king's ministers, and the king were far less flexible. In their efforts to reorganize an expanding empire they were prone to innovate and to tamper. Worse yet, they could become downright pig-headed about it.

In brief, the fathers of American Independence were not revolutionists within the meaning the word has acquired since the French Revolution and its several European sequels. They were conservatives seeking to preserve what they had so long enjoyed.

In England, the problem was one of consolidating and getting a strong grip on all of the vast amount of territorial loot that had fallen into British hands from the crumbling of the Dutch, Spanish, and French colonial empires in the expensive, bitter, and worldwide hostilities of 1754–63. The wealth Clive and his lieutenants brought back from India convinced a suddenly avaricious and almost bankrupt mother country that much could be milked from colonies. Spain had done it, why not England?

The population of Mother England in 1750 was hardly seven million. The European populations of England's sixteen North American colonies approached three million. Why should those distant colonial Englishmen enjoy such freedoms from governance and such light taxes when the mother country had expended so much for their acquisition, expansion, and protection? Something had to be done to reverse the flow of wealth. The king's mercantilist ministers in Parliament knew exactly how it could be done. Their dismal efforts are of record in all school histories. The colonials of the thirteen older colonies knew their rights and proceeded to fight for their preservation.

Dr. Daniel J. Boorstin, in his delightful and analytical volume, *The Genius of American Politics*, startles his readers with a chapter heading, "The American Revolution: A Revolution without a Dogma." His concept of the conservative revolt within the colonies is so clearly sustained, there is no need for repetition here. It is also noteworthy that years earlier the University of Michigan's famed Claude H. Van Tyne had reluctantly arrived at the same conclusion after spending most of his scholarly life in studies of every phase of the war between the mother country and her colonies.

Following the clash of arms at Lexington and Concord in April 1775, the several royal governors were individually deposed by sundry local committees and sent to sea and safety within the historic formula which had removed Governors Andros and Nicholson back in 1689. Heads did not roll as in the French Reign of Terror. Royal charters for Connecticut and Rhode Island permitted local election of governors. Those old charters continued, redesignated as state constitutions, until 1818 and 1843, respectively. Maryland's deputy for the Calvert heirs, Governor Robert Eden, left the colony in the interest of public welfare. In Philadelphia,

John Penn sat as lieutenant governor for the proprietary families, namely, his father and an uncle. Briefly in house arrest, Penn saw his Quaker government quietly expire in the face of a "Supreme Executive Council." This was two months after the signing of the Declaration of Independence. The state bought the proprietary rights.

The royal governor in Boston and his loyal retinue left with the British Army. General Washington's besieging artillery on Dorchester Heights forced the withdrawal by the Royal Navy in March 1776. After Washington took command the previous summer, the war had all the territorial-nationalistic characteristics of conventional warfare, with the aim of independence—social, economic, and political—plus ample room for expansion. Admittedly, these war aims were not officially proclaimed until July 4, 1776.

This does not negate the bitter fact that a limited amount of unconventional warfare can exist alongside and contemporary with its conventional neighbor. Not all of the wealthy Quakers were happy about the expiration of John Penn's governments. Others, not so wealthy and therefore probably more devout, were equally unhappy and likewise gun-shy. But they could adopt postures of passive resistance that moved others to violence. They could, without too much strain on conscience, subsidize others who were willing to shed blood for the king and mother country. Many Quakers did "march forth in a warlike manner" to join the "Military Associators," a Philadelphia euphony for the Volunteer Militia Companies or National Guard units that were becoming the Pennsylvania Line of Washington's Continental Army. Such Quakers were promptly read out of the Church, but this bothered the Quaker Military Associators very little. They merely consulted their collective quakings and organized a warlike branch thereof. Needless to say, feelings were bitter in Pennsylvania.

Elsewhere, there was less indulgence in abstractions. A citizen was for the king or for independence, but many were disinclined to do much about it either way. Many were Loyalists, or Tories, because they considered the British Army and Navy the inevitable winners. Well they might. At least thirty-eight regiments of British Regulars and six regiments of Hessians appeared upon General Henry Clinton's Order of Battle Lists. He was able to organize only six "provincial regiments" in America. One of these was of displaced Irishmen in America who were needful of employment or were "impressed." There is reason to believe that perhaps

60,000 Americans bore British arms for a period, brief or long, during the seven years of hostilities. An unknown number of them undoubtedly served at different periods, brief or long, in the armed forces of both sides. Some of the most abhorrent aspects of the war are found in the small military operations in which a locally recruited Loyalist regiment or battalion was pitted against neighbors in Patriot guerrilla forces.

It was in civil affairs that the readily recognized Tories, or Loyalists, truly suffered. They publicly took oaths of allegiance to the new governments or were denied the rights of citizenship—voting, office holding, even the security of person and property in some communities. Free speech was denied; entry into or continued practice in the professions also could be, and at times was, denied. Being jailed or put in house arrest, with parole, was a common experience.

During the seven years, probably 200,000 Tories vanished from their old colonial towns and cities. Deaths from natural causes and/or violence could account for some. Confiscation of property and banishment was the unquestioned fate of some. The majority appear to have become voluntary exiles. The greatest density of Tory populations was along the coastal estuaries and in the tidewater cities and towns. Some went to England directly or by way of Canada. A larger percentage settled in Canada. The British government eventually disbursed over nine million pounds to Tory claimants for property lost. For those Loyalists who lived through it, it was unconventional warfare indeed.

Be it said in defense of the Patriots that they had little choice. The committed Loyalists were constantly spying for and cooperating with the British Army. In some tidewater areas they had their own militia units. In civil affairs they had futile programs and plans for regaining control of local and state government machinery through violence. They connived with Spaniards in Florida. They allied themselves with the Indians. They succeeded in setting up a rival royal government in one state, Georgia, but its authority seldom extended beyond the British Army's patrols.

It must be admitted that in a conventional war for national goals, there are limits beyond which unconventional warfare on the home front cannot be tolerated without losing the main struggle. In a way, the Tories sealed their own fate. Before the war ended, those not in English army uniforms were either covert or inactive.

Historians could well use some detailed area studies of the home front civil warfare in the turbulent era of 1775–83. Such could better reveal the anatomy of representative regional situations. As for the field as a whole, it has been well ploughed.

Shay's Rebellion, 1786, in Massachusetts was rabble-rousing civil warfare in its most alarming form. It is an oft-told tale and merits no repetition here. It was unique in that its target was the probably corrupt and certainly ruthless judicial system, rather than the usual and far more powerful executive branch. It jolted the Congress of the tottering Confederation into calling the Constitutional Convention. The Convention's work filled the vacuum in regulation of interstate monetary relations, national defence, and foreign affairs that had been created by severence from the mother country. The new Constitution clung tightly to colonial and wartime experience. It was void of inspiration, theory, or imagination. The presidency created was no more than a super-colonial governor; the Congress a replica of a composite of colonial legislatures. The Supreme Court, sometimes said to be America's only original contribution to the machinery of popular government, was no more than a substitute receiving agent for judicial appeals that once went to Britain's Board of Trade, the English higher courts, and the king in Privy Council.

Shay's vicious and telling onslaught against the judiciary could have been a factor in the Convention's amazingly protective instinct for the federal judges. Thanks to life tenure, no matter how old, unwell, senile, or decrepit, they quickly became America's only governmental nobility —nonhereditary, of course, but nevertheless a privileged and powerful nobility. Not even George III, or his most arrogant ministers, ever wished anything like that for them.

The Whiskey Insurrection of 1794 need not detain us long. It has already achieved a bigger place in history than it perhaps deserves. There are as many detailed and differing accounts from varied viewpoints as there are biographers of Albert Gallatin, Thomas Jefferson, and George Washington. That is somewhat more than a few. But these accounts do offer at least one overlooked lesson. Washington called upon a few states to provide about fifteen regiments to an aggregate strength of over 12,000 men, in order to bring law, order, and tax collections to the unhappy, agrarian frontier counties. Washington was immediately denounced. A tyrant, in using sledge hammers against harmless insects, had destroyed the mansion of democracy.

Lincoln, in 1861, confronted by the same problem in seven Southern states, using the same formula and acting under the same laws, called for nearly a hundred regiments to an approximate strength of 75,000. State governors north of Maryland and the Ohio River heavily oversubscribed the requisitions. Lincoln accepted 90,500. This was just enough to trigger strength for the opposition. Immediately the sledge-hammer armies of the South began destroying the Union. It has been often cited as Lincoln's greatest blunder. The lesson: No matter what a governor or a president does when faced by insurrection, he is going to be wrong, come the journalists and the historians.

Violence, strife, competition, tragedy and disaster make news. Seldom, if ever, has placid contentment ever splashed itself across the front page of a daily newspaper. Files of nineteenth century metropolitan newspapers reveal many riots and alleged "insurrections." Such events as apprentices and sailors wrecking "bawdy-houses" can be dismissed as lacking political or ideological significance. But an amazing number were justified by self-association with and sublimation to a "higher cause." Volunteer militia regiments were frequently called. State constabularies were so rare that the Texas Rangers were unique. National Guardsmen handled the grim jobs.

Religious differences offered an excuse for many riots in the history of this nation. Hostility between ethnic groups frequently consolidated with religion to produce a real Donnybrook. Election year riots, complete with noble claims alongside libelous banners, could produce heavy casualties. Usually all they amounted to was that the "Outs" wanted in, and the "Ins" wanted to stay in. Riots for better wages were comparatively rare prior to 1877.

An odd but generally forgotten mass reaction to the early Abolition Movement was tumultuously hostile mobs. Nowhere were they worse than in New York in 1834 and 1835. No less than a regiment of National Guard infantry was required to breach the barricades for the protection of lives and property. The Abolitionists, William Lloyd Garrison in particular, had sought funds for their cause in the more cultured and enlightened England. The flattered Englishmen donated, though probably not as much as the riots cost the taxpayers. But vilification of America for British money was not to be tolerated. Furthermore, there may have been a smouldering fear of competition from cheap labor should slaves become free. The Nat Turner Insurrection and his atrocities of 1831 had created a poor image of such freedmen as prospective neighbors and fellow workingmen. Times were hard and job-protection was cause for worry. In 1835 the New York City stone-cutters staged a first-class street brawl in protest against public buildings being constructed from stones prepared by convicts in Sing Sing. They whipped the police but lost to the Guardsmen.

In the slave states, the Nat Turner Insurrection more tightly riveted the shackles of slavery. Quite by accident, Turner's hallucinated, irresponsible rampage came so closely on the heels of some more successful, and even more ghastly, slave revolts on a few Caribbean islands and in Venezuela that a greatly magnified fear swept over the entire slaveholding part of the nation. The growing movement for voluntary freeing of slaves by manumission in Virginia, Delaware, Maryland, and Kentucky was smothered in horror. Changes in the quality demands of the world tobacco market had put the old tobacco plantations out of business. In those states, owners of unprofitable but growing slave families were facing grim decisions. It was either write off the parental legacy in human bondage as a losing proposition or try to salvage the estate by selling the unwanted slaves "down the river." From South Carolina to Louisiana, the insatiable world demand for cotton was creating plantations of unprecedented size and prosperity. The anti-Abolitionist riots and the Nat Turner Insurrection brought a happy boom in business for the unscrupulous transporters and dealers in slaves.

The "Irrepressible Conflict" between the North and South was on the way. All reasonably informed and rational people, North and South, knew that slavery was written into the Constitution. Federal judicial decisions, including the Supreme Court, said as much. As an academic question, in 1856, the right of secession by one or more states was generally conceded. Those who actually advocated secession as the solution of a regional problem, or problems, were considered extremists. No one confirms the foregoing better than William Lloyd Garrison and his fellow Abolitionists. On January 27, 1843, Garrison submitted, and the Massachusetts Anti-Slavery Society adopted, the following resolution: "That the compact which exists between the North and South is a covenant with death and an agreement with hell, involving both parties in atrocious criminality, and should be immediately annulled." In 1854 Garrison was still hammering on the same theme. He punctuated an address by burning a copy of the United States Constitution and offering the plea, "So perish all compromises with tyranny!" When the South actually took the path to secession, Garrison and his followers viewed it with satisfaction. It saved them the burden of doing it (and for revolutionists troubled waters offer good fishing).

Charles A. Beard repeatedly called the Civil War the "Second American Revolution." To Crane Brinton, author of *The Anatomy of Revolution*, ". . . the American Civil War is really an almost classical example of an abortive territorial-nationalist revolution." We likewise have here a classical example of how far apart two highly competent historians can be when they choose to view the same war from different angles.

I can most readily agree with Beard, but not for the reason that he had in mind. Beard was thinking of America's war of 1775–82 as the First Revolution. I have already pointed out that it was a War for Independence, so that long-existing forms of popular government might be preserved. De Tocqueville was quite right in 1835 when he wrote, "The social condition and the Constitution of the Americans are democratic . . . but they have not had a democratic revolution."

The long-range result of the Civil War was indeed revolutionary; thus Brinton is wrong in calling it an abortive revolution. It was the South's efforts to secede that were abortive. The Southerners were not revolutionists; they were die-hard reactionaries, and they were most particular in the legalisms of their secession. There is merit in their insistence that they "fought to preserve the Constitution as it was conceived by its Authors." Brinton, of course, considered them revolutionists because they early adopted a new Constitution of the Confederate States. What he missed was the fact that it was the same old Constitution, with a few clarifying, reactionary paragraphs and a change in the length of the presidential term, which reflected their experience as practical politicians within the Union.

It was Lincoln who reluctantly sowed the seeds of the ultimate, all-out revolution that Beard discerned, though Professor Woodrow Wilson had identified the end result as revolutionary long before Beard popularized the idea. Lincoln dedicated his administration and his life to the preservation of the Union. To him, it was far more important than the Constitution. Thus he became the reluctant revolutionist. At the time of his death, an embittered Congress, completely radicalized toward the South, was challenging his control. They embraced the "Conquered Provinces" theory and consummated the ultimate revolution by adding the Civil War Amendments, particularly the Fourteenth, to the Constitution. It was done at the points of bayonets.

The foregoing paragraphs, apparently an exercise in semantics, are written not for the sake of semantics but to clarify the roots of the most prolonged and bitter civil, or unconventional, warfare in American history. This guerrilla warfare began in "Bleeding Kansas" in 1856 and became of major importance with John Brown's raid. It continued in the Border States, alongside the conventional warfare of the armies, through 1861–65. It ended in 1877, when President Hayes definitely abandoned all applications of the Conquered Provinces theory. The revolutionary and complete erosion of "states' rights" under the antislavery Fourteenth Amendment has continued into our own era. This is the revolution that Wilson and Beard identified. Not all the states have been "conquered provinces." Under the expansion of implied powers that have nothing to do with slavery or race problems, all of the "states" are now actually mere provinces of an increasingly monolithic national state.

But let us return to the civil warfare that mobilized the conventional armies and continued guerrilla techniques behind the lines. The two capitals of Kansas, proslavery and antislavery, are part of a long and well-known narrative. The emergence therefrom of "Old Ossawatomie Brown" as an enemy of slavery who could get results, was most tragic. John Brown's Harper's Ferry raid was financed by New England Abolitionists, such as the wealthy Gerrit Smith, who was fully aware of Brown's murderous plans. The raid is a popular saga that needs no summary here. It is enough to insist that the passions that radiated from Harper's Ferry and John Brown's trial and execution did much toward destruction of political parties and moderation candidates through the vital election year of 1860.

President Lincoln, for better or worse, shelved in silence the most burning issues of his November election until his inauguration the following March 4. It was then that the preservation of the Union unfolded as his one and only aim. Lesser aims, such as the future of slavery, had to grow from the primary purpose. He was the fortunate beneficiary of the Websterian, broad construction approach to the Constitution. But Lincoln was to find it necessary to exercise "implied powers" far beyond the exhortations of New England's great liberal. Indeed, Lincoln, the reluctant revolutionary, was to violate the Constitution ruthlessly in order to hold his own in the civil warfare of the Border States.

The mobilization of their armies, North and South, in the spring of 1861, and the Blockade Proclamation gave Lincoln the conventional war that we earlier recognized. The mobilization also reduced the width of the would-be neutral zone between the North and the seven states of "Secessia." All eight of the slave states still in the Union when Fort Sumter was fired upon, April 12, 1861, refused to provide any regimental quotas of volunteers for suppression of the Cotton States. For this there were New England precedents from 1812. Four of the eight (North Carolina, Virginia, Tennessee, and Arkansas), notwithstanding potential guerrilla pockets of strong Union sentiment in the Appalachian and Ozark mountains, fell from the neutrality fence of indecision. They joined the Confederacy. This left the Lincoln administration to cope with four slave states. Delaware—small, at a geographical corner, and with a population of only a hundred thousand—could be ignored. The remaining three—Maryland, Kentucky, and Missouri—with combined populations totaling a tenth of the entire nation, were something else. They continued to refuse to send regiments to either side. But they announced a strong willingness to fight the first that violated their neutrality by marching across their soil to get at the other. These "neutral borderlands," largely proslavery, were to become Lincoln's first major problem. They at once drove him to unconstitutional transgressions of the first magnitude. These states soon were the scenes of unconventional, or guerrilla, warfare in its most hideous form.

Happily, the tide of events engulfed Maryland, strategically the most important of the border slave states, before Lincoln had to do much about it. Its governor was a states' rights Democrat but a Union man at heart. He was also an indecisive procrastinator. The Secession Season came and went while Governor Thomas H. Hicks continued to wrestle with conflicting doubts as to his official duty.

He knew a legislative call to special session would create a convention, dominated by the same legislators. They would "absolve the bonds of Union" in the same language with which their fathers had ratified the Constitution in 1789. The inrush of Northern regiments to defend Washington following the mobilization call gave the Union so much muscle in Maryland that an "ordinance of secession" was no longer practical. But Maryland regiments were to fight in both armies. When invading armies were not living off the country, "partisan bands" were to harass the land. Secret and hostile clubs in every town provided spies for both North and South. Martial law was anywhere and everywhere as often as the provost marshal saw fit. Conspirators planned murders, one of which finally reached the White House; civil warfare was at its worst.

It was the mountain counties of western Virginia that offered the most unexpected surprise. Their delegates came home from the Secession Convention in Richmond with complaints. Their state had been "dragooned out of the Union." Organizing a rump convention to meet in Wheeling was an easy, political maneuver. On the Ohio River and but a few miles from the Pennsylvania boundary, no secession claque could bother them. They also had the blessings of Governor Dennison of Ohio. He had regiments Lincoln had declined. Thus, a pleased President Lincoln was informed that because of Virginia's "illegal secession" from the Union, the mountain counties were legally seceding from the remainder of Virginia. To that end, a rival and lawful government had been organized, complete with a governor and legislative body. Could the administration find some money to pay salaries? The inconsistency of their major premises on secession rights was too much for Lincoln. He welcomed the movement but called it a step toward "the Restoration of Virginia." He found the money for them. Governor Dennison, with the aid of Governor Morton of Indiana, sent regiments to liberate the counties when Virginia threatened subjugation. The eastern valleys of West Virginia suffered guerrilla warfare until 1865.

In 1863, an increasingly radicalized Congress welcomed West Virginia into the Union as the "35th State." Nothing could have been more unconstitutional than splitting a state when the Original Document is viewed within the intent of its framers, but Lincoln could hardly have won the war without such revolutionary audacity.

The situations were so similar in the border slave states of Kentucky and Missouri that they can be summarized simultaneously. Both had proslavery governors and legislatures. Both factions in each state viewed one another with smouldering hatreds and burning suspicions. All were giving ostentatious lip service to complete neutrality. They became stranded on that philosophical but shifting sandbar. Thus, neither the Unionists nor the Secessionists were overt. The odds favored the Confederacy. The Davis administration confidently did nothing. For Lincoln, it was a long spring and summer of watchful waiting. He dared not do anything until he had military muscle to sustain an open political move for the Union. For this, Lincoln had his contacts.

In Kentucky it was a U. S. Naval lieutenant, William Nelson. The opening guns of April found him at his Kentucky home, awaiting sea orders that never came. In July he received guns for 5,000 men and a commission as an army brigadier general. He secretly recruited regiments from among the many Union sympathizers in the mountains and valleys of Eastern Kentucky. Union forces in Cincinnati, Indiana, and Illinois were concentrated along the north bank of the Ohio River.

In Missouri, Congressman Francis P. Blair, a Mexican War veteran, and Captain Nathaniel Lyon, an army ordinance officer in charge of the St. Louis arsenal, covertly began recruiting and arming Unionist regiments. Their city manpower base was a large, antislavery German population. Many of them were refugees with military training or combat service in Europe's revolutions of 1848. In a surprise move, they marched on Jefferson City and ousted the proslavery governor and the legislature —literally a coup d'etat. The deposed, erstwhile neutral Secessionists reassembled in New Madrid as a state convention with plenary powers. They seceded the entire state out of the Union, and sent two senators and eleven congressmen to the Confederate government in Richmond. These worthies were seated and served in the Confederate Congress the full four years. Missouri's New Madrid government moved into and out of the state with the tides of warfare. The Unionist government retained the state capitol and their congressional seats in Washington. Thus Missouri was well represented, North and South. Both state governments gave cloaks of legitimacy to their own guerrilla partisans and pillagers. The formula for "Bleeding Kansas" was being repeated.

Much the same thing happened in Kentucky. Confederate troops from Tennessee occupied (September 4) and fortified the high bluffs on the Mississippi at Columbus. This put the Union forces in motion. Out of Ohio and Indiana they poured into the Bluegrass counties and chased the proslavery authorities out of Frankfort. Brigadier General Nelson advanced out of the mountains. Brigadier General U. S. Grant, with Illinois regiments and two gunboats, occupied Paducah. The no-longer-neutral governor ordered his adjutant general, Simon B. Buckner, to drive Grant away from the river. Instead, Buckner convened a secession convention in Bowling Green. They did exactly the same as the dislocated convention in New Madrid, Missouri. Thus Kentucky too had congressmen seated North and South and a shadow secession government that spent most of its time on wheels and issuing blank commissions to whoever thought he could organize a guerrilla band. William C. Quantrill's original commission as captain appears to have come from this dubious source, though most of his operations were Missouri based.

President Lincoln had eliminated the wide "neutral zone" that had separated the growing western armies of the Union and the Confederacy.

They could now go about their conventional warfare. But Lincoln had also created a bitter civil warfare zone from Dover, Delaware, to the Indian frontier in Kansas. Moreover, the northern and southern boundaries of the Border States were not to remain the latitudinal limits of the zone. As victorious Union armies pressed southward, they necessarily left guerrilla pockets in their rear. Line-of-communications regiments sapped their strength. North of the Ohio River, entire tiers of counties in Indiana and Illinois, not to mention a few in Ohio, were ripe for the underground Copperhead Movement. War weariness revitalized die-hard Northern Democrats such as Fernando Wood, long-time Tammany boss, intermittent mayor of New York, and organizer of the briefly powerful Mozart Club; and Congressman Clement L. Vallandigham of Ohio.

The extent to which conspirators from the Border States exploited and expanded this ready-made field for unconventional warfare within the nonslavery Union states may never be fully known. It is an unpleasant subject. Dr. Frank L. Klement, biographer of Vallandigham, knows far more than he has written into his book. James D. Horan, a tireless researcher and able author with a nose for unused sources, has likewise probed deeply into this murky morass. Their findings invite further explorations. More was happening there than has met the eye. And some very disagreeable things are visible, such as the Confederate fire-bombing of conspicuous buildings in New York City on November 26, 1864, of which Fernando Wood probably had prior and criminal knowledge. Thoroughly infiltrated by informers, the ambitious and expensive Northwest Plan of the Sons of Liberty, geared to election day, November 8, 1864, fell on its face in Chicago.

Civil warfare is conducive to secret societies. Both sides took recourse to fraternal networks. By casual signs, passwords, and phrases, strangers might determine whom they could trust. Since membership lists were also secret, some bold operators easily become double agents. Extremely timid souls occasionally joined both fraternities, enabling them to be right every time. Southern sympathizers rapidly gravitated into an existing order, the Knights of the Golden Circle. It originated from a promoter's pipe-dream in Cincinnati, 1854. Weirdly reactionary, it became militantly activist in 1861. Easily infiltrated, the Knights changed their name in 1863 to American Knights. By 1864 their membership was predominantly Northern Copperheads. In search of a better image, the name was changed to Sons of Liberty, with ex-Congressman Clement L. Vallandigham as supreme officer. But the "Knights" and "Sons" were clearly the precursors of the Ku Klux Klan, the Knights of the White Camellia, and lesser lodges that were to continue the civil warfare through the twelve years after the conventional warfare had ended at Appomattox.

The Unionists countered with the same techniques. The best-known were the Union League Clubs, openly active in patriotic works and charities. A few survive today as exclusive local social clubs. But in areas of strife and blood-letting, they were covert, and a part of the militant-survival mechanism. Southerners had bitter memories of the Union League Clubs. Their introduction among the blacks by the Freedmen's Bureau was to create an instant flowering of the Ku Klux Klan. Unionists in some western towns organized independent vigilante societies, which occasionally took the form of quasi-military units. Such was the character of George W. Hoyt's secret Society of Red Legs. It alternated between being a one-lodge fraternity and a tightly organized company of Northern guerrillas, or "Jayhawkers."

"Yankee Bushwackers" and "Rebel Bushwackers" were widely accepted terms. For themselves, the South's guerrillas much preferred softer words, such as "Partisan Rangers."

Some individuals switched allegiances at will. In the absence of fingerprints, standardized forms and, central records, desertions were a major problem for both of the conventional armies. Guerrilla bands always welcomed deserters. Colonel John S. Mosby, one of the few Partisan Rangers to write his memoirs, reports that a deserter from a New York cavalry regiment became one of his most trusted lieutenants. Mosby was covered by a Confederate rank for a part of his service, pursuant to Confederate legislation of April 21, 1862, until it was repealed on February 15, 1864. Such commissions were intended for officers who could infiltrate Union lines and recruit bands in their rear or in the Border States. Mosby apparently did not get news of the repeal. He insists that he operated as a partisan "right up to Appomattox."

In both North and South, guerrilla pay, rations, and clothing came from plunder. Any excess loot was distributed as a bonus. Following a raid, units disbanded for concealment within the population until the rendezvous for the next operation. Army wagon trains, military warehouses, horses in remount stations, and payroll detachments were prime targets. Railroad stations, steam trains, banks, department stores, and farms and plantations owned by hostile families were legitimate targets when none better were available. Grudge fights between hostile bands were common, ambushes, or "dry gulching," the favored tactics.

Appomattox, April 1865, demobilized the armies. The prime wartime targets vanished, but the banks and railroads were still there. They were feeling the impact of guerrilla traditions and techniques as late as 1890. The James Boys, out of Quantrill's Battalion, with Cole Younger and his brothers, were the most notorious practitioners of the bank and train techniques.

Back home and under President Johnson's restored Ten Percent Governments, most Southern taxpayers and all the returned soldiers found themselves without votes. The black freedmen were the voters. But the whites, by intimidations and the Black Codes, further radicalized congressional thinking and legislation. The result underwrote the continuation of unconventional civil warfare throughout the former Confederacy, and to a considerable extent in Missouri and Kentucky.

The congressional Radicals, unbridled by Lincoln's untimely death, accepted the "conquered provinces" concept of the prostrate South. It called for complete "reconstruction" before "readmission." It turned out to be a job for bayonets. As viewed by the South, the federal troops were an army of occupation, supplemented by an organized militia of Negroes, charged with denial of the vote to all whites who were unwilling to swear an oath to support the Republican Party.

Aside from reformatory zeal, the Radicals hoped that their Reconstruction policies would create a political coalition of poor whites, professional men, small tradesmen, artisans, and freed blacks to guarantee a grateful Republican majority in the ex-Confederate states through many, many election years to come. Such a coalition, radical congressmen reasoned, could and would reject the "slavocrat" leadership that had led their people down the path to disaster in the Civil War.

But Radical thinking in Washington was far removed from realities in Dixie. Southern whites, both rich and poor, still admired and had confidence in their former Confederate leaders. Not even the poorest whites were ready for a political alliance with a segment of the population most of whom could not read or write. Thus the Reconstruction governments were delivered into the hands of a few native whites, who took the oath and were slandered as "Scalawags," and Northern adventurers who were more appropriately called "Carpetbaggers."

The Freedmen's Bureau, largely staffed by former Union army officers, was the strong right arm of the Reconstruction governors. In 1866–67, its field workers began urging the freedmen to create and join Union League Clubs. This was just enough to dump all of the simmering fat right into the fire. It was easy for the voteless whites to rationalize that good businessmen and competent property owners could survive the astronomical budgets, incredible bond issues, and exhorbitant taxes of Negro legislators led by irresponsible Carpetbaggers, but this Union League idea added most alarming thoughts of the long-dead Nat Turner and the late and equally hallucinated Old John Brown.

Within weeks the veterans who knew so much that was adverse about the Union League Clubs were turning to the counter-formulas they had known. In New Orleans and the deep South, the Knights of the White Camellia, with many secret "Castles" or local chapters, were fully formidable before they were known to be in existence. From Missouri to the Carolinas, the Ku Klux Klan grew from a saddle club of frivolous pranksters in Pulaski, Tennessee, in 1866, to an "Invisible Empire" of 550,000 "ghouls" the following year. The total of all the active-duty muster lists of the Confederate army in the month Gettysburg was fought was no more than 400,000 officers and men. The Knights are believed to have had a larger membership than the KKK, and were certainly more lasting and powerful. It was the name and terminology of the Klan that captured the headlines. In the North, all underground resistance in the South came to be credited to the Klan. Actually, ex-General Nathan Bedford Forrest was the first and only KKK "Grand Wizard." He and his Grand Council of "Ten Genii" in Memphis, Tennessee, early discovered they had little or no control over the secret doings of the several "Grand Dragons," each of whom commanded, in theory, the "dens" of his state. The Dragons found themselves in the same boat as the Grand Wizard and his Genii. The "Cyclops" of each den appears to have been a tight-lipped free-wheeler who did as he pleased and let his superiors in the KKK learn about it in the newspapers, if ever.

In January 1869, General Forrest ordered the disbanding and end of the Invisible Empire. He resigned from its leadership. There appears to have been lip-service obedience to his order by all dens and actual obedience by some. How many opted for knighthood and a castle with the White Camellia or joined hands with the "Pale Faces," "Men of Justice," "Order of the White Rose," and "Constitutional Guards," is anyone's guess.

Most of the Carpetbag governors and their senators in Washington argued they could stamp out these conspiracies if Congress would restore to their states authority for organizing volunteer militia companies, a right that had been revoked because the Ten Percent Governments had abused it. Congress gave the authority on March 2, 1869. Some governors did not use it; most of them did. In response, the secret and night-riding fraternities really went into high gear. They now felt compelled not only to intimidate the Republican voters, white and black, away from the polls, but also to overawe the armed and drilling black National Guardsmen. Warnings to disappear, disappearances, mysterious deaths, bodies hanging in public places, floggings, ambushing by day as well as night, and occasional crossroads battles between opponents on collision courses finally escalated into opposing forces of battalions in battle array. This usually happened after an election when both candidates were "elected." For a period, Louisiana had three "governors," each with a little private army.

There were battle array showdowns in Jackson, Mississippi, and Little Rock, Arkansas. Both whites and blacks disdained secrecy or lodge disguises. In each case, one candidate backed down to avoid open bloodshed. Each then accelerated the smaller night depredations. In New Orleans the battle was joined, with 27 killed and 105 wounded treated in hospitals. The number treated in homes is unknown.

The Force Act of April 20, 1871, commonly called the Anti-Ku Klux Law, provided heavy penalties in federal courts, allowed suspensions of Habeas Corpus, and permitted summary arrests, both military and by federal marshals and their deputies. It resulted in 5,000 arrests and over 1,250 convictions, largely in South Carolina, but it was utterly ineffective. The previous year a law had put the election of all federal officers under complete control of federal supervisors; this was an important factor in the election of a Republican president in 1876. A byproduct of the Anti-Ku Klux Law was the creation of a congressional committee to investigate and report. The resulting thirteen volumes of testimony, with frequent exhibits, are of great value to historians. The accumulated evidence harshly indicts both sides.

A publicity body blow that jolted and really hurt the Carpetbag regimes came from a most unexpected direction. James S. Pike was a rock-ribbed, Whig-Abolitionist editor in Calais, Maine, until his pungent and honest pen put him in big-time journalism with Horace Greeley's *New York Tribune*. He visited the South in 1873 to write an early example of instant history. His *Prostrate State: South Carolina under Negro Government* shocked a vast public and continues to shock those who search libraries for a copy. It has a bit of the weakness often found in the writings of an unhappily disillusioned idealist. Nevertheless, it is honest, forthright reporting based upon all resources then available, including interviews and first-hand observations. What he saw was indeed scandalous. Subsequent scholarly research has sustained his indignation.

Pike's book joined other exposés that tarnished the Republican control of Congress: the Credit Mobilier scandal; the Senatorial "Mulligan Letters"; "Boss" Tweed's ring in New York. By 1876, all but three of the ex-Confederate states had been restored to the Union. Their conservative senators and representatives were seated in Washington, the citizenship abridgements of nearly all ex-Confederates had been removed, a decade of young voters had come of age, and winds of change were blowing across the nation that election year. Both candidates had reform records.

On the popular vote, Tilden, a Democrat, received 50.94 percent; Hayes, 47.95; splinter candidates, 1.11 percent. The electoral vote was something else. Tilden had 184, only one short of a majority. The decision went to the House of Representatives. With each major candidate getting nineteen challenged electoral votes from four states, the cliff-hanging decision went right up to March 1877. The incredible happened: Hayes received all nineteen of his challenged votes and was inaugurated.

Eighteen of the disputed votes (the other vote clearly belonged to Hayes) were from South Carolina, Louisiana, and Florida. They were still being reconstructed by officials kept in office by bayonets. Southern Democrats in Congress found themselves in a balance-of-power position. Rightly considering Hayes the more sincere and more honorable man, they joined Northern Republicans to dump the North's Democratic candidate. Opposition charges that Hayes had stolen the election vanished when decoded telegrams revealed that Tilden's nephew and other Democratic managers had been trying to buy at least two of South Carolina's Republican electors.

But Hayes had sensed the winds of change long before the election. He was completely out of sympathy with the radical and revolutionary liquidation of Civil War problems. He withdrew military support from the three remaining carpetbag governments, whose electors had put him in office.

In the twelve years of unconventional warfare, the ex-Confederates had actually regained most of the statehood rights lost under the revolutionary "conquered province" theory. State and federal courts sustained their position. The coercive amendments, however, remained for the ultimate revolution that so few recognized until six decades later. Moreover, the underground organizations of both sides vanished as quickly as they had mushroomed. Through the decades that followed, the descendants of the freedmen have progressed, albeit laggingly, in culture, understanding, education, and civic responsibility, and American conservatives have accepted, without further civil warfare, revolutionary judicial opinions inherent in the Civil War amendments. However, many such opinions abridging states' rights have had nothing to do with racial problems.

For reasons other than peace in the South, 1877 was a significant year. The Great Railroad Strike of that summer rudely introduced America to a new kind of strife. More than thirty thousand National Guardsmen and Regulars were needed to contain it. It was more economic than social and more industrial than civil. It took the mobs away from the county court houses and state capitols to create tumult in the mines, the shops, and at factory gates. For such national phenomena, "industrial warfare" seems to be the most widely accepted term.

The Civil War technology was a great stimulus to ocean-going steamers. East-West passages after 1870 were scheduled within eight days instead of the uncertain weeks or months of bucking the westerlies in the old square-riggers. Continental Europe's "armies of labor" were pouring into America—ten million between 1870 and 1900. Within those three decades the population of the United States jumped from 38,500,000 to 76,000,000. Whether times were good or bad, jobs were hard to find and too often were merely seasonal. Wages fluctuated downward as often as upward. Seldom could they be considered affluent.

These burgeoning facts reminded all that there were grave problems in human affairs other than in the erstwhile Confederate States. It was the beginning of a seeding time of ideas for economic betterment, but the swelling armies of European labor were bringing their own philosophic seed with them. The newcomers quickly identified problems to discuss in an ideological context. Some earlier arrivals, such as the European refugees from the revolutions of 1848, were prepared to lead the discussions. The Anglo-American legacies of civil strife were being prepared for a ferment with a difference.

By way of blending the old legacies into those that followed, a few observations are in order. At the city hall and county courthouse levels the heritage was, and continues to be, highly permissive of local disorders that are well geared to or sublimated by an understandable idealism or emotional thrust. But once a mob and its leaders appeared to be rocking the boat merely for the fun of it, or indulging in the doctrine of propaganda through violent deeds, the city halls and lower courts could strike back with astounding rigidity. The stiff reactions normally met with the warm approval of the urban populations that spawned the riots.

Chicago's Haymarket Affair, 1886, came during the blending era. Four Anarchists, including two editors, were hanged. The bomb-maker received the same sentence but cheated the gallows with a death-cell suicide. Three others received long prison sentences. Five men from among a night-shrouded mob of over a thousand could not have thrown the single bomb that killed seven and wounded a known sixty. Judge John P. Altgeld, a political enemy of the trial judge, became governor a few years later and pardoned the three prisoners in language but little short of a charge of legal murder by the trial judge. Altgeld's reward was political oblivion; the trial judge moved upward to the state supreme court. In 1886, the masses of voters in the city, state, and nation, rightly or wrongly, were with the trial judge.

Bombings, incendiary and explosive, and street killing of policemen or elected officials are unacceptable practices in urban civil warfare. Nothing will destroy a sublimated ideology or movement more readily. "Propaganda of the deed" is recognized in America as a discredited European importation. There is a built-in certainty of evolutionary, gradual, corrective changes in American governmental processes that confuse, confound, and baffle the European type of revolutionists. They are much better students of French history than of American.

The United States government has never had to cope with but one powerful, home-grown revolutionary ideology and movement patterned after the all-out French style of going-for-broke. The Abolitionists had the skill, the education, the provocative and persuasive ability, and the affluence in time and money to play the game. They would win or destroy the Union. By 1856 they were growing older, their time was running out. History correctly records, however, that they won the game; by April 1865, the Abolition amendments to the Constitution were guaranteed. The Abolitionists joined in hosannas for having helped to save the Union. But the Abolition victory had not been a game of revolutionary muscle, French style. As with any game, it was a matter of skill.

The best of players, however, often fail to collect their bets. Not an

Abolitionist of 1856 lived to see the American blacks move into the full citizenship they had a right to expect in the bright dawn of April 1865. Most Abolitionists died unhappy over their stringhalted cause. America's built-in gradualism for corrective changes had cheated them. But most real revolutionists of all countries die with a feeling of being robbed of something by somebody. It is a characteristic of the game.

III

ARMED FORCES IN PEACETIME, CIVIC ACTION, CIVIL WAR, AND REVOLUTION

WHEN A CIVIL WAR occurs it means that the government has failed in its management of crucial problems, that a major conservative segment of the population has become disaffected, and that in most cases a significant part of the army is mentally ready to desert. If civil war breaks out, it implies that a critical point of popular dissatisfaction has been reached and that internal peacekeeping has failed.

Historically, peacekeeping in Britain was usually the job of the sheriff or the local landlord. The latter was usually a justice of the peace. He called out the militia when normal means failed. Under the Stuarts, however, the worthy country and city gentlemen who kept the peace became at odds with the royal government, and a full-fledged civil war broke out. Even after its end, the continued presence of strong religious feelings, drunken rioting, and political furor led in 1715 to the passage of the Riot Act. This gave the local magistrate the power to disperse a duly-warned mob by force, and force since 1660 had come to mean a detachment of the regular army. This situation persisted until the 1820s, when the army, after the so-called Peterloo Massacre, once more began to be looked down upon and to be not only suspect as a means of keeping order but also detested by the new urban working classes. The position was eased by the

The author is grateful to his colleagues at Kansas State University, Eugene Friedmann in Sociology, Alden Williams in Political Science, and George Kren in History, for their suggestions.

50

creation of a police force, a logical outcome of the medieval watchman system. While Anglo-Saxon countries have generally followed the tactic of calling out troops only when civil authorities have been unable to handle a situation, elsewhere the patterns have been a little different and solutions somewhat slower in appearing. In France, Germany, Italy, Spain, and other countries the gendarmerie arose as a semimilitary force, while in certain autocracies, notably Austria-Hungary and Russia, the secret police and sometimes also the clergy were employed to keep people in line; but when they did get out of control, the army was employed. Such actions, including the turning back of the bonus-marchers in Washington in 1933, were regarded as normal and proper. Nor did insurgency succeed while the army remained loyal to the state.

Edmund Burke, reflecting in 1790 on the then-nascent French Revolution, pointed out that it would inevitably destroy every authority but the army. Significantly, he did not mention the navy, even though he was an Englishman, because in internal affairs the army is the service most directly involved. Even in modern times, neither the navy nor the air force is in a position to cope with internal conflicts. The very nature of peace-keeping involves keeping one group from assaulting another. Because these groups are rarely well armed, this function calls for men on the spot. Moreover, it usually calls for numbers of men either lightly armed or not armed at all. The force required is more often of a psychological nature in which uniforms symbolize authority and power. The defence of authority can be accomplished by far smaller numbers, provided they are both legal and potentially lethal, than can the assault upon it, especially if the attack is by an ill-organized mob. In the twentieth century, however, the problem has been made considerably more difficult by the rise of paramilitary organizations trained in the use of both physical and psychological brutality and often equipped with cheap war-surplus or stolen weapons. The emergence of these organized forces has, however, often been possible only with the tacit, if not the official, acquiescence of the authorities, or at least of the army.

Military Involvement in Politics

To understand why the military become involved in politics, certain related questions should first be considered. Firstly, what conditions make a political system unstable or fix unsteadiness? Secondly, are institutional mechanisms adequate for anticipating the problems of transition from peace to war and back again? Is it more difficult to demobilize than to mobilize? Thirdly, how much is official action normally affected by an individual's beliefs as to the consequences to his career of certain decisions? And fourthly, can we distinguish between the causes of civil wars and those of revolutions?

The stability or instability of a state depends to a large extent on whether or not the government knows its mind, has sufficient force available, and is willing to use it to stand behind the laws and to enforce them, and on whether or not rebellious-minded people regard retribution as certain or are willing to gamble on its not being effective. While sound administration calls for the intelligent anticipation of trouble, wise governors are prepared to overpower hostile forces within as well as without the state. But wise governors must also be aware that a generally repressive or backward regime, corrupt, despotic, and inefficient, invites trouble and national instability. Conversely, an unstable situation can be made secure by a careful combination of the imposition of authority and intelligent reforms which deflate the opposition, even by stealing its ideas. At the same time, such action must placate conservatives who fear a threat to their positions, though their own actions may have created the hazard. If a weak leader with ignorant or unscrupulous and unfeeling advisers can create instability, a strong leader, unafraid of naked power and aided by realistic and sensible aids, can both restore and improve the situation, thus preventing civil war.

There is some reason to believe that immediately after a war, a country experiences a period of instability such as does not exist during mobilization. The reasons for this are clear. Mobilization is generally something for which military and civilian staffs have made contingent plans. Because it is aimed against an exterior threat, internal quarrels are usually submerged in the face of the need to man the barriers against a common danger. At the same time much is done to develop a belief in victory to create military élan. Demobilization, however, usually presents problems far less conspicuous, less anticipated, and perhaps clouded by the oppression of defeat. A short war may not involve enough men to disrupt the economy at the end of the war by flooding the labor market with demobilized men seeking jobs. A major war, however, not only disrupts the labor market by refilling industrial places with a second generation of workers, but is apt to fill the ranks of the armed services with young men who have never held jobs. If these men are demobilized without an economic or educational plan to absorb them into industry or agriculture, a ready-made force of able and destructive malcontents is created. Moreover, demobilization is not only a period of uncertainty and rumors but one in which the tight camaraderie of the services falls apart. Men know neither their units nor their officers as rapid transformations of the services take place. Failure to handle both the physical and the politico-psychological sides of demobilization can be dangerous to the stability of the state.

After a civil war, there is a double demobilization problem, for even the loyal veterans are usually supported inadequately, if at all. As for the rebels, the defeated area will have been the more devastated, and will lack capital and the means to employ the newly available but psychologically shocked manpower. This is not always so, of course. If the area is treated as Germany was after World War II, the purge of defeat may prove to be a blessing in disguise, accelerating modernization and thus healing the sore, as in West Germany in the 1950s and 1960s. The result of defeat is more likely, however, to be similar to the plight of the South after the American Civil War. Defeat, moreover, usually means a reexamination of loyalties. It can result in leaderlessness, as in the case of the German officer corps after the flight of the kaiser in 1918.

The problem of demobilization in a defeated state is further complicated by the distraction, if not collapse, of the government by resentment against it for losing the war, and by a mass exodus from the services of men who may quickly become the willing tools of those preaching against the regime. The new government may be, as in Germany in 1919, faced not only with the distractions of peacemaking and of learning how to govern, but also with the stigma that it has betrayed the country. World War I in particular created among many a distrust of politicians; other wars can do likewise.

There is also the question of individuals' perceptions of the consequences of their actions. On the road to war some harmony between the military and political groups is likely to be achieved. Politicians who have for years refused to heed the pleas of their military advisers for preparedness may in the imminence of war be clamoring for action. (Contrarily, politicians such as Hitler may on occasion be strategically right in advocating attack before their military advisers believe the national forces are prepared for it.) The immediate prewar months are the time for action and a chance to enhance a military career by attracting the notice of politicians. After a war, however, the situation is likely to be just the opposite. Whether the war has been won or lost, the politician wishes to look out for his own career, and that is best done by economizing, relegating the services to a minor role, and emphasizing whatever the public wants in the way of the good old days and a better life. On the whole, by the time peace comes, the soldier's brief moment of glory or opportunity is past, while the politician's may be just beginning. Yet it can also be noted that politicians who have run wars may not survive in peace, especially in a democracy. Thus they, too, may be put out to pasture, and unless they are, like Winston Churchill, strong opportunists or national heroes, they may never make a comeback. Sometimes they remain as leaders of dissident minorities, but rarely have they been successful.

A period of national uncertainty such as existed in the United States in 1788, 1828, 1840, 1848, 1868, 1888, and 1952, may well see the emergence of a father figure known to political scientists as "a man on horseback." The rise of the military-leader-turned-political-chief is not infrequent and takes place when the public feels uncertain, is tired of disorder or afraid, or when the political parties lack an appealing ideology. A general is accepted because as a shining military hero he usually lacks political taint and appears to offer prestige and security once again. De Gaulle in France is a modern example, as was Eisenhower in the U.S., Ojukwu in Biafra, and Gowon in Nigeria. In new nations the officer assumes power because, among the educated people in the state, he has experience in administration, supply, and the maintenance of national security. Among the visible alternatives, all too commonly, are men trained in law who have spent their lives fighting the old regime and thwarting its system and thus are antiadministration, and are too immersed in principles and precedents to be practical. Moreover, the officer has, in all likelihood, inherited standards of incorruptibility from the former colonial administration as opposed to the graft which postcolonial chaos brings.

A thesis or wave theory (it has been called Higham's Law) can be developed that the typical pattern for armed forces begins in a long period of peacetime equilibrium, when all is settled and routine, when the emphasis is upon punctiliousness, red tape, and inescapable economies. It is a period in which the slightest *faux pas*—military, political, or social— may well blight a career. Thus it is a period in which dullness and stability, routine and training, the letter rather than the spirit of discipline dominate. The oscillating international, political, or military situation may call forth a change short of war which can be characterized as rearmamental instability. In this period of uncertainty, when resupply, reinforcement, and reorientation are all in flux, uncertainties creep in and careers may be rapidly accelerated, especially if the services are expanded with or without conscription. This phase may last well into the war, presuming here that conflict follows, though how quickly it is transformed into wartime equilibrium depends upon the tempo of the war and the casualty rates. Once the war takes a settled course, a good deal of stability returns to the services and the career patterns become reasonably discernible. The fourth stage is demobilizational instability. Here, as opposed to the uncertainties of expansion during rearmament, there are the far worse fears of a shrinking service, reductions in rank, and lack of clear guidance as to the future size and budget for the service, future enemies, and the planning necessary to meet the threat they offer. While nations normally have mobilization plans, demobilization plans are often hastily made and sometimes inadequate. In a defeated country or area, such planning is faced with great reluctance if at all, and then rather hopelessly. Here military and political views may well be miles apart. Civil war is more likely to occur during demobilization or peacetime than during war.

The thesis stated above assumes a cyclical system with a recurring pattern of wars. However, more and more the cycle is, in many countries, being broken by a lack of wars and attenuated periods of peace and military stagnation. Increasingly, as in much of the nineteenth century, rather than eventually preparing for a major conflict, the services are involved at the most in a small series of peacekeeping actions. It is true that they may have to maintain a major striking force, but it may never be used. Increasingly, their visible functions may become ceremonial, though still important symbolically. More serious, however, is the problem in countries unlikely to face a major war again. This might be labelled a fading peacetime equilibrium. The problem of the armed forces is the problem faced by all organizations when their primary purpose has been fulfilled—how to justify their existence. One answer may be that as a military career ceases to have anything but a monetary value, normal redundancy may take care of the problem until the national force, regular or cadre, vanishes into either an internal police or a supranational constabulary, such as has been proposed for the United Nations.

Armies in new states face also the problems of tribal loyalties, languages, and lineages. Tribal rebellions may become civil wars. Gifts and graft may become the normal way of doing business. This leads to cynicism and the corruption of both the state and discipline within the armed services and, if coupled with severe casualties and lack of military success, to defeatism. The syndrome may be augmented by the intervention of troops from more advanced nations, who increase the cost of living by their higher pay and greater spending power as well as by the value of their stealable equipment. Under such conditions, a black market usually flourishes. Compounding scarcity with items of high resale value, it encourages theft and discourages thrift and honesty. More than this, well-trained and disciplined outsiders may look with scorn upon the less victorious or noisy efforts of their allies and gradually usurp the fighting, thus crippling the pride and *esprit de corps* of the local army. And in a civil war, confidence and ability are psychologically most important in the popularity battle.

The army is, as noted earlier, the force most generally involved in domestic disturbances. It is also the service most likely to become entangled in politics. There are many reasons for this. The army's officers are basically patriotic and loyal, though at times myopically selfish. As previously noted, however, an army not in combat has to justify its existence, if only artificially. Loyalty to country becomes the safest focus, and, as with any product, the salesmen eventually come to believe in it.

It is essential for a military man in any service to feel that he is the defender of the state and its leader and to love its symbols and all they represent. They may stand more for a social order, representing the good old days, than for anything else as far as he is concerned. The closer he gets to retirement the stronger his convictions become. And the higher his rank, the more likely he is to attempt to command that faith and the more righteous he feels about it. At the same time, the system tends to enforce a tremendous loyalty, an *esprit de corps*, to the particular service to which he belongs. In addition, because a fighting man must believe that he will win, an officer also expects that the country or system behind him will be loyal to the utmost degree. Because most officers have in the past come from agrarian families, a certain political distrust of urbane politicians and urban workers complicates their thought patterns. Their view of these matters has often been simplistic: those who do not think and act as they do are unreliable and probably disloyal. This sometimes aligns them with the extreme Right. Occasionally, as in a recent American case, it means that their ideas and those of some millionaires are closely aligned in support of their own concept of the country. Their desire for a strong national base for military operations may cause them to intervene in domestic politics so as to insure that the army can be the protector of the state, even to the extent of denying usurpations from the Right as well as the Left. This also means that they may take progressive action, as in modern Turkey, to protect the country from politicians' neglect of military-industrial preparedness. And in a sense, in this they may be innovative rather than counterrevolutionary. The recent case in Greece, in which the army misjudged the young king, is of considerable interest because here the monachy provided an authority which could not easily be overthrown without bringing on a serious challenge to the idea that the army's action was patriotic. It may even be argued that a monarch who is also the commander-in-chief serves a most useful purpose as a stabilizing influence, whereas an elected president is always tainted by belonging to a party and is politically ephemeral in tenure. Interestingly, despite claims that the 1968 Greek vote was rigged, the results indicated that the "silent majority" preferred military management with stability and freedom from corruption. It is also worth noting that nearly a quarter of the world's governments in the 1960s were military.

This raises a question: Is the army as politically important in countries like the United States or Britain, where the political parties do not quarrel interminably, as it is in Spain, France, and Latin America, where the factions are always in flux except when a dictator, often with military backing, takes over?

The military establishment is based on order and discipline, not simply because of the anonymity that uniforms create, but because of the nature of the human material employed and the necessity of giving clear orders, simple to obey. Thus the military mind is repelled by disorder and by the factionalism of politics, and longs to set national affairs straight. Discipline is clear and impartial; chaos is militarily intolerable. Order is, moreover, a shield against the unpleasant, making even war tolerable. Thus as governors military men suffer because they are acting as neither professional ministers of state nor professional soldiers. So they fall between two stools, being lost politically, professionally, and socially.

The army also gets into politics by reason of some of its functions. At times it becomes involved in disaster relief, public health projects, educational programs, and public works—all involving grassroots politics. In the less stable countries the army is also involved in protecting regimes and in overturning them when it feels they are no longer patriotic or pertinent, so that it can function as it feels it should.

The subtle influence of wives in modern armies, in which there is an increasing proportion of married officers, has yet to be determined. It can be expected to exist, as it does in ordinary civilian life. It is not unreasonable to assume that, especially in peacetime, wives are status-conscious, ambitious for their husbands, and powerful. Crane Brinton's studies of revolutions have shown that certain queens played a disastrous role in their husbands' troubles. And there is an abundance of business literature on wives. So we cannot deny the same influence to service wives with their husbands' promotions and their own security on their minds.

Not all of these points would be potentially dangerous if armies were not also afflicted with problems caused by long periods without wars. During an extended peace, an army is apt to become bored, creates artificial standards of conduct or honor, and engages in simulation. In the protracted absence of an object, training frequently becomes unrealistic and meaningless. To maintain a public image, an army puts on drill displays which become an end in themselves. Since drilling can best be handled by NCOs, the officers have more and more time on their hands for sports, social life, and politics. In the peacetime campaign for budgetary survival, military lobbying is intensified and there is an increased awareness of menaces from abroad. If service intrigues are well controlled by various fraternal or familial arrangements, then scope exists for dabbling either subtly or openly in national affairs. In well developed constitutional democracies the chances of a *Seven Days in May* situation are slight. In less developed countries, where the military does considerably more than the U.S. Army Corps of Engineers, often in fact playing a constabulary role, the need for political engagement is present, if seen only as a patriotic role. The power elite tends to create for itself something of a feudal system, which the location of army bases may well enhance. In the more backward or autocratic countries the officer corps, often drawn from the aristocracy, rather naturally and paternalistically regards the peons and privates as a labor force to be ruled, while distrusting the city masses as anarchic and their leaders as schemers. The idea of military control over the state thus comes fairly readily.

Reasons for the Inaction of the Other Armed Forces

If these things are true of armies, they are far less a problem in navies and air forces. Naval forces are on a healthier routine, struggling with the sea rather than standing tedious guard duties in remote areas. Naval bases are usually not far removed from major cities, while naval units are more self-contained and have a tighter discipline. But more importantly, naval personnel are out of their element ashore and lack the requisite arms, notably trucks and tanks but also small arms, with which to undertake operations, let alone the training for work ashore. Naval officers tend to sail rather than hunt, race horses, or play polo; they have fewer social opportunities and are less likely because of their duties to be able to keep up with intrigues ashore. Thus a navy is often for just these reasons the silent service.

Many of these same points apply to an air force, which in addition tends to lack tradition, maturity, and power. Air force officers, especially in poorly maintained forces, may reach high rank at a junior age but without necessarily commanding the respect of their equals in the older services or in civilian life. But much more important is the fact that an air force is even less equipped than a navy for ground operations, especially in populous areas. In relative immunity to mobs and small arms (though not artillery), naval vessels can exert a limited threat by merely anchoring off a key location. But this is not true of airplanes; to be a visible threat they must stay airborne. They are vulnerable, too, for their bases are easily overrun by ground forces. True, occasionally an air force general, such as Barrientos in Bolivia, manages to become president, but that is rare.

Marines are a special case. They are usually trained for landing parties and amphibious assault, and their brief participation in these has overshadowed their more normal peacetime activities. Used afloat as shipboard police, they have also long been employed diplomatically for temporary occupations and peacekeeping duties. There is a tradition that the use of marines is unlikely to provoke hostilities, whereas the landing of soldiers constitutes invasion, an openly hostile act. Because of their special role, marines are accustomed to working with civilians. However, in most countries the force is so small that it cannot undertake major political action, even though it sometimes has an elite role in guarding the government.

Problems Involved in Civic Action or Civil War

All of the factors discussed above provide background for an appreciation of the problems involved in civic action or civil war. Force, when used against the government, may be reactionary, even when it appears to be revolutionary. It is an historical truism that revolutions do not succeed unless the army is either won over or chooses not to act. Usually the army is not committed against the government unless it believes that the politicians are betraying the trust imposed in them and are ruining or endangering the country. Whether the army is placed in control or seizes power, it is not always happy in that position and, at least in the democratic countries, is usually most anxious to hand back authority to the politicians as soon as it judges the situation safe enough to do so.

Generals and colonels, normally contented professionals, do not like to be openly political; they prefer that the basic orders be given by someone else. It might perhaps be argued that staff colonels become engaged in revolutions more often than generals because, not yet at the top, they have more to gain. A revolution or a *coup d'etat* is, in countries passing through long periods of peace, the quickest way in which they can place themselves in high command. When, however, they do cross the Rubicon, they frequently find that power is not so easy to grasp or to hold as they had thought. Even civic action presents many problems.

In any country the question may arise: When shall armed forces be called in to handle civil disturbances? This is a crucial question both for statesmen and for the military man on the critical spot. In all likelihood, the answer will depend upon a variety of circumstances: the location of trouble, the state of the police and the courts, the forces to be opposed, and the troops available. It may depend upon whether or not the civil authority has already been defied or even beaten, upon whether the government's intent is to placate the insurgents, and upon the nervousness or fatalism of the authorities. It may be governed by the state of communications, both for instructions and for reinforcements. It is controlled in part by the ability of the government to predict what will happen under all combinations of circumstances and may be complicated by hesitation by civil authorities to call for aid because of their fear of loss of face and their reluctance to use the army to solve a civil problem.

In some countries the solution for the civil governor is made easier by the existence of a militia, in the U.S. by the presence of the National Guard. Generally, reluctance to call out the militia has been due not to fear of its loyalty so much as to its general unpreparedness and its associated unreliability.

Once the civil authorities have decided that military aid must be sought, still other problems arise or remain. The mere presence of troops may be sufficient to quiet the populace, but if that is not enough, then the question of control arises. Military power is generally not so constituted that it can work within normal civil limits. If the courts are open and functioning, martial law cannot be employed, nor can troops be given free rein. Thus the critical question in the employment of troops may be one of legal consequences rather than the physical violence that is likely to result. Once control is handed over to the troop commander, martial power prevails—preferably, from the army standpoint, under conditions of martial law. The suspension of legal rights is an admission that civil government has been temporarily withdrawn, if indeed it has not altogether broken down.

From the military's point of view, action can only be effective if justice can be summary. Moreover, the military tend to associate lawyers with politicians, if not with troublemakers. In emergent countries lawyers often spearhead the new political movements and are thus automatically unpopular with the conservative classes from which the officer group normally springs.

It is, however, a mistake to assume that the ordinary, politically unambitious officer wants to take over civil powers. On the whole, dealing with civilians is the last thing he wants, for he knows he may be assaulted by the press and made the thankless political scapegoat for any casualties which occur, thus ruining his career after order and the civil government have been restored.

After World War I the rise of radical ideologies helped make the army and the officer class suspect in any case. The war was demoralizing and destroyed much of the social adhesive that had made the caste system work, just at a time when the Socialists and the new democratization in Europe were providing an alternative approach to control of the problems of industrialization and urbanization. Thus, the soldier might win at the barricades and lose at the polls.

There are some very real practical problems involved in handling crowds, looters, and partisans. The military, like the police, are easily identifiable because of their uniforms; civilian activists can attack and disappear. This inhibits the use of firearms by soldiers, for they do not enjoy the same legal protection as do police, yet their training is in killing and not in passive control. Guerrillas always have the advantage in this respect, as they demonstrated in Ireland in 1916 and 1921 and more recently in Vietnam. For the military, the problem is and remains how to tell the rebel from the civilian and how to persuade the populace not to shelter or support guerrillas. The whole problem is vastly more complex where the soldiers do not know either the local language or local customs.

An even more practical point, depending upon whether or not a riotous crowd is openly armed, if only with poles, is with what weapons to equip the troops. Rifles and bayonets may draw blood. An inexperienced or nervous soldier can start general firing. Moreover, a rifle wrested from a soldier is a piece of state property whose loss must be investigated even if recovery is effected. In India the British found that against natives armed with ironshod lathis or poles, a pickax handle was a better guarantor of peace. In New York the police have found a backing horse effective. Heavier weapons than light firearms may be necessary against barricaded rebels. But most artillerymen or tank specialists have not been trained for such action, and in any case the legal burdens of damaging property act as a restraint against their effective use. Thus civil actions are not the same legally as street fighting against a declared enemy. Unless troops are well equipped with walkie-talkies, it may be very difficult for the commander to exercise the proper calm, decisive control of all his units that is particularly desirable when operating within his own country.

In the 1970 tragedy at Kent State University in Ohio, the confrontation of National Guardsmen and students was almost inevitable, but the tragic results of that conflict were not. Had the troops been armed with pickax handles, the results might have been quite different.

The Army and Reform

The action taken after the troops have been successful in restoring peace will depend upon the nature of the insurrection and the impact of external affairs upon the general state of the country. Former colonial traditions may hold sway, or the new government may be from the army itself, the latter especially likely when continual unrest appears coupled with a loss of national prestige. The middle class, anxious as ever about its status and property, may support the army or its figurehead, as in Germany in 1933, so as to reestablish stability. Real revolutions, as opposed to the armed *coups d'etat* so common in such chronically unstable areas as South America, involve political, economic, social, and ideological change and have such widespread results that the army cannot help but be affected. The aristocrats in the army command may make it the guardian of stability, but the middle class in its artillery and engineers keep it in touch with progress. In recent years many army officers have had training and service abroad, and thus have become aware of imperfections and needs for reform in their own country, particularly if they feel the country is threatened by outside forces. Close to the land and to industry, they know how change should be achieved and why modernization is essential for military strength. Thus aware, they tend to be angered by the inability of self-seeking, legal-minded political leaders to administer a program. Ultimately frustrated, they are led to seize power in an attempt to wage war on backwardness with efficiency, coupling disciplined employment of the masses with land reform. They realize that progress in their sort of country can come only from an authoritarianism which harnesses the resources available. Thus, if an army seizes power, it is likely to do so for what its officers honestly believe are patriotic reasons. The result may not be so simple as they thought. The public expects victory from soldiers, but only achievements from politicians. Unfortunately for themselves, officers are less able publicists than are politicians, and their task of making the army popular is far from easy, especially when achievements—as for example, a checking of monetary inflation—take time. Though less technically traditional, the navy and the air force lack the manpower to undertake change in the hinterland.

In many areas of the world today violence remains a national rather than a personal matter. Border clashes, civil wars, tribal uprisings in Southeast Asia, Africa, and Latin America make it obvious that armies in these areas are unlikely to fade away for many years. The civil war in Nigeria destroyed all authority but that of the army and left General Gowon with awesome questions to answer. Will the army give up power in due course?

Conclusions

In concluding, it is necessary to reemphasize that armies are usually far from happy to be thrust into civil war, revolution, or even civic action. All too often such situations prove to be instances of having a bear by the tail; if the army kills or cages the brute, societies for the prevention of cruelty to animals will condemn the action. If, however, it lets him go, he may turn and tear both the army and the country to pieces. The commander on the spot has to act on what he knows at the time and what he believes will happen. He would rather be told what to do by a well-informed government. If the government fails in its duty, however, he may seize power to preserve the state in which he believes.

The common myth that the use of troops in civic actions is a new phenomenon brought to the fore by totalitarian states of the twentieth century will not hold historical water. Even in democratic countries like the United States there is a long history, if not a tradition, going back at least to the Whiskey Rebellion of 1794, of using military force to maintain internal peace and even the Union. Given this, then, we need to scrutinize the traditions, training, equipment, and experience of troops used in these circumstances, at the same time seeking a further understanding of their roles and problems in peacetime and of the motives that may lead their officers to employ them in revolutionary action. Peacekeeping has many facets.

The trouble with all generalizations is that there are exceptions to them. This has been a chapter of generalizations, but they may at least awaken thought and stimulate the examination of other occasions to see it theoretical patterns hold true. The stimulation of such thought is satisfaction enough.

IV

THE LATIN AMERICAN LEGACY
The Background for Civil War

JAMES C. CAREY

NOT COUNTING the four emerging ones, Latin America is composed of twenty nations, some of which are as different from one another as France is from Germany or Switzerland from Portugal. Though there are numerous common currents from the Spanish legacy, and some from the French and Portuguese, one cannot speak of either *a* legacy or *a* background except in a very general manner.

Though Latin America is notorious for its turmoil and military governments, these phenomena have been given little research. Apart from the works of Edwin Lieuwen, John J. Johnson, and a few others in the United States and Britain, the number of studies available in English is miniscule compared to those on revolution and civil disturbances elsewhere. Part of the explanation lies in the simple fact that publishing on these matters could be very dangerous. The possibility of direct retaliation of the military upon the writer, or reprisals against his family, is not something to be treated lightly. One of Peru's best-known historians told this writer of difficulties in this respect. In various ways the military governments South of the Border have been able to shield themselves from the careful critical examination which serious scholars would have wished. It appears also that until recently *Latino* students have not relished the drudgery or have lacked the necessary funds for collecting and assembling the data involved in careful research.

It is also well to make a distinction between the northern and southern parts of this hemisphere. The *Anglo* armed forces, unlike the *Latino*, have not aggressively sought political responsibility. Historically, Latin

American dictators have been military men, and most civilian dictators of the early national period appropriated some military title for their personal use. (The term "militarism" is loosely used in Latin America. The lack of sound research is one of the explanations for the confusion which arose from the practice of lumping many, if not all, forms of violence under this term.) In March 1955 (a high point of recent decades in numbers of military presidents), thirteen of the twenty principal republics were ruled by men from the armed forces. As of this writing (1971) almost half of the Latin American nations have military men as chiefs of state.

How do background conditions help explain the evolution of *Latino* military influence? Spanish heritage and colonial patterns tended to elevate the higher clergy and military leaders into power centers above society. A third power center, the civilian landlords, although possessing great prestige, did not enjoy such legal benefits. Military officials, like the clerics, basked in special privileges called *fueros*, with courts independent of the civil courts. The favored legal tradition extended back into early Spain, when kings depended upon clerics and military officials to win back the land from the Moors. Their campaigns, often fanatical and referred to as part of the *Reconquista*, were scattered across seven centuries. This left an inheritance of confused political-military jurisdictions, with an ensuing institutional interdependence of the two. The discovery, exploration, and settlement of vast and geographically different expanses of the New World further strengthened the military. Spanish and Portuguese transference of feudal and aristocratic patterns to the New World was greater than was *Anglo* transference in this respect. Chronology helps explain this—Iberians were active in exploring and colonizing almost a century before the English were.

Generally speaking, Latin America and Spain have experienced long confused periods of quasimilitary preparedness followed by ill-defined stages of demobilizational instability. Martial law, quasimartial law, or some type of protracted "state of siege" has often persisted. From the beginning, civilian and military have not been as neatly divided as they have been North of the Border. The persistence of internal confusion also explains why the *Latino* military have often been involved in matters normally reserved to the civil powers in much of the Western world. Often this latter condition has prevailed because an adequate regular police force was lacking.

The throes of establishing nationhood added to the chaos. The wars of independence (1810–25), fought to bring separation from Europe, were longer and bloodier than that waged by the thirteen British colonies in North America. The many-faceted independence movement (or movements) of Latin America was weakened by civil wars within, as for example in Mexico, Peru, Argentina, and Chile. Mexico's surge for independence contained two civil wars—Peninsular versus creole and white versus Indian. Then, due to various complicated factors which included the lack of homogeneity in the *Latino* national societies, the wars of independence did not secure many of the basic social changes which were gained by the *Anglos* in the American Revolution. Internal social reforms were so delayed that for over a century segments of Latin America struggled to achieve what the *Anglo* had held prior to 1776 or possibly what he had gained between 1776 and 1800. For instance, the question of "who should rule at home" (as well as that of "home rule") was not answered in Mexico until after 1910, in spite of various bloody nineteenth-century attempts. Using liberty of the individual as a standard, the North American *Anglo* was free before independence, while the *Latino* was not free even after independence. Although *Latino* wars of independence were costly and left bitter factionalism, they turned out to be nearly sterile with respect to basic reform.

Other philosophical differences between *Anglos* and *Latinos* are found imbedded in history. Society in Anglo America tended to develop a more positive attitude toward the state, while in Latin America the citizen viewed the state with wariness if not outright suspicion. Centuries of history lie behind these distinctions of the "good" state and the "questionable" or "bad" state. (In a real sense, England and the United States have concentrated their greater internal problems into one short civil war apiece.) The *Latino* early faced something which never seriously confronted the *Anglo*—a concern and effort to absorb the indigenous population. The indigenous conceptions of state and government were quite different from those held by the Iberians. This often resulted in bicultural societies, or even tricultural when a mestizo culture stood apart. Under these conditions, attempts to develop a broad sense of civic responsibility in the *Latino* citizenry have faced serious obstacles.

Following the long, confused wars of independence, an epidemic of *caudillismo* spread. The *caudillo*, an aristocratic leader, was invited to step in and establish order. The green young nations came into existence at a most inopportune time, one when the Concert of Europe in the age of Metternich was trying to hold the line of the past. The world was far less hospitable to young republics in 1820 than it had been forty-five years earlier when the United States set out on an independent path.

The *caudillo*, the aristocratic man on horseback, propelled himself, or was propelled, into this complicated socioeconomic scene. Postwar chaos, ethnic divisions, illiteracy, and populations lacking experience in self-government were some of the factors which invited the strong man to take charge. An ultraconservative state with a corrupt and ineffective government was the ultimate result in most cases. Some of the *caudillos* were men with positive missions, but this did not necessarily benefit the people in the long run. The more charismatic leaders developed their particular brands of *personalismo*, some as brutal tyrants and some as benevolent despots. Almost all of them had had military or quasimilitary experience, and the great majority favored the continuation of a praetorian military caste. *Caudillo* governments tended to be unenlightened. And although in many cases order was maintained, it was accomplished at a price to be exacted in the violence of the future. The ill will and the delay in making reforms piled up a bloody debt for the twentieth century. *Continuismo* (the administration in power continuing to hold on to power) became a political way of life, and the party, faction, or *caudillo* went to great lengths to stay in office.

Mexico's Antonio López de Santa Anna (1795–1876) often comes to mind as a prototype for the *caudillo*, the crafty manipulator who practiced graft, chicanery, and tampering with the constitution while holding back social progress. When these methods failed, there remained the possibility of using the military force to help shaky administrations retain control of Latin American governments. Unfortunately the military, usually the army, was for sale, or the military leaders were vulnerable, for many aspired to political posts. Such ambition was a cause of numerous barrack revolts, palace seizures of the *golpe* or *cuartelazo* type (sudden attacks by military officials), in addition to involvement in political party coups. Quite often, if not usually, such changes in administration signified merely a variation in leaders. The cry was for revolution, but the result was often limited to a change in administrative personnel under the same oligarchic structure. In a few instances where reform was too long delayed, the result was near destruction of the military establishment, as in Mexico during the decade of 1910 to 1920 and in Bolivia following the Chaco

War and the loss of disputed territory to Paraguay with the peace treaty of 1938.

From early nationhood a search was taken up, usually in vain, for a balance between orderly government and liberties for the individual. The attempts at republican government in areas lacking a qualified citizenry often resulted in chaos. The ultraconservatives then moved toward heavy-handed controls and the ultraliberals clamored for greater freedom. At times the governmental pendulum swung back and forth between tyranny and anarchy. As a rule, order was maintained when a strong leader, with the support of the military, moved to restrict individual liberties. In this manner, social reform was hampered throughout the nineteenth century. The twentieth century has seen a few innovations as the military drifted away from its rigid attachment to the status quo; in some countries such as Cuba, Argentina, and Peru it has even come to sponsor social reforms in recent years.

In Latin America, despite its reputation of political volatility, military coups have seldom led to civil wars. It is possible that foreign investors, especially those from the United States, encouraged the idea that "instability" was especially high from 1880 to 1936, as it afforded an excuse for outside intervention to protect foreign investments and personnel. One thing is certain, the total number of years of intervention and occupation by United States forces is considerable for the period 1900–1933 in Cuba, Mexico, Haiti, Nicaragua, Panama, and the Dominican Republic.

As elsewhere, there is no simple means of distinguishing between civil disorder and civil war in Latin America, although there seems to have been much less of the latter. Customarily we consider it to be disorder when only a small segment of the population or a limited geographical area of the nation is involved. When a large area with something approaching one-third or more of the population takes up arms in an attempt to take control of the government or is in contention with another domestic army, it is thought to be a civil war. As a rule, national authorities over much of the world are inclined to use a minimum of force to put down civil disorder. On the other hand, while conducting civil wars, the two or more sets of authorities within the disrupted nation usually concentrate their efforts on destroying the effectiveness of the other army or armies. In such cases, the overuse of firepower is of less concern than while dealing with civil disorder. Conditions in Latin America have made it more difficult than in the United States and much of the rest of the Western world to distinguish between civil disorder and civil war. In this, as in most matters, it is not wise to generalize about twenty or more nations. Strictly speaking, only Mexico, Nicaragua, Colombia, Cuba, and the Dominican Republic have had civil wars in this century, while Guatemala, Bolivia, and Haiti have had protracted periods of disorder, armed revolution, or insurrection. (Of course, this categorization does not imply that civil war has resulted in greater social change than has armed revolution.) Bolivia seems to fit into either category. Civil wars in four of the five nations mentioned above followed a long period of strong-arm government by one man: Porfirio Díaz in Mexico (1876–1910); José Santos Zelaya in Nicaragua (1893–1909); Fulgencio Batista in Cuba (1934–44, 1952–59); and Rafael L. Trujillo in the Dominican Republic (1930–61).

It is risky to generalize about *Latino* disorder and civil war. Where nations have had chronic military interferences in politics, it might appear that civil war and excessive civil disorder are less common, but, in fact, strife has followed long "orderly" periods of tyranny. In a category of considerable militarism and little chronic disorder we include Paraguay, Argentina, Peru, Brazil, Panama, Ecuador, Honduras, and El Salvador. To the contrary, militarism has been at a low ebb in Mexico, Costa Rica, Uruguay, and Chile for at least the last thirty years, and still internal order has generally prevailed. Militarism has been dominant in Haiti, the Dominican Republic, Bolivia, Cuba, and, until recently, in Venezuela—areas where disorder has been common in the twentieth century. Furthermore it appears that in places such as Paraguay, Panama, and Nicaragua the last few decades would have been very disorderly but for a combination of circumstances of which a powerful or efficient military force is not the least. Since World War II only Uruguay, Costa Rica, Chile, and Mexico have been free from serious military meddling in civilian affairs. Of the four, only Mexico has had a radical shift of pattern since the first decade of this century.

The amount of military action in a country or the amount of money it spends on the military does not appear to be closely related to either the degree of internal security or the degree of military influence exerted on national policy. This, of course, does not take into account how efficiently monies are used or other factors which might influence the net result. Nicaragua, with considerable military influence for the first third of this century, is a nation where the army often plays a decisive role in politics, either directly or indirectly. Mexico's twentieth-century "Revolution" was accompanied by the bloodiest civil war in Latin American history, and in the long run this resulted in greatly reducing the influence of the military. A brief examination of budgets supports the above statement with respect to other nations. In terms of the percent of the gross national product used for the military we find that Peru is highest, with the Dominican Republic, Haiti, Paraguay, Argentina, Ecuador, and Brazil following in that order. At the bottom of the list we find Costa Rica, followed closely by Mexico, or possibly by Uruguay, for which we have inadequate statistics. El Salvador, spending a proportionately low amount of its national product for the military, has a very influential military establishment in relative terms, but so does Paraguay with one of the more sizable military budgets. Again it is difficult to draw meaningful generalizations for all of Latin America. The total picture of each nation's development in these matters is a unique and complex cultural web, and thus matters connected with the military, national security, or civil disorder are not especially meaningful when analyzed independently in quantitative terms.

In addition to the unique factors in each country, there are basic historic developments of a general nature which help explain the nature and significance of civil disorder and civil war South of the Border. Of course the concentrated ownership of capital goods and the persistence of feudalism have greatly contributed to this. For long periods of time, disorder may have plagued a nation and necessitated considerable military action, while other principal conditions common to civil war were not in existence. A vicious circle developed, especially wherever the police force was impotent. A strong military was required to maintain order, but the maintenance of order had a sedative effect upon social reforms. The longer social reforms were delayed, the more difficult it became to maintain order. A result of all this was that distrust of central government increased.

A condition usually in evidence in troubled times has been the intense feeling of bitter rivalry between those in office and those aspiring to office. *Latinos* have been noted for their mistreatment of political prisoners, something which did not lack for infamous precedents in early Spain or in the wars of independence. Various heinous social crimes have been treated lightly when judged to have been motivated by *machismo*, but political opponents could expect little or no sympathy, even though they were charged with nothing more than organizing political opposition to the administration in power. Latin American nations have had their disgraceful prisons where political prisoners were tortured, horrendous examples being El Frontón of Peru, Belén or Vera Cruz of Mexico, and Cuba's prison on the Isles of Pines. (This is by no means a complete list.) The principle of political amnesty has not been given much consideration until quite recently. So, when two internal factions have contended for power, the mistreatment of one group by the other has invited repayment in the same nefarious manner. It is possible that part of the fuel which has kept certain movements alive has been the effort to persecute the opposition or would-be opposition. The APRA (*Alianza Popular Revolucionaria Americana*) and the army in Peru are a case in point. After Colonel Luis Sánchez Cerro's disputed election in 1931, APRA gained the enmity of the army, which in turn ruthlessly crushed an incipient revolt at the Peruvian city of Trujillo. Down to the present the two have carried on a feud which has meant that part of the time APRA has functioned as a clandestine movement. The intrigue of underground activity was probably an asset in the early attempt to form a political party. But in recent years the armed forces have prevented APRA from inaugurating a president, even when it had the strongest and best organized political party.

Guerrilla war, often associated in one way or another with psychological-political action, seems to be preferred in Latin American civil wars, where systems and organizational structures are not as highly valued as in the United States and much of western Europe. It is worthy of mention that our word "guerrilla" is of Spanish origin, although the practice of guerrilla warfare is much older than the Spanish word. The rough mountain terrain and difficult jungle areas of Latin America provide an invitation for guerrilla tactics of both a military and a nonmilitary character. The personal nature of *Latino* guerrilla activity encourages the creation of Robin Hood images, such as those of Doroteo Arango (Pancho Villa) or Emiliano Zapata in Mexico, Fidel Castro of the Sierra Maestra days, the young priest Camilo Torres Restrepo, who was hunted down and killed in the mountains of Colombia (1966), and, of course, the much-publicized "Che" Guevara. Although a civil war does not necessitate the use of guerrilla tactics any more than guerrilla warfare signifies that it is a civil war, in Latin America most civil wars have had strong guerrilla characteristics. Preference for guerrilla fighting and for the patterns of war which call for a minimum of military professionalism (not always coexistent) are two factors which contribute to the confusion which often exists.

Contributing also is an emotional element which builds about the revolutionary leader an aura of romantic idealism. He becomes both a nucleus and a symbol. The colonial and early national habit of building loyalty around the man and his personal characteristics rather than to the nation may have helped prepare such a backdrop. If in the United States, in the period 1783 to 1800, Jefferson and Hamilton had been able to build two strictly personal parties, we might have found the nation split into two irreconcilable camps. Surely deep factionalism of this sort has played a disruptive role in Latin America. Often it has bred a bitterness of greater intensity, especially in the small nation. But even in an area as large as Argentina there is the example of Juan Manuel Rosas and those opposing him; there, as in the Mexico of Porfirio Díaz and his opponents, the most bitter factionalism evolved around *personalismo*. Fidel Castro's "History Will Absolve Me" statement reflects the idealistic tones: "When men carry the same ideals in their hearts, nothing can keep them isolated: neither wall of prisons nor the sod of cemeteries. For a single memory, a single spirit, a single idea, a single conscience, a single dignity, will sustain them all." Charisma builds myths, and myths do carry some weight. Some of the legend and lore which have been built up around Zapata and Guevara, to name but two, continue to have influence, especially in areas where agrarian reform is a live issue.

Under these conditions, charismatic leadership plays a tremendously important part in moving society, while political party organization may be neglected. An example of a leader making use of his military image years after his fighting was over is Alvaro Obregón, who would in effect say to politicians, "Follow me and my guns here in the presidential palace, or leave me." In that instance, as is often the case, the revolution had built up some of its own mystique and the mystique carried over from fighting into the world of political action. The revolutionary intrigue, which had broken the monotony of the old life, became attractive and may have contributed to the unstable status quo in the limbo between civil war and civil disorder. Such limbo is extended in time span because Latin Americans tend to wage both civil disorder and civil war in a rather disorganized manner. The *Latino*, in contrast to the *Anglo*, simply does not care for efficient operation in these any more than he does in many other matters, especially if it is depersonalized efficiency. Often these factors have resulted in a sort of domestic cold war in which those out of office struggle to get in.

Once the "outs" defeat the "ins," there is no assurance that administrative machinery will operate smoothly. Commonly the former opposition forces find themselves coming to rule without knowing how to proceed with government. The years of clandestine political activity or guerrilla campaigning are apt to result in personnel becoming less, rather than more, familiar with the needs of leadership roles in government. Opposition and destruction symbols which have been significant in the field of guerrilla tactics have to be replaced with ones which encourage planning, promoting, and building. These call for the development of very different approaches from those which the political exile or social outcast might have used when he was "out in the cold." The frame of mind which develops around the guerrilla-*politico*, who can afford to trust only men of similar political faith and shared experience (usually quite disagreeable), makes it difficult for him to expand mentally to the intellectual and social horizons which the new conditions demand. Some men seem to be fitted principally for the work of "blasters," and although they have positive goals, these are quite limited. They see their main contribution to be the task of clearing away the old. Is it surprising that Patrick Henry, Sam Adams, and others of the *provocateur* category did not adapt to the new political leadership needs in the United States after 1783? Pancho Villa and Emiliano Zapata, even if they had had a background of formal education, would probably have been unqualified to step from the military field to civil administrative posts, even if they had escaped early death. Alvaro Obregón and Lázaro Cárdenas did make such transitions with considerable success, but they had not been caught up in an extended period of guerrilla experience. Even the erudite, mild-mannered Víctor Raúl Haya de la Torre of Peru was persecuted so long, so motivated by opposition political tactics, and lived so long in forced exile that it is doubtful he could have accomplished much, even if he had been inaugurated. This is mere speculation, since the climate of opinion had been one of persecution and exile rather than guerrilla campaigning. Juan Bosch of the Dominican Republic, coming to office in 1963, is another instance worthy of mention in this respect. He entered office with widespread good wishes from home and abroad, and yet within the year was exiled. In this case, as probably in many others, the new chief executive should not have to carry the blame for failures due to institutional rigidities handed him by the departing tyranny. Somewhat related, but more complex, was the case of Plutarco Elias Calles (1924) in Mexico, who pushed his personal program aggressively. And it seems apparent that Fidel Castro experienced many of the typical problems of the former revolutionary leader who suddenly comes to power.

In many instances the victory of one side or the other is not complete, and in such situations there is apt to be a smoldering civil war which never quite bursts into full flame. In this confusion a loose guerrilla activity has often flourished, one which has been political, social, and economic, as well as military. Zapata of Mexico, Sandino of Nicaragua, and Castro of Cuba are but three guerrilla chieftains who led revolutionary civil movements of note. Every Latin American nation has experienced something similar, at least in a lesser form, at some time. For instance, from 1913 to 1915, during the Mexican three-cornered civil war, there were three armies, made up mainly of civilians. The Carranza-Obregón forces had to contend with the armies of both Zapata and Villa. Each of the three forces could count on occasional assistance from other quasi-independent bands of armed men. This, the largest civil war of the twentieth century in Latin America, gave rise to the greatest chaos, as political action lagged behind the violent semiorganized developments.

Mexico's experience may be indicative of the quality or strength of individuality in those who have followed the Latin-American guerrilla traditions. *Latino* guerrillas usually are not willing to organize sufficiently nor are they prepared to discipline themselves to the point where they are especially effective in dealing with political factions. This may be one explanation of the success which dictators have had in holding on to power. At the same time, the prevalence of internal confusion of whatever nature has likely been an invitation to foreign intervention of one form or another. On various occasions the United States has intervened upon an imagined or real possibility that the civil unrest might bring about the involvement of outside nations. Washington has reacted hurriedly when it appeared that an unfriendly outside nation might gain a powerful foothold in the western hemisphere. For example, the activities of Germany in Haiti and the Dominican Republic (1913–14) and of the Soviet Union in Guatemala (1954) encouraged United States intervention and counteraction. The Cuban missile crisis of 1962 brought an ultimatum from Washington, but did not lead to further interference on the part of the United States.

United States military intervention followed by occupation has taken place during the twentieth century in Mexico, Cuba, Haiti, the Dominican Republic, and Nicaragua. Temporary interference of lesser importance has occurred in other places in Latin America. The intervention in Mexico (both at Vera Cruz in 1914 and in the Pershing punitive expedition in 1916) invited open war with Mexico, but such was avoided. In Nicaragua the intervention forces got bogged down in a confused civil war between conservatives and liberals. The United States Marines found themselves in the position of putting down the liberal uprising (1912) while helping maintain conservative Adolfo Díaz in the presidency, and they remained involved off and on until 1933. In no place South of the Border has the United States found it a simple matter merely to withdraw after having intervened. Within the Latin American nations, political and economic conditions have had a way of becoming very complicated once the northern forces were sent in.

Cuba and Colombia experienced smoldering civil wars, again movements which grew out of the impetus to reform. These were wars which had the sympathy of sizable segments of the populations, even if active participation was not provided. The Cuban reform movement which brought on civil strife was led by a dynamic young man. Fidel Castro's military campaign, with only a few participants, started in December of 1956 after his return from Mexico. It spread rapidly. From March 1957 to New Year's Day 1959, the island, one way or another, was involved in a guerrilla civil war of an economic, political, and social nature. A five-year class war in Colombia (1948–53) was touched off by the assassination of liberal leader Jorge Eliécer Gaitán. It climaxed when General Gustavo Rojas Pinilla joined the movement, promising reforms. The liberals were soon disillusioned as Rojas Pinilla's tyrannical administration moved away from the social changes he had endorsed. In 1958 a liberal-conservative civilian coalition was able to heal enough of the political wounds to head Colombia back toward orderly constitutional and progressive government.

The short, bloody civil war (1965) in the Dominican Republic has not been adequately studied. It is still too early to see clearly all of the major implications. In its origins there appears to have been something of a counterrevolution to the successful anti-Bosch forces, which had been thwarted in carrying out a widespread reform program. Preliminary developments indicated that delayed reactions to the Trujillo regime were involved. If this indication is valid, then of course the faction of

General Elías Wessin y Wessin was following in the Trujillo traditions and Lieutenant Colonel Francisco Caamaño Deñó, of the Bosch program, was pointed away from such traditions. The bitter civil war lasted slightly more than four months (April 24–August 30, 1965) with limited sporadic outbursts for another four months. Many Latin American leaders have resentfully noted that the Organization of American States was not notified of the intervention of United States troops until their landing was in progress.

Where Castro-Communism is active outside of Cuba, it does not appear to be a distinct new call to take up civil war and in this way be principally concerned with promoting a foreign ideology. Rather it is phrased as an appeal for stepping up the guerrilla-type revolutionary movements which seek rapid social reforms. In Brazil, Peru, and Panama, where reform-minded military coups have recently taken place, these governments are not as much at odds with Castroism as are the old, hard-line military dictators in Paraguay or Nicaragua. As concerns the United States stance in most cases, it appears that Washington has been quite willing to extend military aid to the countries which claim that the aid will enable them to better combat the spread of Castroism in any form. It is very difficult to determine the need for such aid in many cases, and it is very questionable whether the aid is so used. However, there seems to be little doubt but that the extension of military aid results in a strengthening of Latin American military establishments—even if it only affords them more sophisticated means.

Recently an extremist tactic has been added to the bag of tricks used by left-wing terrorists who hope to exert pressure on governments—the seizure of foreign diplomatic envoys for use as hostages to gain the release of political prisoners. This activity has been most pronounced in Brazil, the Dominican Republic, and especially Guatemala. From January 1968 to March 1970, at least six United States envoys were kidnapped and held as hostages in return for the release of partisan prisoners. It is too early to assess the significance of this maneuver in the constant struggle between the "ins" and the "outs" of Latin American politics. On the surface it seems to be but one of the various innovations which continue to appear.

Up to this point, we have concerned ourselves mainly with problems of political confusion, the common incidence of domestic disorder, and the frequency of military intervention into civilian affairs. And, although historically the military has been a block on social progress, it would be questionable to conclude that such is the case today. Each nation needs to be considered separately in this respect. It would be unjust not to point out that even before World War II the armed forces South of the Border were becoming active in frontier exploration, communications development, public works, and even welfare operations. Medical science and understanding of jungle problems have been advanced by campaigns into the interior of various nations. Civil action programs of the armed forces are known over most of Latin America. On the surface it would appear that such programs would help unify a nation; it follows then that this should lessen the chances of civil war breaking out. But even if such is true, it does not signify that domestic unity will not be used in pressing for advantages with a neighboring country, as Chile did with Bolivia leading to the War of the Pacific (1879–83) or Peru with Ecuador in the 1940s. But almost the opposite has occurred also when an international incident has been used to try to consolidate the position of the home government, as, for instance, in 1932 when the Peruvian dictator, Sánchez Cerro, seized a Colombian outpost. It is also true that some military interventions into domestic politics have been made in order to remove military leaders from control of government. Although the net result has been of dubious value, it was the armed forces which greatly helped in terminating the Getulio Vargas regime in Brazil (1945) and in ousting Juan Domingo Perón from Argentina (1953).

What is the sum of all this? Little which emerges distinctly, for it is extremely difficult to distinguish between civil disorder and civil war in Latin America. On reflection it seems that a nearly constant state of unrest has been common in much of twentieth-century Latin America. This state, however, has usually been one of political uprising and/or low-level simmering insurrection of a political-military-guerrilla nature. Often the motivating forces have been energized by groups desirous of achieving some long-overdue social reforms. Gradually the reform movement has gained, and this in turn has reduced the outbreak of open civil war—but it has not lessened the chance of a continuation of the state of unrest. The latter will come about only if and when the governments are more completely modernized.

Another explanation of chronic unrest and relatively uncommon civil war is the significant role which the military has played. When men of the armed forces are in contention for top leadership positions in government, they are usually aware of their vulnerability unless they already have the support of the military. Even in a country where the armed forces are at a low level of professionalization, one segment of the military does not relish fighting against another segment for purposes of furthering an officer's political ambitions. In the main, individualism has been strong and professionalism weak on the Latin American military scene. Only Mexico has had a bitter, protracted civil war in this century. Nicaragua, Cuba, Colombia, and the Dominican Republic have experienced bloody episodes where strong civilian armies were in contention. In all these cases with the exception of Colombia, the strife came at the end of a long period of despotism. Also, it is noteworthy that preceding or during the civil wars the United States militarily intervened in the five countries. In another category are Bolivia and Guatemala which, in armed revolution, came very close to civil war. In these two nations, armed civilians were joined by reform-minded members of the military: Bolivia (1943) and Guatemala (1944).

Each nation has a unique political-military history, and each national situation must be studied independently if the study is to have real significance in specific terms. A much more careful examination is needed which will spell out the interrelationships in each country among the military, the church, the financiers, the landed proprietors, and industry, as well as with all the other power centers of society. It is quite possible that the partially submerged political wars and the quasimilitary revolutions have been an important deterrent to large-scale military actions. Also, since civil wars have come where social reforms were sought but repressed, the amount of civil war to be expected in the future will be determined in part by how rapidly the Latin American governments can peaceably modernize.

V

DIPLOMACY FROM THE INSIDE
Russia in the Civil War of 1918-1920

ROBERT D. WARTH

AMONG THE numerous civil wars that have so far occurred in this century, Russia fought the bloodiest and most consequential. The cost in human lives can be only vaguely estimated, and material losses in destroyed property, barren fields, and economic and social disintegration cannot be accurately measured. At least two or three million died on hundreds of obscure battlefields, while executions, pogroms, hardship, disease, malnutrition, and climate accounted for an even more grisly toll. Waged in the aftermath of a losing war against the Central Powers and as a delayed reaction to the Bolshevik Revolution of November 1917, the civil war broke out in the region of the lower Don in the early months of 1918 and concluded (except for minor diversions) with Baron Peter Wrangel's defeat in the Crimean Peninsula in the fall of 1920.

The conflict was waged with the utmost ferocity by both sides, although the problems of draft-dodging, malingering, mutiny, and desertion among the rank and file were not exclusive to either army. In no internecine struggle since the religious wars of the sixteenth century could the combatants have been more ideologically polarized, each convinced that the other represented the ultimate in political if not personal depravity. But unlike a foreign war, in which patriotic hatred of the enemy is accepted as just and natural in the defense of one's country, in a civil war "it is only the fanatics and simpletons whose minds are proof against the suspicion that there may be something wrong in tearing one's own nation apart, killing one's compatriots and looting their houses."

The struggle between "Reds" and "Whites" was further complicated by the intervention of Russia's former allies, chiefly Great Britain, France, the United States, and Japan, in three widely separate areas: Murmansk and Archangel in North Russia, the Black Sea and the Caucasus, and Vladivostok, the major port on the Pacific. The motives leading to intervention were based on false premises, largely relating to the maintenance of a second front against Germany. But the Armistice of November 1918 rendered these arguments obsolete, and the continued presence of Allied troops on Russian soil was explained in a variety of ways, none of them very convincing to the soldiers involved or to the war-weary public, and denounced as the rankest sort of double-talk by the Bolshevik leaders. The whole episode was a blunder of major proportions, clearly in violation of the accepted principles of international law. Yet the version favored by Soviet spokesmen, that intervention was a calculated conspiracy by capitalist imperialism to extirpate communism in its infancy, is too obviously a product of Marxist ideology to sustain full credibility, although there were indeed Allied politicians, diplomats, and generals who advocated precisely this solution to the "Bolshevik menace."

Paradoxically, the ravages of the civil war were repaired in time, while the comparatively moderate impact of foreign intervention left a more durable legacy. For at least a decade the Soviet government anticipated a renewed assault by the capitalist powers, but when the belated invasion actually came in 1941 the enemy was Nazi Germany rather than the relatively inoffensive Western democracies which had been the *bête noire* of the fledgling Communist state. The cold war brought renewed Soviet fears of aggression. Both propagandists and scholars (sometimes it was difficult to separate one from the other) recalled to the public mind the circumstances of military intervention. The United States, the most reluctant of the powers to interfere in Russia's internal affairs, was now portrayed as a ringleader if not the actual instigator—an instructive example of the present molding the past for political ends. It would be only a slight exaggeration to say that since 1917 a "cold war" of sorts has prevailed between the Western democracies and Soviet Russia except for the outwardly cordial but often inwardly troubled Grand Alliance of World War II.

Allied support in arms and equipment was more vital to the Whites than manpower, and it was chiefly Great Britain, though less enthusiastic about intervention than France, that provided the wherewithal to sustain the civil war. As a British military observer attached to Alexander

Kolchak's Siberian army confided in his diary, "It was a bit of an eye-opener to stand for an hour and see platoon after platoon, company after company, battalion after battalion march past carrying British rifles, wearing British tunics, overcoats, equipment, underclothing, puttees and boots. A British band played them past to British tunes." Allied troops occasionally gave armed assistance to the Whites, especially in the Arch-angel area and at Odessa on the Black Sea, but on the whole they were few in number, poorly motivated, and prohibited as a rule from combat assignments. Their mere presence, however, lent credence to the Bolshevik charge of capitalist aggression and identified the Whites, already vaguely associated in the peasant mind with the landlord system and the old regime, as lackeys of foreign imperialism. Many patriots whose natural convictions were non-Communist or even anti-Communist gave at least token allegiance to the Soviet government as the lesser of evils; of the 48,000 former officers who served in the Red Army, a substantial pro-portion must have been half-persuaded that the Reds were fighting for the independence and national unity of Russia.

So bitter was the conflict that neither side contemplated a negotiated peace with the other. But on several occasions Lenin and his colleagues, on the Marxist premise that the Allies, as predatory capitalist powers, could be bought off with appropriate territorial and economic concessions, offered a tentative peace settlement. President Woodrow Wilson con-sidered this approach insulting and refused to dignify it with a reply. His credentials as an idealist and man of peace had been secured (in his own estimation) with the Fourteen Points address on January 8, 1918. The sixth point called for the evacuation of Russian territory, economic as-sistance, the "independent determination of her own political development and national policy," and a "sincere welcome into the society of free nations under institutions of her own choosing." Allied policy was to make a mockery of these promises and assurances, as the peace settle-ment with the Central Powers did with so much of Wilson's well-meaning rhetoric. Yet at the time of the original address the Bolsheviks were still at war with Germany and welcomed the Fourteen Points as additional ammunition to sap the morale of the enemy. And their anxiety about Germany resulted, ironically, in the opening wedge of Allied intervention on Russian soil: the landing at Murmansk of 300 British and French marines in March 1918 with the tacit consent of the Soviet government.

Since the Armistice on the western front would presumably destroy the argument of war necessity for the presence of Allied troops in Russia, the Bolsheviks began a "peace offensive" with a series of diplomatic notes and proclamations. In December 1918 Maxim Litvinov, the deputy commissar for foreign affairs, was sent on a mission to Sweden to help publicize the Soviet case through a neutral channel. The results were meager until he dispatched a masterly Christmas Eve message to Wilson, then in Paris for the forthcoming peace conference. The provocative tone that Soviet spokesmen had used heretofore—a kind of revolutionary braggadocio—was replaced by an appeal to the president's "sense of justice and impartiality." Whatever he might think of Russia's "new social system" surely did not excuse the "sending of foreign troops to fight against it, or for arming and supporting classes interested in the restoration of the old system of exploitation of man by man." Litvinov had at last struck the right psychological chord, and Wilson responded by suggesting to his Allied colleagues a temporary truce in Russia and an invitation to all factions to send representatives to Paris. The French objected to the presence of Bolsheviks (they would "make no contract with crime," they haughtily declared), but Wilson sent an emissary, William H. Buckler, to sound out Litvinov in Stockholm.

Meanwhile the peace conference convened to hammer out a series of treaties with the defeated Central Powers. Neither White nor Red Russia participated, despite the heavy sacrifices made by that nation during the war. But a variety of anti-Bolsheviks, most of whom had direct contacts with the White movement, maintained a self-appointed political lobby in Paris, the so-called Russian Political Conference, with marginal results as far as influencing Allied policy was concerned. They had greater success in creating a facade of unity among the White factions competing for power in Russia and continued to act as the political voice of anti-Bolshevism throughout the conference.

Nothing came of the Buckler mission beyond a report that the Soviet government was conciliatory and apparently sincere about peace negotiations. But the British prime minister, David Lloyd George, had taken up the charge, proposing rather inelegantly that Bolshevik representatives be called to Paris "somewhat in the way that the Roman Empire summoned chiefs of outlying tributary states to render an account of their actions." In deference to French objections (Premier Georges Clemenceau feared that Paris might be contaminated by revolutionary propaganda) the proposed confrontation was shifted to the Turkish island of

Prinkipo near Constantinople. The scheme was also amended to include representatives of the White movement. Wilson personally drafted the invitation on his own typewriter, and, though slightly altered after consultation with his colleagues, it contained much the same blend of sincere altruism and political naiveté that characterized most of his pronouncements on Russia. Unable to reconcile the sordid reality of the Russian situation with his own highminded idealism, he simply ignored the fact of intervention and blandly claimed that the powers recognized the revolution "without reservation" and would not "favor or assist any of the organized groups now contending for the leadership and guidance of Russia." An invitation was extended to all the contesting parties to send three representatives to Prinkipo by February 15, 1919, "provided, in the meantime, there is a truce of arms amongst the parties involved." This scrupulous "equality" was frankly discriminatory against the Bolsheviks, who exercised sovereignty over the largest territory and population but were limited to a three-man delegation, while the same number was permitted for each of the dozen or more groups who could claim "political authority or military control" anywhere in the former Russian empire.

The proposal was made public and immediately raised cries of outrage from the anti-Bolshevik *émigrés*, and the leading Western newspapers, especially in France, condemned the idea of consorting with a group that was politically beyond the pale. The White regimes, reacting with anger and dismay, scorned the invitation. The head of the North Russian government at Archangel, for example, replied that it was "morally unacceptable" since the Bolsheviks were "venal traitors in international affairs and brigands, robbers, and murderers in internal affairs." Only the shaky governments representing the Ukraine and the Baltic republics of Latvia, Estonia, and Lithuania responded favorably—on condition, however, that their independence would be recognized and that they would be granted representation at the Paris Peace Conference.

The Soviet government replied positively, although *Pravda* editorialized in a sarcastic vein about the hypocrisy of the Allied offer and questioned the impartiality of the proposed settlement if the mediators were already supporting one of the parties to the dispute. Lenin advocated a "second Brest-Litovsk," referring to the unfavorable peace treaty that Russia had signed with Germany in March 1918. Despite opposition within the party, his will prevailed, and the Soviet response sought to appease the

Allies with major concessions: recognition of Russia's foreign debts (previously repudiated); a grant of mining, timber, and "other" rights; a territorial settlement, with possible cession of areas held by Allied troops; and, in deference to fears of Communist activity, a guarantee of noninterference in the internal affairs of the Allied countries. The note failed to mention a cease-fire, and by implying that the Allies could be bribed with concessions, the Bolsheviks offended both Wilson and Lloyd George. It was a psychological blunder, yet, as in Chicherin's note of the previous November, fully in accord with the Soviet image of capitalist imperialism. "I am sorry," Lenin telegraphed War Commissar Leon Trotsky, "but you will have to go to Wilson." Perhaps recalling his experience as chief negotiator at Brest-Litovsk, Trotsky begged off the assignment, and Lenin apparently did not insist.

Distracted by other matters, the peace conferees in Paris failed to exert pressure on the Whites, who were bitter but generally resigned to some type of negotiations with the enemy. But the French were bent upon sabotaging the Prinkipo scheme, and on February 5, 1919, Sergei Sazonov, a former tsarist minister of foreign affairs and one of the leaders of the Russian Political Conference, wired Kolchak's regime at Omsk in central Siberia that the plan was "doomed to failure" and that "France intends to continue to support us with supplies and will not withdraw her military units in Russia." Increasingly confident that Allied assistance would be maintained—for the Whites could easily have been coerced into participating in whatever negotiations the powers had in mind—the Political Conference drafted a formal rejection after consulting the anti-Bolshevik governments of Siberia, South Russia, and Archangel. "Any meeting would not only remain without effect," the note maintained, "but might possibly cause the Russian patriots as well as the Allied nations irreparable moral harm."

By mid-February Wilson had returned to the United States for political fence-mending, Lloyd George was in England to deal with labor problems, and Clemenceau was soon thereafter laid low by an assassin's bullet. The Prinkipo proposal died of malnutrition as the Allied "second team" grappled with the Russian question. While Winston Churchill, the British war minister, tried in vain to win support in Paris for more substantial aid to the Whites, including volunteer troops and military specialists, a new plan germinated. William C. Bullitt, a young State Department aide in Wilson's entourage and eventually the first American ambassador to the Soviet Union, was sent on a secret mission to Moscow to consult the Bolshevik leaders and sound them out on peace terms. The Soviet position was serious but not desperate. The Red Army was holding its own, although neither Kolchak nor General Anton Denikin in South Russia had begun a spring offensive. Famine, however, was already stalking the cities. Lenin still favored the "second Brest-Litovsk" strategy, assuming that any territorial or other concessions would be recouped in time and that in any case the spread of communism to the West would take care of the problem. Shortly before Bullitt's arrival in Moscow a group of delegates, theoretically representing world communism, had founded the Third (Communist) International, and revolutionary expectations ran high in Bolshevik circles. After talks with Lenin and Georgi Chicherin, the commissar for foreign affairs, Bullitt received a formal statement on March 14 outlining terms that would be acceptable to the Soviet government if made by the Allies no later than April 10. In several respects they were even more generous than the Prinkipo concessions, though no economic inducements were offered. The Bolsheviks promised to recognize the territorial conquests of the Whites, to accept responsibility for Russia's foreign debts, and to participate in a mutual political amnesty provided the Allies withdrew their troops, ceased their assistance to the Whites, and lifted the economic blockade of Soviet territory.

Bullitt was impressed with the apparent stability of Bolshevik rule, and in his formal report he appeared—at least to his critics—overly sympathetic to the Soviet cause. But his personal views made little difference, for Wilson and Lloyd George, now back in Paris, had passed on to the problems of Germany in his absence, and they simply ignored the Soviet proposals with which the importunate young diplomat confronted them. Wilson refused to see him, and Lloyd George publicly denied that a Soviet peace overture had ever been made. No decision had been reached to send more troops to Russia, but Kolchak's spring "push" was already under way, and the Allies contemplated no diminution of their aid. A White victory would render the Bolshevik peace strategy obsolete.

Aside from the Red Army, an uncertain and largely untested military force, the Soviet regime wielded a potentially formidable weapon in the ideology and political reality of a functioning Communist government. To its leaders, Soviet Russia was not so much a viable state in the international community as a bastion from which the Bolshevik virus might leap across frontiers and strike silently at the capitalist enemy. With the benefit of over a half century of hindsight the specter of a Red tide overwhelming the democratic West seems highly exaggerated, yet it would be wrong to conclude that Lenin and his colleagues were simply deluded visionaries, so divorced from reality that they substituted Marxist dogma and wishful thinking for a sober and objective appraisal of their revolutionary prospects. Many if not most of their extravagant public statements were designed to boost party morale and cannot be taken at face value. They nevertheless had implicit faith in the inevitability of a European revolution and invariably looked to Germany as the key that would unlock a Communist chain reaction. That assumption had been temporarily drowned in blood in January 1919, when the German Communist party precipitously sought to emulate the Bolshevik example by seizing power in Berlin.

Suddenly and from an unexpected quarter Moscow's expectations were fulfilled, or at least partially confirmed, when the Hungarian Soviet Republic was proclaimed. Béla Kun, an obscure journalist who had absorbed Bolshevik principles while a war prisoner in Russia, assumed power in Budapest on March 21 and inaugurated a curious 133-day experiment in Communist rule. The Bolsheviks naturally greeted their new "comrades" with enthusiasm and assured them that the "proletariat throughout the world is watching your struggle with intense interest and will not permit the imperialists to raise their hands against the new Soviet Republic." But revolutionary rhetoric could not compensate for Russia's geographical separation from Hungary nor disguise the plight of its own regime. Lenin, who maintained intermittent contact with Kun by radio, was pessimistic about the small and isolated Danubian republic, warning that the "imperialists" could crush it almost at will. His forebodings were realized some three months later when external pressure and his own mistakes forced Kun to flee to Vienna as Red Hungary collapsed.

Moscow's ideological radar continued to record false and misleading data about the revolutionary consciousness of the European proletariat. Again it was rewarded by events that tended to substantiate the Marxist canon as viewed through the Bolshevik prism. Close upon the news of Communist success in Hungary came startling developments in southern Germany. A Soviet republic was proclaimed in Munich on April 7, and immediately the prophets of the German revolution regained confidence. Once more the Bolsheviks hailed an unexpected accomplishment by revolutionary colleagues. Lenin, speaking on April 11 to the Central Council of Trade Unions on the tasks of mobilizing against the Kolchak offensive, referred to the "Soviet republics in the heart of Europe" and to the recent evacuation of mutinous French troops from the Black Sea port of Odessa. "The Soviet form of government is becoming irresistible," he maintained, and "we may say without exaggeration . . . that our victory on an international scale is absolutely certain." But events in distant Bavaria were even more confusing than those in Hungary, and Lenin was unaware of the insubstantial base upon which the German "Soviet republic" rested. It had been founded on a wave of utopian radicalism by intellectuals and "coffee house anarchists" who judgment had been paralyzed by the example of Hungary and the anticipated rising of Viennese workers. Both Moscow and Budapest endorsed the regime, seemingly unprepared and perhaps unwilling to examine its revolutionary credentials too closely at a time when allies of any description were in such short supply. The local Communists, unaware of the Bolshevik stamp of approval, dismissed the incident as adventurist folly, and when their foresight had been validated in a week's time, they proceeded to step into the political vacuum with a cabinet of their own. The move was taken with misgivings but in the belief that revolutionary honor required a common front with the workers, then prepared to defend Munich from right-wing military units. By early May the Bavarian capital had gone the way of Berlin and became a stronghold for nationalist zealots—notably Adolph Hitler's Nazi party— for the remainder of the Weimar era. The episode passed so quickly that the Bolsheviks were spared both the elation and the depression that attended the Hungarian affair.

The failure of the Prinkipo plan and the Bullitt mission did not entirely scotch further efforts to seek peace. A new scheme appeared from unofficial sources: Fridtjof Nansen, the famed Norwegian explorer and humanitarian, and Herbert Hoover, chairman of the American Relief Administration and later president of the United States. Nansen previously had been approached by White leaders in Paris to sponsor a fundraising organization to assist their cause, but had declined, pleading ignorance of the Russian situation. Hoover wished to extend his relief program to Russia, primarily as an anti-Bolshevik measure, since wellfed Russians would presumably repudiate the "murderous tyranny" installed in Moscow. He persuaded Nansen to head the commission, and the Allied statesmen in Paris were asked to confer their blessing upon it. The reply, drafted by subordinates, expressed cautious approval without indicating how a "cessation of all hostilities," said to be an "obvious" precondition for relief activities, might be obtained. Released to the public the next day (April 17), the letter stirred up a storm of abuse among the Whites and their supporters, akin to the unflattering reception that had greeted the Prinkipo proposal. The White Russian lobby in Paris, encouraged by the French, genuflected toward the humanitarian aims of the plan but denounced the substance of it as a means of giving moral and material assistance to the Bolsheviks on the eve of their collapse. From both Omsk and Archangel came protests that the Soviet government would use the food to feed the Red Army.

Nansen experienced serious difficulty in transmitting his proposal (the government radio stations in western Europe refused him their facilities) but eventually his message reached Moscow. The Bolshevik answer, which was not received in Paris until May 15, was signed by Chicherin and reflected an improved military position on the eastern front against Kolchak. The latter, though personally honest, presided over an incredibly corrupt and incompetent regime, and in retrospect it seems remarkable that his army was able to sustain an offensive that carried it beyond the Urals into European Russia. The Red Army saved Kazan and Samara, the key cities on the upper Volga, and by the end of May was in a position to counterattack.

At a time when the Allied governments—certainly the Western press— were expecting the momentary fall of Moscow, the Bolsheviks hardened their stand. No longer did they seek to placate the Atlantic powers with concessions. Chicherin thanked Nansen for his generous offer but pointed out that his "benevolent intentions" had been used by the Allies to serve their own political aims. They had instituted an economic blockade, and their aid to the Whites had made possible the turmoil and deprivation from which all Russians were suffering. An armistice could be arranged only after a general discussion of Allied policy, and he reiterated his government's willingness to enter negotiations. More specifically, Nansen was asked to name a time and place where the details of the relief measures could be worked out.

The Allied statesmen gave only perfunctory attention to the latest Bolshevik overture. Official silence prevailed, and insofar as they concerned themselves with Russian matters it was to consider recognition of Kolchak's supposedly victorious regime. Due to the efforts of the Russian *émigrés* in Paris, the Whites had contrived a surface unity by this

time, acknowledging Kolchak as Russia's "supreme ruler." Late in May
the Allies confronted him with a series of demands in a note that flagrantly
misrepresented the reasons for the collapse of the Prinkipo conference
and again denied any intention of interfering in Russia's internal affairs.
Since his future success depended upon largesse from abroad, he could
but respond with good grace to what he must have regarded as an affront
to his dignity. Disregarding the advice of his reactionary staff for that of
General Alfred Knox, the senior British officer (who in turn was coached
by Churchill), the admiral replied that he would indeed hold free elections after reaching Moscow, assume responsibility for Russia's foreign
debts, grant independence to Poland and Finland, and permit autonomy
to other nationalities. But his acceptance was carefully qualified: a constituent assembly would ultimately make the final decisions. The Allies,
in no mood for nitpicking, declared themselves satisfied, for they had
gained "for the record" a statement demonstrating that Kolchak was a
democratic ruler and not a military dictator. He was promised further
aid, but, his drive on Moscow having been repulsed, he was denied official
recognition for the time being.

Kolchak never regained the initiative. The dry rot of defeatism, compounded by "moral decay, cowardice, greed and treachery" (to use the
admiral's own words) sapped the strength of his army. By midsummer
the retreat verged upon a rout. Knox, a fervent supporter of intervention,
advised his government early in August that it was "useless to send any
more military assistance to Siberia unless we have some guarantee that it
will be used with ordinary common sense." The Red Army's preoccupation with other fronts spared the Omsk regime from a coup de grace
until the late fall.

The beleaguered Reds were by no means assured of victory when the
Kolchak debacle began. Denikin's summer offensive, too late to coincide
with that of his Siberian counterpart, picked up momentum, and by October his Volunteer Army was only 250 miles south of Moscow. The French
withdrawal left no sizable body of foreign troops in South Russia, although the British had occupied parts of the Caucasus—notably Batum
on the Caspian and Baku on the Black Sea. The opening of the Turkish
Straits after the defeat of the Central Powers allowed easy access to Russia's Black Sea ports, and the British had sent a military mission to
Denikin, followed by generous quantities of war materiel. The White
advance was greatly assisted by a British tank battalion and two squad-

rons of the Royal Air Force. Both units were originally assigned for instructional purposes but, given the combat psychology of professional soldiers, were drawn into battlefield operations.

Deniken's approach to Moscow raised political questions similar to those that had troubled Allied relations with Kolchak. But Denikin thought of himself as a soldier, not a politician, and avoided nonmilitary problems by deferring to Kolchak's nominal leadership. The anti-Semitic predilections of many Volunteer Army commanders was another source of difficulty, for pogroms against Jews—often indiscriminately linked with the Bolshevik cause—became a regular feature of the advance into the Ukraine. British protests, especially from Churchill, arrived in a steady stream but appeared to make no difference in the number and severity of anti-Semitic excesses. The inability or unconcern of the British mission to do much about the problem did not extend to matters that were more directly military. Guidance from London was imprecise, but Denikin was prevented from seizing territory claimed by the Menshevik republic of Georgia. His conception of a united Russia was incompatible with independent or autonomous territories on the borderlands of the former empire, and the whole question of the Russian nationalities (other than an independent Poland and Finland) was never thrashed out by the Allied governments. The Bolsheviks, too, had trouble on this score and eventually "solved" it by the expedient method of a federal structure within a centralized governmental system.

On October 20, 1919, the Red Army took the town of Orel south of Moscow. Overextended along a 700-mile front and far from its supply bases, the Volunteer Army, once obliged to retreat, began to disintegrate at a more rapid pace than Kolchak's Siberian army. In Petrograd, the former Russian capital, the Bolsheviks were also victorious on October 20. There the Northwest Army of Nikolai Yudenich was repulsed on the outskirts of the city by the Seventh Red Army. His troops had been supplied by the British during the summer after a virtual ultimatum by Allied representatives in Estonia had compelled the formation of a "democratic" government for Northwest Russia. Lenin had recommended abandoning the city to strengthen Moscow's defenses. But Trotsky stressed the symbolic value of Petrograd as the cradle of the Revolution, and his presence during the siege lifted the morale of the defenders and proved the validity of his judgment.

By November 1919 the Red Army had triumphed on every major

front. The Allies, at last convinced that proxy armies could not accomplish what their own were unwilling and unable to do, completed the process of withdrawal. Force, Lloyd George acknowledged in the House of Commons, had "failed to restore Russia to sanity." Allied troops at Murmansk and Archangel had already been evacuated during the late summer. Somewhat later the British withdrew from the Caucasus, as did the token force with Kolchak. Only in the Russian Far East did foreign troops remain during the winter of 1919–20. There Soviet power, except for Red partisan units, was unable to penetrate. The major obstacle was Japan, whose army of some 73,000 in the Maritime Province was less anxious to succor the Whites than to carve out a sphere of influence. It did, however, protect and supply several White commanders (hardly more than brigands) who made it their business to despoil the civilian population east of Lake Baikal.

The 9,000 American troops departed from Vladivostok in February–March 1920. With great difficulty they had maintained a neutral stance among the contending factions, and, despite their vital role in keeping open the rail link between the Pacific and the Siberian Whites, Kolchak complained bitterly about their failure to participate actively in the anti-Bolshevik struggle. The Czech legion, whose supposed plight at the hands of the nefarious Reds in the summer of 1918 had precipitated intervention at Vladivostok in the first place, was delayed even longer by a shortage of transport. The last units left the harbor in September 1920.

The process by which the Soviet government levered Japanese troops off the mainland was a prolonged exercise in diplomatic gamesmanship, for the Red Army, battle-hardened against the inferior White armies, carefully refrained from a test of strength lest the Tokyo militarists order a full-scale invasion. But Moscow's anxiety about the security of its east Asian patrimony was interrupted by a variety of domestic concerns and by a struggle with Poland in 1920 that might be considered the last—or perhaps next to last—of the wars of intervention against revolutionary Russia. Poland's rebirth had been made possible by the Allied victory, and France in particular looked to a strong Poland as the eastern anchor of the Versailles settlement with Germany and a major link in the *cordon sanitaire* against Communist Russia. Soviet weakness presented the Poles, with the tacit consent of the French, the best opportunity since the seventeenth century for territorial aggrandizement at Russia's expense. The Bolsheviks were exhausted by the civil war and offered a generous boundary, well to the east of a fair ethnic line. The Poles spurned serious negotiations and struck in the spring of 1920. Counting on the assistance of the Ukranian nationalist leader Simon Petlyura, they seized Kiev on May 7. Military success concealed a costly political blunder. The Ukranian peasants, disenchanted with Reds and Whites alike, were not disposed to rally to an alien invader who would restore the landlord system. Petlyura's help proved ephemeral, and the Poles were driven back with ease. The Bolsheviks then made a political miscalculation of their own by attempting to export revolution by force of arms. They rejected British mediation as the Red Army drove to the gates of Warsaw. The attack faltered, perhaps fortunately for all parties, for the prospect of a Communist Poland would not have been accepted passively in London and Paris. The Bolsheviks, having gambled and lost, were content to make peace on unfavorable terms, leaving the question of territorial redress to be solved by Stalinist methods of *Realpolitik* in conjunction with World War II.

The dying convulsion of the White movement came just as the Red Army's counteroffensive against the Poles picked up momentum. The remnants of Denikin's beaten army, ferried by British ships to the sanctuary of the Crimean Peninsula, were taken over by Baron Wrangel. In Trotsky's astringent phrase, the "German hireling of the French loansharks," Wrangel was an able field commander, probably the best of the White generals. His resources, however, were limited and his campaigns beyond the Crimea were only temporarily successful. While France recognized his government and gave him material support, Britain blew hot and cold, reluctant to disavow him but clearly weary of the prolonged civil war. A truce with Poland in the fall, allowing the full weight of the Red Army to be shifted to the Crimean area, disposed of the last of the major White leaders.

Japan's withdrawal from Russia's Maritime Province furnished an epilogue to the civil war. The Bolsheviks, halting their troops at Lake Baikal, created a "front" government in eastern Siberia to bluff the Japanese. Labeled the Far Eastern Republic and founded by Alexander Krasnoshchekov, a Bolshevik sympathizer who had lived in exile in the United States until 1917, it was officially created in the spring of 1920 at Verkhne-Udinsk near the eastern shore of Lake Baikal. Moscow recognized its own appendage after a month's delay, and Tokyo, puzzled by this hybrid regime within its sphere of influence, made cautious soundings in hopes that it might be manipulated as a weapon against the

Bolsheviks. By midsummer, as Red partisans infiltrated the Japanese-held Trans-Baikal area, Tokyo agreed to withdraw its troops in return for the "neutrality" of Moscow's satellite republic. Yet two more years elapsed before Japan was persuaded to leave the Maritime Province, all the while fighting a diplomatic delaying action with Soviet Russia and the United States. The Far Eastern Republic, free from the taint of Communism, maintained a lobby in Washington during the conference there on naval limitation (1921–22) that was far more effective than any diplomatic approaches the Soviet government could have contrived.

As Japan's dwindling number of White freebooters were defeated by Red forces, Tokyo entered negotiations with Far Eastern Republic representatives in August 1921. But its exorbitant demands, including a permanent buffer state in eastern Siberia, discouraged a settlement, and the final evacuation in the fall of 1922 came about because of a change of government in Japan. The concluding act in this prolonged diplomatic charade came in November when Moscow formally absorbed its "stalking horse" into the Soviet state. Ironically, the unfriendliness of Soviet-American relations prevented either the Kremlin or the State Department from acknowledging the significant role of the United States in maneuvering Japan out of eastern Siberia.

If any meaningful lessons can be drawn from the Russian civil war, one certainly stands out: the senseless futility of foreign intervention and the bankruptcy of leadership that permitted this sordid spectacle to drag on for some two years (four in the case of Japan). Mixed motives—the twisted logic of Wilsonian idealism that entangled the United States, the counterrevolutionary "realism" of Britain and France, old-fashioned imperialism on the part of Japan—combined with inept diplomacy and confused public opinion to bestow a flavor of bizarre unreality upon this polluted backwash of World War I. If one ignores the human and material destruction brought upon the Russian people directly by the Allied armies or indirectly by their propping up the White regimes, it can be argued, of course, that intervention, as blundering and half-hearted as it was, effectively "quarantined" the Bolsheviks. Hard pressed to survive, they were unable to penetrate westward either by political pressure or by military action. But the Soviet leaders were sufficiently harried by domestic problems without the added burden of civil war, and after Brest-Litovsk they had looked forward to a breathing space that would allow them to put their own house in order. Moreover, in the absence of a major internal threat or external aggression it would have been unnecessary to create a large army so quickly, and without adequate military strength there could have been no artificial expansion of Bolshevism, however tempting such a prospect might have been.

It would be equally wrongheaded to argue, as some Soviet apologists have done, that the legacy of hostility between East and West stemmed primarily from Allied bad conduct following the Bolshevik Revolution. A major contribution was certainly made during these years, but the messianic flavor of the Communist creed and the ingrained antipathy of the Bolshevik chieftains to capitalist governments would not in any case have allowed a normal relationship to flourish.

Armed intervention in the domestic affairs of another country, particularly a great power, is a risky business and can seldom be justified except by a strained—and usually mistaken—interpretation of the national interest. The attempt to crush revolutionary France in 1792 is the most obvious analogy to the Russian case, and the boomerang effect of that ill-considered venture reverberated throughout Europe until 1815. In more recent times the United States has been the principal intervening power, usually against the threat or supposed threat of communism. Except in the peripheral case of Greece and Turkey in 1947, where no combat troops were used, these endeavors have become increasingly fruitless. The quagmire of Vietnam, though quite different in many ways from the Russian civil war, serves as a contemporary warning of the dangers inherent in a policy of military intervention.

Suggestions for Further Research

Most of the intellectually respectable work on the Russian civil war, particularly the diplomatic story, has been done by Western scholars. Soviet historians have operated under varying degrees of political constraint, and of course the Stalin era was the most notorious in its ideological requirements and the least productive in objective scholarship. Perhaps the most obvious need is a general treatment of the civil war that will take into account published work, both primary and secondary, that has appeared since World War II.

The number of monographs on various aspects of Allied intervention is already staggering, but the opening of new manuscript and archival sources tends to raise the rate of obsolescence in the older studies. Among the major intervening powers, France and Japan have been somewhat neglected; of the major White commanders, only General Yudenich lacks a biography or other specialized treatment. Nevertheless, a moratorium might well be declared on further work dealing with the Allies' Russian diplomacy until significant new material emerges.

The Russian archives are generally unavailable, even to Soviet historians, and substantial advances in our knowledge of the internal history of the civil war must await the day, presumably in the far distant future, when these resources will be opened to independent investigators. Meanwhile, Western specialists have scarcely exploited the resources available outside the Soviet Union, notably those at the Hoover Institution in Stanford, California. For example, we need to know more about the Red Army and its leaders (apart from military campaigns), the economic and social background (especially the peasants and their attitudes), the various partisan groups, and the lesser-known White commanders and non-Russian nationalist leaders.

IV

INTERNAL POLITICAL PROBLEMS AND LOYALTIES
The Republican Side in the Spanish Civil War

EDWARD E. MALEFAKIS

THE SPANISH CIVIL WAR has often been described as "the last great cause," the last instance in our increasingly complex world when moral issues were sharply drawn and men of good will could unreservedly support the cause of freedom against the encroachments of totalitarian fascism. This was the feeling of many of those who lived during the conflict. Because of the peculiar inability of World War II (in truth a much more profound and clear-cut moral crusade) to arouse similar emotional involvement among intellectuals, the feeling persists.

However one chooses to explain this great outpouring of emotions which the Western world channeled into the Spanish Civil War, the fact remains that it was not a struggle between united, homogeneous blocs. Rather, probably more than any other civil war of this century, the Spanish conflict was characterized by internal divisions, particularly on the Republican side. It resembled less a medieval morality play, with its emphasis on the struggle between undivided good and evil, than Greek tragedy or modern drama, with their protrayal of the protagonist as his own chief enemy, unable to triumph because he is unable to gain ascendancy over himself.

That this was so should not be surprising, given the history of Spain in the years immediately preceding the Civil War. The nonviolent overthrow of the monarchy in 1931 by a coalition of middle-class progressives and Socialists did not bring a solid national consensus in favor of the

Republic that followed. From the start, what was then the largest working-class group in Spain, the *Anarchosyndicalist Confederación Nacional del Trabajo* (CNT), sought to overthrow the new regime by means of a second, social revolution which, going far beyond the reforms advocated by the Republicans, would completely destroy capitalism, traditional forms of government, and all other manifestations of what it considered to be the eternal oppression of man by man.

The intense opposition of the CNT might have been contained had the left Republican-Socialist alliance which gave birth to the Republic been maintained. This did not occur, however. The middle-class left Republican parties proved unwilling to accept the implications of the social policies they had so bravely proclaimed in 1931. The underdeveloped Spanish economy was unable to solve the perennial problem of unemployment, now aggravated by world depression. Above all, the Socialists abandoned their acceptance of parliamentary democracy, partly because of its slowness in bringing about reforms, partly because of the fear engendered by the fascist victories in Germany and Austria in 1933–34, and partly because the first electoral test of the Republic after the initial enthusiasm for it had waned went against them.

In the autumn of 1933 the Socialists abandoned their left Republican allies as weak, incompetent, or treasonous. Instead, they unsuccessfully attempted to create a working-class bloc with the CNT and, in October 1934, launched a hopelessly badly organized revolution against the Center-Right government that had taken power. Defeat in the October Revolution split the Socialist movement. One wing, headed by Indalecio Prieto, worked to reestablish the former Socialist commitment to reformist tactics, with its corollary of close cooperation with the left Republicans. The other wing, headed by Francisco Largo Caballero, sought its remedy in renewal and intensification of the revolutionary spirit.

Had the Center-Right been more flexible and far-sighted, the divisions within the Left might have kept it from recapturing power almost indefinitely. As it was, reactionaries gained control of the Center-Right bloc in 1935 and by their purely negative policies forced the Left to reunite temporarily into a Popular Front coalition during the elections of February 1936. Those elections won, the old divisions within the Left immediately reasserted themselves. The Popular Front cabinet, composed exclusively of left Republicans, could rely on full support only from middle-class progressives and the Prieto Socialists. The Caballero Socialists, the CNT, and the Communists (who now began to assume importance for the first time) vacillated between advocacy of the immediate overthrow of what they considered to be still another "bourgeois" regime, and toleration of that regime until conditions were ripe for full-scale social revolution. This ambiguity was never resolved during the six months between the elections and the Civil War, in great part because the working-class Left was once again unable to unite within itself. The CNT demanded as the price of union a complete break with all parliamentary forms and an exclusive reliance on insurrectionary tactics. Neither the Caballeristas nor the Communists were willing to accept these terms, partly because their grounding in Marxist philosophy left a greater residue of caution among them than the millenarian CNT possessed.

To summarize, on the eve of the Civil War the Spanish Left was doubly divided. Its working-class components were separated from its middle-class components by their desire for social revolution. The working-class groups in turn were themselves divided by the intensity with which they pressed this revolutionary goal and the tactics by which they sought to achieve it.

As though these divisions were not enough, the middle-class Left was also divided because of the regional question, uniquely important in Spain. The failure of the country to modernize itself during the nineteenth century had given rise to separatist tendencies in its two most industrialized regions, Catalonia and the Basque country. Both joined the Loyalists so as to preserve or secure their regional autonomy against the Nationalist determination to restore a unitary Spain. Yet the bond that tied them to the Republic simultaneously separated them from it, since their fear that the regional principle would also be violated by their allies frequently led them to excessive insistence on their right of autonomous government.

The divisions within the Spanish Right need not concern us in as much detail for several reasons. First, although they existed, they had never become so profound during the peacetime Republic, partly because the Right had usually been on the defensive rather than in power. Second, the army, an organization without specific ideological commitments and not previously involved in daily political life, immediately established its ascendancy over the Right when it rebelled against the Republic on July 18, 1936. In so doing, it reduced to secondary importance the hatreds between monarchists and conservative Republicans, as well as those between these more traditional groups and the small fascist party, the Falange. The main danger of internal conflict for the Nationalists stemmed from rivalry among the leading generals. This danger was avoided by the astuteness of Franco, the early deaths of his two main competitors, Sanjurjo and Mola, and the continuous success of Nationalist arms on the battlefield. The unwillingness of Hitler and Mussolini to risk alienating Franco by supporting their ideological counterpart, the Falange, during the coup by which Franco won control of that movement in April 1937 removed the only other threat of serious internal discord. Consequently, the Right was able to maintain far greater unity during the Civil War than it had previously. Rivalries there were aplenty, but none achieved major political significance.

The outbreak of war had quite different effects on the Left. In one sense it diminshed factional strife: for the first time since 1931, a common enemy had appeared against whom all Republican factions could join. This was more than counterbalanced, however, by the fact that the insurrection momentarily destroyed the central state apparatus and left power in the hands of Anarchist and Socialist groups. This power was used to launch a profound social revolution which, because it was conducted more or less independently in each locality and lacked a single ideological impulse, transformed Republican Spain into a veritable mosaic of separate and often competing authorities. Within days after the military insurrrection there were several different levels of government in the Loyalist zone: the central government in Madrid; the autonomous Catalan and Basque governments in Barcelona and Bilbao, respectively; an almost fully autonomous CNT-sponsored Regional Council in eastern Aragon; somewhat less independent Socialist or Communist regional councils in Asturias, Santander, and Valencia; and finally, hundreds of local village and town antifascist committees that often claimed the right to independent action. The same pattern characterized the Loyalist military forces: rather than a single army under unified command, there was an unstable mixture of increasingly outnumbered regular army and police units which had remained loyal to the Republic, and steadily expanding, self-assertive militias spontaneously created under Anarchist, Socialist, Communist, left Communist, and sometimes even left Republican auspices.

The history of the Civil War on the Loyalist side was in large measure one of trying to come to terms with this extraordinary fragmentation of political and military power in the latter part of July 1936. Two predominant points of view emerged very quickly. One maintained essentially that victory could be achieved only if the war was fought primarily through conventional means, defined in three ways. First, the power of the central government must be restored. Second, a new army must be created through conscription and must operate on hierarchical principles under unified command. Finally, the social revolution that had occurred must be checked and even partially reversed so as to enlist the support of the urban middle classes and small peasant proprietors within Spain as well as that of the bourgeois governments of England and France, the most logical suppliers of arms to the Republic.

As one would expect, this viewpoint was strongly advocated by the middle-class left Republicans and the Prieto Socialists, the two moderate groups of the Popular Front coalition. Its most energetic and effective champions, however, were the Communists, whose seemingly uncharacteristic stance stemmed from a complex mixture of foreign, domestic, and ideological considerations. The chief goal of the Soviet Union during the mid-1930s was to escape, through rapprochement with the Western democracies, the threat to its existence posed by Hitler. Consequently, Stalin sought to transform the previous Communist reputation for universal, unrelenting class antagonism into one of working-class reasonableness. Domestically, the Spanish Communist party, because of its relatively small size and lack of a fully developed union apparatus in 1936, found that the principal gains in the social revolution of late July had been made by the Anarchists and Socialists, not by itself. Moreover, new left Communist groups, particularly the POUM, had gained strength in certain localities, from which they launched Trotsky-like attacks against the Stalinists. As to ideology, spontaneous, undirected popular revolution had been deprecated in the teachings of Lenin from a very early date; moreover, the Russian Revolution seemed to reaffirm the necessity of a vanguard party exercising strong control over the people.

This curious coalition of middle-class Republicans, moderate Socialists, and Stalinist Communists was opposed by an even more complex de facto alliance of the Anarchists, the POUM, and many left Socialists. For these groups victory could be won only if the war was fought entirely by revolutionary means—that is, by abandoning conventional political, economic, and military organization and relying instead on the new types that had appeared. It would be futile to try to win over the Spanish middle classes or England and France by checking the social revolution, they asserted;

rather, the revolution must be carried further so as to inspire the Spanish masses to still greater efforts.

For all three groups, this position was a continuation of their policies of the preceding few years, when they had worked to overthrow the peacetime Republic through a second revolution, as well as an expression of their determination to hold on to the great gains they had made in late July. For the Anarchosyndicalists, an ideological motive was added. The very essence of Bakunin's teachings, and the point ultimately at issue between him and Marx, was the romantic conception that man had survived whole and good despite the sufferings to which the feudal and capitalistic systems had subjected him. Therefore, not only did Bakunin believe in the efficacy of spontaneous revolution, he also thought that as soon as it had triumphed traditional forms of government could be dispensed with so that men would be free to establish looser, more humane forms. The Spanish Anarchists, having gained this freedom in several regions where they were principally responsible for frustrating the military insurrection, were unwilling to return to centralized control, whoever might exercise it. They made their stance most strongly in eastern Aragon, whose Regional Council was led by CNT extremists, and where rural collectives sprang up by the hundreds after July.

As had been the case in the immediate prewar period, the two-fold division in the Spanish Left did not erupt into open conflict, even though the rival factions now possessed their own militias and, to some extent, their own territorial bases. The internal struggle as newly defined continued to be waged mainly through propaganda and political maneuvering. The revolutionary side held the initial advantage because its mass following and enthusiasm enabled it to fill most rapidly the power vacuum created by the military insurrection. But the tide gradually began to shift in the late summer and early autumn of 1936 for two fundamental reasons: steady military defeat, and the Communist switch to the antirevolutionary side, at least in the context of Spain.

Defeat on the battlefield during this period was in large part the price paid for the fact that many of those who collectively came to be known (more outside than inside Spain) as the Loyalists were more loyal to their particular ideology or revolutionary achievement than to a commonly defined Republic. The recent attempt of Noam Chomsky to revive the Anarchist interpretation of the war may have validity for later periods and in the exceedingly important sense that without the social revolution the Republic might well have collapsed without a fight instead of resisting the military insurrection. However, for the critical period from July to October 1936, when the basic military positions for the rest of the war were being decided, a major reason for the Republic's failure to take advantage of the opportunities open to it was the inability of the newly dominant Anarchist and left Socialist groups to wage an effective struggle of their own, and their simultaneous refusal to accept the revival of alternative forms of organization that might have proven militarily more efficacious.

The army insurrection in itself, without reference to the social revolution it set off, disorganized the Republic but did not render it completely helpless. Of the seven major Spanish cities, five remained in Republican hands. The two most industrialized regions were also Republican. The gold reserves and most other financial assets were Republican. The air force and navy remained primarily Republican, as did the large, semi-militarized police forces. Finally, the army itself was by no means united behind the insurrection of some of its generals; more than half of the units stationed on the peninsula seem to have remained on the Republican side.

Against this array, the Nationalists had two material assets of similar magnitude at the very start: command of the units stationed in Spanish Morocco, by far the best in the army, and support of most of the rural population of northern and north central Spain. Yet since the army in Morocco was rendered ineffective for more than two weeks by its inability to cross the Straits of Gibraltar and the northern rural population was far smaller than that of the Republican zone, the true advantage of the Nationalists during this period was probably psychological: their single, desperately held sense of purpose as opposed to the divided allegiances and multiple purposes of their opponents.

The Republic's inability to implement its potentially greater power was partly inherent in the situation and could not have been entirely overcome under any circumstances. The insurrection inevitably sowed suspicion as to the loyalty of all officers; defections and a handful of treasonous acts deepened the distrust. Yet the army and police strength left in the Republican zone might have been used more effectively, and a larger number of initially neutral officers might have been won over had not the ideological presuppositions of the Anarchist and Socialist militias led to their being branded "fascist" almost automatically. Similarly, in many areas, particularly Barcelona, social revolution was inherent in the very act of resisting the insurrection and could not have been avoided. But once successful in these places, revolutionaries diverted precious military resources in ridding themselves of "class enemies" and in imposing the new order upon populations to whom it did not come so naturally. Some scarcity of weapons was also unavoidable, but thousands of rifles that might have been used on the fronts were instead stowed away in CNT headquarters or strutted around the streets by militiamen celebrating their momentary triumph. All this was not without effect on Republican foreign relations. Given the overriding English and French desire to avoid conflict during the 1930s and the aggressive assertiveness of Germany and Italy, an international alignment unfavorable to the Republic would probably have developed in any event. Yet the revolutionary chaos among the Loyalists and their attendant lack of military success enabled each country to overcome, sooner than it otherwise might have, its initial doubts as to what course to follow.

In short, had the Spanish Left not been so disunited before the July insurrection and by the social revolution that immediately followed, it is conceivable (though admittedly not very likely) that the outcome of the French army rebellions in Algeria in 1960–61 might have been anticipated: the relatively weak opposition in the metropolitan country might have been suppressed and the strong force in the trans-Mediterranean colony therefore rendered permanently ineffective.[1] As it was, by August 5 sufficient troops had been transported from Morocco with German and Italian aid to alter completely the military situation on the peninsula. Instead of the weak Nationalist forces of the north, which had been able to do little more than maintain their positions during the preceding two and a half weeks, the Republicans were suddenly confronted by small but effective units that immediately launched an offensive. Against this force the true extent of their lack of preparation revealed itself. Within a month much of Andalusia and nearly all of Estremadura, two vast regions of southern Spain where the Anarchist and Socialist peasant following was most numerous, had fallen to the Nationalists. In another month they had taken San Sebastian in the north and penetrated deep into south central Spain. As the Nationalists approached Madrid in October, resistance stiffened. Only when they actually reached the outskirts of the capital in early November and were stopped short by its defenders, however, did it

---

[1] The major differences between the two situations were that the rebellious French generals had won no territorial base in France as well as Algeria, held insecure control over their own forces and the native population, and confronted a powerful leader in De Gaulle. Nevertheless, the analogy helps illuminate some of the reasons for Republican failure in the Civil War.

become clear that they were faced with a true war rather than a military promenade. In the three months between August 6, the start of the Moroccan army's offensive from Seville, and November 7, its first setback in Madrid, the Nationalists conquered approximately 25,000 square miles of territory. In the next three months, to the start of the Malaga offensive on February 3, 1937, they conquered not much more than 250.

So profound a setback could not but alter internal political relationships in the Republican zone. The extreme revolutionary position eroded, and the position of those who called for sacrifice of ideology and particular revolutionary achievements in favor of greater unity grew stronger. All factions were affected to some extent. The Largo Caballero Socialists drew back from their revolutionary intransigence, accepted leadership of the Madrid government in September, and thereupon lent their support to the drive to create a new, hierarchically organized Republican army. Despite cries of treason from many of their followers, several CNT leaders abandoned their ideological principles and accepted posts in the Catalan government in September and in the Madrid government in November. The Communists gained enormously in strength, both because their units, having shunned revolutionary delirium, had proven most effective in the fighting, and because the Soviet Union had emerged in early October as the Republic's chief supplier of arms. With the Communist increase in power and the growing left Socialist acceptance of centralization, the regional councils in Santander and Asturias which these two forces dominated became more closely linked to the central government. The same effect was achieved in Valencia when that government, fleeing before the Nationalist onslaught, transferred itself from Madrid to the Mediterranean coastal city.

Yet if these changes, together with continuous Soviet aid after October and the appearance on the battlefield of the International Brigades in November, converted the Republicans into a much more formidable military force than before, the Loyalist side continued to be handicapped by its internal divisions. Republican strength approximated its potential only in the central zone around Madrid, where Anarchist influence was weakest and regionalist sentiment did not exist. Elsewhere, the situation was far different. In the northern war zone, the autonomous Basque government continued to operate more or less independently of other Republican forces, whether those immediately adjacent to it in Santander and Asturias or those in the central zone, from which it was cut off by Nationalist territory. Only once did this populous, highly industrialized region launch an offensive, which lasted for six days; otherwise it vainly guarded its strength and was preoccupied by its own internal conflicts. Catalonia participated more actively in the war effort, but the gap between its actual and its potential performance was of even greater importance since the area was even more populous and industrialized than the Basque region.

In Catalonia, because it had not been so directly affected as Madrid by the great Nationalist advance of August–October, and because of its different internal political composition, the inner transformation that had taken place in the central zone did not occur to the same degree. The Communists and Socialists achieved a closer union there than elsewhere and greatly increased their prewar following, but the superiority of the CNT had been so great that they were not yet able to impose their policy of centralization, particularly since the POUM supported the CNT revolutionary line, and the middle-class Catalan regionalists, seeing their autonomy threatened by both groups, played a vacillating role. In consequence, the Catalan sector of the front (which lay in Aragon, some miles west of Catalonia proper) continued to display the military ineffectiveness characteristic of the Republic as a whole in the months immediately after the July insurrection. Internal conflict was rampant; offensives were infrequent and poorly executed; and the CNT and POUM generally refused integration into the new Republican army and insisted upon retaining their special prerogatives and separate structure. Under these circumstances, the manpower and extensive material resources of Catalonia were rendered meaningless, even though directed against Nationalist forces that were much smaller and more poorly equipped than those ranged against Madrid. After an entire year of intermittent combat, the lines on the Aragon front remained essentially what they had been in July 1936.

There are two possible explanations for the next major political transformation in the Republican zone, the events of May 1937 in which the rivalries between the Republican forces burst into several days of street fighting in Barcelona and left the Communists the dominant force. The more popular explanation emphasizes the ruthlessness and duplicity of the Communists, characteristics certainly not foreign to them. Having gained a strong position by their discipline and influence over the arms supply from the USSR, it is said, the Communists, though unable to assume open command because they feared to alienate England and France, decided to take over de facto control of the Republic. This they achieved in three ways: by honeycombing the Republican army with their political commissars, by reducing the power of the CNT and destroying completely the POUM (more because it was "Trotskyite," the argument runs, than because of its specific actions within Spain), and by substituting a more pliable leader, the moderate Socialist Juan Negrín, in the central government when Largo Caballero sought to resist them.

The other, less ideological explanation is that the ambiguous situation that arose after the Nationalists had been stopped at Madrid in November 1936 could have continued only so long as the war remained stalemated. Once the Nationalists began to move again, with their rapid conquest of Malaga in February 1937 and the opening of their offensive on the northern front in April, the same kind of transformation that had been experienced in the central zone earlier would have to be imposed upon Catalonia. The May events, in essence, were a desperate attempt to prevent further defeat by forcing Catalonia to shoulder more of the war effort. They may have been hastened by Communist fears that the CNT and POUM would stage a coup of their own, perhaps with the support of the Caballero Socialists, who were increasingly resentful of the growth in Communist power. But primarily the Communists sought to create a more effective war machine rather than secure personal dominance as such.

Insofar as these two motives can be separated (for they are by no means mutually exclusive), the second seems the more plausible, though the savageness of the suppression of the POUM leaves room for doubt. The Communists could not have won the Barcelona streetfighting in early May or ousted Largo Caballero from the premiership in the latter part of that month had they not enjoyed the support of the Prieto Socialists and the reluctant acquiescence of many CNT leaders (who, while refusing to join the new Negrín government, did not try to turn their massive following actively against it). The same was true of the changes that occured in the summer of 1937 as an aftermath to these two decisive events. The Communists alone could not have disbanded the semiindependent Regional Council of Aragon, undone the nearly universal collectivization that had existed under the CNT in that region since the 1936 social revolution, nor reduced Catalan autonomy to a shadow of its former self.

Yet having been achieved by force rather than consent, the victory of the Communists had its price. Their chief allies of the prewar period, the Caballero Socialists, now began to tread rapidly down the road that by 1939 would lead them to regard the Communists as a greater evil than the

Nationalists. The Anarchosyndicalists, who had been psychologically buffeted since the autumn of 1936 by the failure of reality to correspond to their theories, now became almost completely dispirited. The Catalan regionalists were in a similar condition for similar reasons. The dominance achieved by the Communists subtly affected even those groups not directly injured by the May events by raising doubts as to their tactics and suspicions as to their ultimate motives.

The Communists were successful in their purpose of integrating Catalonia more closely with the war effort, but they could have enabled the Republic to transcend the new divisions that had appeared only if this integration had led to victory on the battlefield. Such was not to be the case. The Nationalists, because of their conquest of industrial Bilbao in June 1937 and of the rest of the northern Republican zone by October, and because of the steady flow of arms and men they had been receiving from Germany and Italy since the autumn of the previous year, now held material as well as psychological superiority.

Thus while the Republicans were able (as they had not been earlier in the war) to convert Aragon, not Madrid, into the principal scene of battle, the greater military effectiveness that this shift symbolized was no longer enough. The Aragon offensives of August and September 1937, by which the Republicans sought to divert the Nationalist army from completing its conquest of northern Spain, failed in their purpose. The massive Teruel offensive of December–January won its initial objectives but so exhausted Republican forces that it enabled the Nationalists to stage a breakthrough unmatched since their drive of August–October 1936. In four months, from early March to early July 1938, the Republicans lost some 15,000 square miles of territory on the Aragon front and saw the Nationalists reach the Mediterranean Sea, splitting the Loyalist zone in two. The valor of the Republican army was proven in late July when, managing to take the overextended Nationalists by surprise, it pushed their forces back some ten to fifteen miles in exceedingly difficult terrain along the Ebro River. But this momentary victory had little effect except to lead to several months of a battle of attrition which the diminishing Republican forces could ill afford.

Communist dominance after May 1937 had led—at a tremendous cost in lives—only to a greater ability to resist, not to a turn in the tide of battle. Thus the Communists, militarily the most formidable of the Republican groups, were no more able than their rivals to create a consensus of loyalties behind their version of the Republic. War-weariness inevitably spread among large sectors of the population as defeat followed defeat, the hope that England and France might change their policies became more untenable, and even the Soviet Union first reduced and then entirely stopped its flow of arms. Aside from the battles mentioned, there were three major milestones in the Republican descent into hopelessness. Prieto's dismissal from the Ministry of War under Communist pressure in April 1938, after the Teruel disaster, narrowed the base of Negrín's coalition government still further. Franco's rejection of Negrín's thirteen-point peace proposal in May raised demands for an alternative government that would negotiate surrender. Moreover, the British and French collapse before Hitler at the Munich Conference in September destroyed the illusion of a dramatic shift in international alignments that had sustained the Republicans during the Czech crisis of the late summer.

Because of the destruction of the POUM and the disintegration of the Anarchists and Caballero Socialists, the opposition to Negrín and the Communists came more from individual middle-class and moderate Socialist leaders than from working-class groups, as it had in the past. The Republican masses might still occasionally express their valor in battle, as on the Ebro, but no longer acted in the streets under the inspiration of some ideological vision. For the urban masses, food shortages and destruction of the revolutionary factory workers' councils in favor of government control ended the enthusiasm of 1936 and early 1937. For the peasantry, which retained control of most of the land it had seized in July 1936, social gains were rendered meaningless by ever greater government crop requisitions and the growing horror of war. In short, a general consensus had finally arisen within the Republic, but it was the consensus of defeatism.

Under these circumstances, the success of the Nationalist offensive against Catalonia in January 1939 should not be surprising. There was no repetition of the saga of Madrid, no stubborn stand as the armies approached the Catalan capital, only steady retreat. Within two months the Nationalists conquered the most populous and industrialized region of Spain, captured vast quantities of military supplies, and forced a major portion of the Republican army to intern itself in France. Because of the sudden change that occurred in the European political scene soon after, the Republican cause might not have been entirely hopeless even after this amputation of its resources. Given the slowness with which the cautious Franco planned each major move, it is conceivable that the struggle might have dragged on until the outbreak of World War II in September, and that the Western democracies then might possibly have come to the Republic's aid (though this was unlikely because of England's generally good relations with Franco and its tendency to regard the Spanish war as a separate conflict).[2] But the will to fight was gone from everyone except the Communists and Negrín.

The final act of the Republican drama was the one which had long been threatening: open warfare among the Republic's component elements. The conflict took the form of an anti-Communist coup in Madrid, headed by a nonpolitical military man, Colonel Casado, and supported by most Socialists and Anarchists as well as by what was left of the middle-class Republican groups. Some 2,000 lives were lost in a week-long battle in early March. Had Franco been more generous, this new tragedy might have been expiated by his agreement to the general amnesty which the Casado forces sought as the basis for peace. Instead, Spain was finally delivered from the horror of war on April 1, 1939, only to be plunged into a new horror of prison camps and political executions by the tens of thousands.

The principal lesson of the Spanish Civil War, insofar as internal political loyalties are concerned, is that a common cause can be maintained only if it has been generally accepted prior to the opening of hostilities. If it has not and either of the combatants is riven, as was Republican Spain, by a multiplicity of social, ideological, and regional conflicts, two consequences are probable. Moments of apparent triumph are unlikely to be converted into full victory because each of the rival factions will try to anticipate the final settlement and secure as strong a position as possible for itself by imposing its particular political vision within the territory under its control. This is what occurred in Spain from July to October 1936. Times of defeat, on the other hand, may enable or compel the faction that can draw upon the widest assortment of politically effective partial allegiances to impose a forced unity upon the others, thus weakening still further their attachment to the general cause and creating new divisions that may eventually erupt into internecine conflict if the forced union is not militarily victorious. This is what occurred in Spain under the Com-

---

[2] This kind of miraculous, last-minute salvation of the Republic was also improbable because Hitler might not have chosen to risk general war over Poland in September had the Spanish conflict still continued.

munists after May 1937. The tragedy of Republican Spain, in short, was that a civil war of its own always lurked within its ranks as it fought the greater Civil War against the Nationalists.

Suggestions for Further Research

Literally thousands of books, pamphlets, and articles have appeared on the Spanish Civil War, yet many basic questions remain unresolved. This is partly because the war was so controversial that most of what has been written is polemic or biased, and partly because professional historians have tended to concentrate on general histories or studies of international repercussions, thus leaving undone the monographic work required for a more exact understanding of domestic politics. In the context of this chapter, three suggestions for further research seem especially pertinent.

First, we desperately need detailed monographic research on the relationship between military effectiveness and revolutionary enthusiasm on the Republican side, particularly in the periods from July to October 1936 in Spain as a whole, and from May 1937 to April 1938 for the regions of Catalonia and Aragon. Were major opportunities really lost in the first period because of revolutionary upheaval? What, objectively, were the consequences of the partial reversal of the revolution in the second period?

Second, a history of the Socialist movement during the war would be extremely useful; this was in some ways potentially the most powerful force in Spain, yet the force that played the most ill-defined and inconsistent a role.

Third, it is time to look again at the history of the Spanish Communist party during the war, using the new insights that the development of national communism during the past decade has given us.

VII

DIPLOMACY FROM THE OUTSIDE
American Intervention in Vietnam

NORMAN A. GRAEBNER

NONINTERVENTION IN THE CIVIL WARS of other nations is a deeply established diplomatic tradition stemming from the assumption that international peace and goodwill demand the acceptance of national governments as a matter of internal rather than external choice. For that reason international law has been concerned less with the nature of governments or the means of their selection than with their capacity to function effectively in the international realm in behalf of their peoples. In emphasizing this principle the United Nations, in its original charter, declared itself in favor of nonintervention and against the exportation of political influence or revolution. Under the prodding of its lesser members the U.N. General Assembly restated the principle on numerous occasions. Still, the United Nations could never provide either the guidance or the machinery needed for any effective response to a civil war situation, whether the struggle for power resulted from a revolution against an allegedly unrepresentative or colonial regime or an externally controlled insurgency.

This perennial concern of the U.N. for the right of self-determination reflects the experience of the twentieth century. Despite its almost universal acceptance in principle, nonintervention has not always governed the conduct of nations. The reason is clear. Obnoxious, threatening, or dangerous foreign policies cannot be separated easily from the ambitions of ruling elites. Thus any government's obligation to defend its citizens' welfare must include the right to influence, if possible, the behavior of other countries at its source. That governments have seldom resorted to direct intervention reflects both a general absence of necessity and the known limitations of success. Most governments of modern times have not pointedly pursued policies designed to injure the interests of neighbors. Established nations, moreover, in large measure follow historic objectives that change little with successive regimes. Secondly, intervention, when attempted, has often proved ineffective or taxing, requiring force to achieve its purposes in direct proportion to the strength, efficiency, and national identification of those it opposed. Even when successful, intervention challenges national pride and integrity.

What mattered in the Indochinese civil war, therefore, was not the legal basis of intervention: nations will serve their interests as they perceive them whether they enjoy the sanction of international law or not. At issue after 1950 were the security interests of the United States. Yet what enemy could have rendered this jungle country, a region of no historic importance to the American people, of such immediate concern? This was a critical question at mid-century, and it compelled Washington both to conceptualize the danger embodied in Ho Chi Minh's revolutionary struggle against the French and to calculate the possible costs of involvement in that conflict. Any subsequent questioning of this nation's Indochinese intervention would simply challenge the wisdom of its successive calculations of the ends or the means of policy. Had American security interests in the Indochinese civil war been sufficient to necessitate intervention, Washington need never have hesitated to expend whatever human and material resources the success of that involvement demanded. At the beginning, this ultimate test of national behavior mattered little.

Ho Chi Minh was the immediate problem. After 1945 he mobilized the communal spirit of the Indochinese countryside and thus fell heir to the nationalist uprising of the Indochinese people against foreign control. The Indochinese revolution was a complex blend of Asian nationalism and communism, fused in the personality and leadership of Ho Chi Minh— an amalgam understood by many Far Eastern specialists in Europe and America but not sufficiently by official Washington. Still, in supporting France's war against Ho, the United States was less than sympathetic with that nation's continuing colonial position in Southeast Asia. Washington's purpose in Indochina and elsewhere was the containment of communism, and Ho Chi Minh was an avowed Communist. To undermine Ho, the Truman administration pressed the French to grant autonomy and the promise of full independence to the non-Communist Indochinese nationalists, hoping that by weakening French authority it might strengthen the nationalistic resistance to Ho.

Still, to Washington officials Ho Chi Minh was not the real enemy. The United States resisted the collapse of the French empire in Southeast Asia under the clear assumption that Ho was a puppet of the Soviet Union and that his revolution, if successful, would further the cause of Indochinese independence less than the cause of Soviet imperialism. Indeed, beginning in 1950 the American rationale for supporting the French in Indochina denied that the Indochinese struggle for power was a civil war at all. In January, both Moscow and Peking recognized Ho's newly established Democratic Republic of Viet Nam. Shortly thereafter, United States officials announced that they regarded Ho's war against the French as a Soviet-based aggression against the people of Indochina. Secretary of State Dean Acheson declared characteristically that the Soviet recognition of Ho's Democratic Republic revealed him "in his true color as the mortal enemy of national independence in Indochina." The notion that Bao Dai, the Paris-chosen native leader of the new Viet Nam state, had better claims to Vietnamese leadership and that he would ultimately triumph over Ho became the prevailing wishful thought in Washington. Yet to those who knew better it was already clear that Bao Dai would win few defectors from Ho's Vietminh.

When finally on May 8, 1950, Secretary Acheson negotiated an arrangement with French Foreign Minister Robert Schuman whereby France and the governments of Indochina together would carry the responsibility for Indochinese security, the rationale for United States aid was clear. "The United States Government," declared Acheson, "convinced that neither national independence nor democratic evolution exists in any area dominated by Soviet imperialism, considers the situation to be such as to warrant its according economic aid and military equipment to the Associated States of Indochina and to France in order to assist them in restoring stability and permitting these states to pursue their peaceful and democratic development." With Mao Tse-tung's victory on the Chinese mainland in late 1949, ran official American rhetoric, Moscow had captured control of a half billion Chinese people in its cause of world conquest; now through Ho Chi Minh the Kremlin would add Southeast Asia to the widening area under its command.

This concept of a Soviet-controlled global conspiracy, sustained by

Stalinist rhetoric, led logically to the concept of falling dominoes. The conclusion, widely accepted in Washington, that the Chinese and Indo-chinese revolutions demonstrated less the force of nationalism than the capacity of the Soviets to expand their power through control of revolutionary élites corrupted beyond measure the nation's attitude toward revolutionary change and thus its ability to distinguish a civil from an international contest of power. What gave special credence to this concept of Soviet expansion through revolution was the theory that Marxism was antithetical to national sovereignty and that communism would gradually destroy the national entity of those states that it controlled and create one Communist-led community. John Foster Dulles, as a State Department adviser after 1950, first developed this theme of conquest through revolution in the wake of the Korean War. He gave the theory its clearest expression in a speech of November 1953, after he had become Secretary of State. "The Soviet leaders, in mapping their strategy for world conquest," he said, "hit upon nationalism as a device for absorbing the colonial peoples." The danger lay, he continued, in the ability of Communist agitators and agents to aggravate the nationalistic aspirations of people so that they would rebel violently against the existing political order. Before a new internally based stability could be created, the Communists would gain control of the nation and convey it into the Soviet orbit. With time, this interpretation of Communist-led revolution, warning the world of the Soviet capacity to conquer without resort to invading armies, became accepted in government and out as a self-evident truth, although it had no precedent in history.

This concept of falling dominoes was, despite its wide acceptance, a puzzling one, for it assumed that the government or the people of one country would pursue the interests of another even at the cost of war and destruction. The Soviets could with a minimum of rhetoric identify their interests with a revolutionary movement, whether Communist-led or not. But Washington has never demonstrated that the Soviets can manufacture revolutionary situations or control whatever revolutionary movements they elect to support. Nor has the Kremlin claimed such power.

Revolution in itself can scarcely serve the expansionist interests of others, for any successful revolution requires both a local base of power and the support of indigenous conditions and issues which enable its leaders to promise better and more effective government as well as a prospect of modernization and social change. All revolutionary élites of postwar

Asia and Africa, in their emphasis on national performance, have been fundamentally nationalistic, whatever the precise programs of economic reconstruction and state-building their ideological preferences may dictate. Such revolutionaries may accept external aid with both hands; they will not accept external control.

Within the context of falling dominoes the Eisenhower administration viewed the French collapse at Dienbienphu in the late spring of 1954 with concern, for to Washington the Indochinese struggle had long ceased to be a civil war. By definition, Ho's impending success would merely open the way for new additions of territory to the Communist monolith in South and Southeast Asia. The French defeat, decisive as it was, did not destroy all French authority in Indochina. Indeed, the French still controlled Saigon and large areas of the South. But the Dienbienphu disaster, because of the symbolic importance which the French had attached to that battle, convinced the Paris government that further military efforts would be futile. Dienbienphu, after all, was only the culmination of a long series of French reverses that reached back a half-dozen years. The United States and Britain made clear during April their determination not to intervene militarily. The Geneva Conference, in session after late April, conveyed to the world the Western decision to accept compromise. Following the fall of Dienbienphu in May, the new French premier, Pierre Mendès-France, committed his government to an Indochinese settlement within one month. Thereafter Western diplomacy, guided largely by Britain's Anthony Eden, sought no more at Geneva than some political arrangement which would permit the French to withdraw from an untenable position with some dignity.

Two conditions suggest why Ho Chi Minh, having broken French resistance, still accepted far less than a victory at Geneva. His successes assured independence for all Indochina, even that portion which continued to oppose him bitterly, but he emerged from Geneva with immediate control of only that portion of the new state of Vietnam north of the seventeenth parallel. Yet Ho could view the future with satisfaction. First of all, his military forces had disposed of the French military presence in Southeast Asia without the necessity of confronting either a British or an American army. The French effort had cost France twice the total of Marshall aid, plus 175,000 casualties and 92,000 dead, among them 40 percent of France's regular commissioned and noncommissioned officers. Ho's forces would increase rather than diminish in effectiveness with the passage of time. Secondly, the Geneva Conference had created only one Vietnam, momentarily divided at the seventeenth parallel, with its political future to be resolved by free elections in two years. This provision seemed to promise Ho the ultimate possession of the South without the necessity of additional fighting.

Thus for those who anticipated a post-Geneva era of stability in Southeast Asia the realities of July 1954 were hardly reassuring. The Geneva Conference had not destroyed Ho's power or compelled him to renounce his intention of unifying all Vietnam under his command. Second, the conference, in establishing the seventeenth parallel division, had attempted to resolve a national struggle for power, aimed at social revolution as much as at freedom from French rule, with an artificial geographic division. With independence, countless Vietnamese south of the seventeenth parallel, whatever their attitudes toward communism, would sustain an allegiance to those in Hanoi who had driven the French from their land. At Geneva, Communist spokesmen promised to withdraw all pro-Hanoi forces north of the seventeenth parallel within 100 days; they withdrew few, if any. Despite Dulles's assurance that the Southeast Asia Treaty Organization, to be formalized at Manila in September 1954, eliminated the danger of falling dominoes, it was obvious to newsmen that Washington's diplomatic maneuvering during the Indochina crisis had not resolved the problem of containment.

Two delegations at Geneva—the American and the South Vietnamese —refused to sign the Geneva Agreement, although both pledged themselves not to upset by force the accords reached there. Those Vietnamese who had supported the French, primarily Indochina's Catholic minority, rejected the consequences of the French defeat. At Geneva they made good their opposition to Ho Chi Minh by gaining a divided Vietnam which, at least temporarily, gave them both a country of their own and the right to recover the large Catholic population in the North through migration. Eventually some 800,000 refugees crossed the seventeenth parallel into South Vietnam, thereby strengthening the claims of that region to continued independence. Still, left to their own devices, the new South Vietnamese leaders had no hope of sustaining themselves against either an election or an invasion from the North—perhaps even a revolution within South Vietnam itself. Their long-term success hinged on their ability to gain external support. This they received from the United States with scarcely a request, for Washington could not view the continuing struggle for power in Vietnam as a purely civil conflict despite the fact that there was, in 1954, only one Vietnam.

Unlike the British and the French, Washington had not used the opportunity afforded at Geneva to terminate its past anti-Communist commitments or to formulate a new policy towards the future of Southeast Asia. Rather it followed the logic of established policy and reaffirmed its goal of containing the ambitions of Ho Chi Minh, substituting for the French the new government in Saigon as the key agency for achieving that purpose. For Dulles the seventeenth parallel had become the line dividing the free from the Communist worlds; that boundary would not be changed, he declared, by any means whatever. Unfortunately that status quo was a political and territorial standstill which recognized two political entities, each allegedly possessing a government in full control of its own region. But such a concept of the status quo denied the existence of a continuing revolutionary process within South Vietnam itself which would challenge the right of any pro-Western Saigon regime to govern the region. Fundamentally, Dulles's decision ruled out any Communist gains in the South, even through the promised elections. As the United States embarked on its program of massive economic and military aid to the Saigon government, observers predicted accurately that this material was not being sent as a free gift to the North Vietnamese.

It came as no surprise when, in July 1955, the Saigon government, with Washington's approval, announced its decision to oppose nationwide elections despite its desire for national unity. "We do not reject the principle of free elections as peaceful and democratic means to achieve that unity," ran its communiqué, ". . . [But] they will be meaningful only on the condition that they are absolutely free." That the Western nations at Geneva had accepted an election procedure when free elections had no chance suggests clearly that beyond extricating the French they had no clear interest in the political future of Vietnam. Saigon's determination to defend itself against Hanoi by avoiding the election was but a hollow victory. For Hanoi it compelled no change in intent; it merely shifted the means of unification from an election to force. The struggle for power in Vietnam had scarcely begun. And the United States, in this burgeoning conflict, had replaced France and England as the guarantors of the status quo in Southeast Asia. No less than in the past, Washington's opposition to Ho reflected less his known ambitions toward South Vietnam than his alleged integration into a Soviet-based Communist plunge into all Southeast Asia. By the mid-1950s the growing American concern for Southeast Asia, including the rationale behind it, was dramatic enough for all to see.

This clear extension of the nation's military obligations to the Asian mainland did not weigh heavily after 1954 on either Eisenhower or Dulles. Indeed, both denied consistently that containment in Asia might necessitate any direct United States involvement in another Asian war. President Eisenhower, confronted early in 1954 with the impending French collapse in Indochina, reminded the press that nothing could be more absurd than the involvement of American forces in another land war in Asia. Secretary Dulles informed the Manila Conference in September 1954 that the United States, with its worldwide obligations, would not commit its ground forces to the SEATO defense area. If the Asian treaty forces, with United States logistical support, proved incapable of halting aggression, the country would simply respond with its weapons of massive retaliation. This theme the secretary reiterated consistently until his death in 1959. This repeated assertion that the United States would not fight in Asia comprised either a gross military miscalculation or a denial that this nation had any interests on the Asian mainland that were worth an American war. For when in the past did the United States refrain from employing its land power when its vital interests were challenged?

After 1954 the United States embarked on two separate yet complementary courses of action designed specifically to sustain the seventeenth parallel without any United States military presence on the Asian mainland. Eisenhower and his advisers had placed their essential faith for South Vietnam's continued independence on the leadership of Ngo Dinh Diem. Unfortunately Diem, who had spent the years of struggle for Indochinese freedom in self-imposed exile, lacked the legitimacy that came to other postwar Asian leaders because of their identification with the anticolonial movements. This serious handicap scarcely disturbed American officials in Washington and Saigon who regarded Diem as the answer to his country's need for honest, reformist leadership. Eisenhower entrusted the burden of successful containment in Vietnam to Diem with his promise of aid in October 1954:

> The purpose of this offer is to assist the Government of Vietnam in developing and maintaining a strong, viable state, capable of resisting attempted subversion or aggression through military means. The Government of the United States expects that this aid will be met by performance

on the part of the Government of Vietnam in undertaking needed reforms. It hopes that such aid, combined with your own continuing efforts, will contribute effectively toward an independent Vietnam endowed with a strong government. Such a government would, I hope, be so responsive to the nationalist aspirations of its people, so enlightened in purpose and effective in performance, that it will be respected both at home and abroad and discourage any who might wish to impose a foreign ideology on your free people.

Thereafter Diem, carrying the major responsibility for successful containment in Southeast Asia, enjoyed wide support in Washington. The administration, for its part, established a crash program with most of the aid earmarked for defense and police; much of the remainder it allotted for economic and technical assistance which included special help for refugees—their transportation and resettlement. The United States, in addition, sent a select mission to train the South Vietnamese army. United States aid to Saigon totaled almost $2 billion for the years 1955–1963. As Diem, with that support, slowly brought some order out of chaos, albeit at the price of sending most of his liberal opposition into exile, the enthusiasm of his American adherents exceeded the limits of reality.

Members of the administration took the lead in acclaiming Diem. In June 1956, Assistant Secretary of State Walter S. Robertson reminded the American Friends of Vietnam in Washington of Diem's achievements: "In him the country has found a truly worthy leader whose integrity and devotion to his country's welfare have become generally recognized among his people. Asia has given us in President Diem another great figure, and the entire free world has become richer for his example and determination and moral fortitude." By 1957 members of government and the press spoke freely of Diem's "miracle" in South Vietnam. When in May the South Vietnamese president visited Washington, Eisenhower greeted him in person at the airport and hailed him as one of the truly outstanding national leaders of his time. In their subsequent communiqué the two presidents anticipated the peaceful unification of Vietnam under a freely elected government.

Unfortunately the evidence for the miracle was elusive. Diem, accused by his enemies of being concerned primarily with the security and well-being of his own regime, had made little effort, despite the urging of his American advisers, to democratize his army or improve the lot of the Vietnamese peasants. After 1957, Communist-led guerrillas began to organize the countryside, taking control of village after village, until by 1960 they commanded most of the territory of South Vietnam. Meanwhile many of Diem's former admirers became disenchanted: the miracle of Vietnam had been a miracle in public relations, but little else. The *Wall Street Journal* concluded in April 1959: "[T]he accomplishment, so far, rests on American aid. Without that aid there would be no Vietnam." Yet Eisenhower could write to Diem in 1960 on the occasion of the Republic of Vietnam's fifth anniversary:

> During the years of your independence it has been refreshing for us to observe how clearly the Government and the citizens of Vietnam have faced the fact that the greatest danger to their independence was Communism. You and your countrymen have used your strength well in accepting the double challenge of building your country and resisting Communist imperialism. . . . Vietnam's ability to defend itself from the Communists has grown immeasurably since its successful struggle to become an independent Republic.

Already terrorism and infiltration had begun to undermine the carefully constructed image of a stable and secure Vietnam. The insurgency spread even more rapidly with the formation of the National Liberation Front in December 1960, dedicated to the liberation of South Vietnam and unification of the country. For a brief period longer Diem continued to play down the Communist threat, for its existence reflected adversely on his leadership and the alleged triumphs of his government. When finally he acknowledged his inability to counter the increasingly defiant guerrilla challenge to his regime, he reminded President Kennedy early in 1961 of the long-standing American commitment to South Vietnamese independence. Kennedy responded by sending additional aid and Vice President Johnson, in May, on an investigating mission. Then in October he dispatched a second mission under General Maxwell Taylor, who reported both the inadequacies of the Diem regime and the need for American personnel to stop the infiltration across the seventeenth parallel, which Washington no longer viewed as a temporary line dividing a single country but as an international boundary line separating two nations. Kennedy in December recommitted the nation to the defense of the Saigon government. But the basic American strategy remained that of undermining Ho's influence in the South through Diem's massive successes.

Washington had, however, prepared meticulously for the possible failure of its political strategy by developing a military strategy as well. After 1954, SEATO carried the military burden of containment, and the inadequacy of that alliance as a guarantor of Southeast Asian stability quickly moved beyond the realm of official doubt. As late as 1962 Secretary of Defense Robert McNamara assured a congressional committee that SEATO's evolution into a sound military organization had eliminated the need for United States ground forces in any foreseeable Asian conflict. On the occasion of SEATO's ninth anniversary in 1963, Prime Minister Sarit Thanarat of Thailand recounted the alliance's successes: "At present it may be said that SEATO is an important fortress capable of making the Communists think carefully before committing any aggression against the area under the Treaty [which included South Vietnam]. Since this organization acts as an effective deterrent to potential aggressors, it has increasingly been attacked verbally by the Communists. This indicates how important SEATO is in resisting Communist aggression."

Unfortunately SEATO, despite the approbation heaped upon it, did not function. Indeed, under the conditions laid down in the initial treaty, it could not function. Its eight members, scattered widely around the globe and including France and Pakistan, two nations with only minor or vestigial interests in Southeast Asia, would never agree on policy. Despite the extent of its military aid program designed to build and sustain Asian armies capable of meeting the Communist enemy on the ground, the United States succeeded in creating no army capable of any performance. The Laotian army, amply supplied with advisers, equipment, and encouragement to underwrite a pro-Western regime in Vientiane, never won a battle against the Communist-led Pathet Lao. It never fought one. Nowhere in SEATO was there any force, other than the mobile striking power of the United States, that could resist the encroachments of Ho Chi Minh. But the United States had no more a commitment than other member nations to action under the SEATO pact. As the chairman of the Senate Foreign Relations Committee declared in 1954, "The Treaty [SEATO] does not call for automatic action; it calls for consultation with other signatories. . . . I cannot emphasize too strongly that we have no obligations . . . to take positive measures of any kind. All we are obliged to do is to consult together about it."

Such foundations for a potentially costly policy were scarcely adequate, for after 1950 the United States government never revealed even the intention to commit material and manpower resources to Southeast Asia commensurate with its declared purpose of containing communism, whether the danger lay in global Communist aggression or in the specific, but limited, expansionism of Ho Chi Minh. The "domino theory," to be at all convincing, had to assume that Ho represented a threat which far transcended his own power. (Certainly Ho commanded no strength to topple dominoes throughout South and Southeast Asia.) Washington predicted disaster if containment at the seventeenth parallel should falter, but it neglected throughout a decade to show the public why this was true.

It mattered little at the time. As long as Diem and SEATO guaranteed successful containment at little cost, the Eisenhower administration faced no necessity to explain what United States policy was really containing. Thus was shaped a dilemma for subsequent administrations. The ends of U.S. policy assumed a global danger of which Hanoi comprised only a minor segment, yet the means of policy, as they evolved during the Eisenhower years, were not even an adequate defense against Hanoi, much less against Moscow and Peking, included in the more abstract phrase "Communist aggression." If the latter two comprised the essential danger to American security interests in Asia, policies aimed at the disposal of Ho's ambitions, whatever their success, would not touch, much less resolve, the dangers posed by the two leading Communist powers. If, on the other hand, the challenge to United States security lay in Hanoi, then the rhetoric of a Soviet-based global danger—the initial and continuing rationale for opposing Ho—had no meaning whatever. No matter what the global pressures that demanded successful containment of communism in Asia, the United States would behave as if the danger conprised no more than North Vietnam's determination to unseat the Saigon regime. Washington never contemplated war with China or Russia to settle the question of South Vietnam.

During 1964, President Johnson faced a critical choice in Vietnam. The limited but growing infusions of aid and advisers during the Kennedy years had not enabled Saigon to recapture the countryside. Indeed, by 1964 the Vietcong, now operating openly, had begun to demolish all government forces sent against them. During the weeks following the November election, the president discovered that he had either to recognize a partial if not a total victory for Hanoi or introduce United States land and air power in sufficient quantities to stabilize the Saigon regime by driving all pro-Hanoi forces, even those which had always resided in South Vietnam, north of the seventeenth parallel. That President Johnson made the latter choice, and ultimately converted the war into an American war, was never a question of international law; it was a question of national policy, to be judged on the basis of the American interest at stake in Vietnam.

No one questioned the right of the United States government to provide assistance to Saigon after 1954 under the assumption that it was a widely recognized government. When facing an insurgency, moreover, such a government might anticipate continued assistance at established levels inasmuch as it had been led to rely on such aid. To lose it at a moment of crisis might have jeopardized its existence unfairly. Nonintervention does not necessarily serve the cause of self-determination when those who oppose an established government enjoy extensive external support. Indeed, counterrevolutionary support of a recognized government might better serve the cause of self-determination than an externally-supported insurgency.

Still, American aid to Saigon had become a subject of controversy before the end of the Kennedy administration. It was already apparent that the vastly augmented military assistance program was holding a tottering regime in power under conditions which could easily bring the United States into the conflict directly. At what point, critics asked, did such aid endanger the very principle of self-determination? Even as the South Vietnamese forces continued to disintegrate, their resources both in quality and in quantity seemed vastly superior to those of their antagonists. But what complicated the issue and negated the possibility of measuring the genuine will of the Vietnamese people with some accuracy was the uncertain level of aid and encouragement which the South Vietnamese insurgents received from Hanoi and whether that aid represented a nationalizing or a conquering force. Washington officials had long agreed that Ho Chi Minh was nothing less than an aggressor. That Hanoi received massive Soviet and later Chinese aid was demonstrated by the volume and character of its weaponry. Yet military aid was never more than a small fraction of the American investment in the South Vietnamese effort. That of the USSR probably never exceeded $1.5 billion a year. The North Vietnamese and the Vietcong, moreover, continued to do their own fighting and dying.

Ngo Dinh Diem, during the nine years that he governed South Vietnam, carried the prime responsibility to build a national administration. But having failed, was he justified in pushing the burden of his failure onto the United States? Historically governments sensitive to the broad interests of their people have resisted revolutions successfully. Some Vietnam critics have argued flatly that any government with widespread support cannot be overthrown and that if it lacks such support no level of external assistance will save it. Indeed, Richard J. Barnet, a well-known student of Asian revolution, has insisted that no regime requiring counterrevolutionary aid to remain in power can achieve lasting success "short of wholesale murder and resettlement of the population." Those who upheld President Johnson's decision to escalate the war questioned the application of such assumptions to Vietnam. Even a thoroughly representative government, they insisted, might easily succumb to a foreign-backed revolution if it lacked an efficient military organization. An insurgency, moreover, which had access to foreign sanctuaries enjoyed a distinct advantage over government forces in any struggle for power. Believing that the special military advantages possessed by the enemies of Saigon scarcely reflected popular approval, the defenders of United States policy insisted that Ngo Dinh Diem and his successors merited no less than equalizing support from the American people.

Hanoi's clear encouragement of the South Vietnamese insurgency raised the central issue in the Vietnam debate: Was the contest for power in South Vietnam a civil or an international conflict? On this question hinged both the scale of the American involvement and its chance for an early success. Countless Americans, many in high positions, refused to distinguish the war in Vietnam from that between North and South Korea a decade earlier. The fact that in both cases the competing halves had *de facto* governments which claimed legitimate control over the entire country, as well as a series of treaty arrangements with the major cold-war blocs, gave both wars the same superficial character. Measured by the Korean precedent, Hanoi had no more recognizable claims to power or influence over the whole than had North Korea. It seemed imperative, in the interest of worldwide stability, that one half of a divided nation not be permitted to unite both halves by force, whether its strategy constituted an all-out attack or a limited and largely covert assistance to an insurgency. In either case, insisted the proponents of United States policy, Hanoi's policies of unification were an expression less of nationalism than of external aggression. As in Korea, therefore, the United States and its allies had no choice but to support the South Vietnamese government against attack.

The struggles for power in Korea and Vietnam, however, were hardly identical. It is possible that Hanoi had directed the South Vietnamese insurgency from the beginning. But the fact that the South Vietnamese revolutionaries would accept the leadership of Ho Chi Minh, declared by Washington the enemy of self-determination in South Vietnam, suggested clearly that for them the assault on the Saigon government comprised the continuation of the old nationalist-Communist upheaval rather than an external aggression. It is unlikely that the Vietcong would have courted death and destruction in their homeland merely to serve the expansionist interests of another nation. North Vietnam, in short, was not for them a foreign power.

Thus in at least two important respects the war in Vietnam was not a repetition of Korea. Unlike Ho Chi Minh, Syngman Rhee, the pro-Western spokesman of Korean nationalism and unity, had contributed little to the independence of the Korean people. United States and Russian armies had liberated Korea from Japanese control, and following their postwar division of the peninsula at the thirty-eighth parallel, Washington had handed control of South Korea to Syngman Rhee. The fact that Ho Chi Minh's revolutionary forces were directly responsible for the liberation of all Vietnam, North and South, from French rule, dictated from 1954 onward that the seventeenth parallel could never equal the thirty-eighth parallel in significance as a boundary separating two nations. Nor did the quality of war in Vietnam have much relationship to that in Korea. The Seoul government had the fanatical support of the South Korean populace; this permitted the United Nations allies in Korea to establish stable battle lines and to conduct the war as a conventional struggle in every respect. In South Vietnam, however, the enemies of Saigon moved freely through the countryside, striking everywhere and anywhere at will, reducing the actual warfare to a primarily civil struggle where success could be measured only by death and destruction, not by territory captured and held.

What interests in Vietnam could cover the mounting costs of the American intervention? Throughout the Kennedy administration, when containment still demanded little of this nation, Washington limited the American interest to that of honoring a commitment to the South Vietnamese government. After President Johnson Americanized the war and sent the human, physical, and social costs of intervention to staggering proportions, Washington assigned the conflict an increasing level of importance until the promising consequences of success and the grave consequences of failure began the resemble those of the great wars of the century. As President Johnson assured the American people in 1967, "I am convinced that by seeing this struggle through now we are greatly reducing the chances of a much larger war—perhaps a nuclear war." Walt W. Rostow, White House adviser, detected an equally magnificent promise of world peace in a Vietnam victory. If the United States, he said, "could get on with the job, the struggle in Vietnam might be the last confrontation of the postwar era." Victory would not only demonstrate at least that aggression, including so-called wars of national liberation, could not succeed, but would also accomplish the essential purpose of guaranteeing self-determination for the people of Vietnam. In short, the Johnson administration promised to limit Communist expansion by winning in Vietnam.

Defeat, in contrast, would presage retreat before the onrush of a confident and increasingly aggressive world communism until a cornered West would be compelled to lash out in nuclear war. Accepting the validity of the Munich analogy without question (although historians of Europe generally rejected it outright) Washington warned the nation to avoid that first fatal backward step which would require new concessions and terminate in international chaos. If the containment of Communist expansion rested everywhere on the credibility of United States power, then world stability required the successful demonstration of that power in Vietnam. As Vice President Hubert H. Humphrey warned in April 1966, "[T]he day that this nation does not honor its commitments, it is on that day that the whole fabric of international law and order is torn apart and breaks down." President Johnson once complained to a Japanese diplomat that the United States, in accepting less than victory in Vietnam, would give up all of its alliances around the world. No nation would thereafter trust the United States again.

Upon entering the White House in January 1969, President Richard M. Nixon accepted the previous administration's rationale for victory in Vietnam. To strengthen his case for continued military involvement he recognized no feasible immediate alternative to inherited policy except total abandonment of the people of South Vietnam. As he explained over national television on May 14, 1969:

> When we assumed the burden of helping defend South Vietnam, millions of South Vietnamese men, women, and children placed their trust in us. To abandon them now would risk a massacre that would

shock and dismay everyone in the world who values human life. Abandoning the South Vietnamese, however, would jeopardize more than lives in South Vietnam. It would threaten our long-term hopes for peace in the world. A great nation cannot renege on its pledges. A great nation must be worthy of trust.

When it comes to maintaining peace, "prestige" is not an empty word. I am not speaking of false pride or bravado. . . . I speak, rather, of the respect that one nation has for another's integrity in defending its principles and meeting its obligations. If we simply abandoned our effort in Vietnam, the cause of peace might not survive the damage that would be done to other nations' confidence in our reliability.

Another reason for not withdrawing unilaterally stems from debates within the communist world. . . . If Hanoi were to succeed in taking over South Vietnam by force—even after the power of the United States had been engaged—it would greatly strengthen those leaders who scorn negotiation, who advocate aggression, who minimize the risks of confrontation with the United States. It would bring peace now but it would enormously increase the danger of a bigger war later.

Official warnings against failure in Vietnam, repeated by administration spokesmen over a span of five years, eventually produced a conditioned response in much of the American public. Members of the "silent majority," in their support of administration policy, agreed that any compromise or withdrawal from Vietnam short of victory would, as one Virginia resident expressed it, "only whet the appetite of our sworn adversaries. The Communists are out for world conquest and we are in their way. We never wanted anything from them—they want this country and don't ever forget it." Such demands for victory, like official statements in Washington, defined neither the nature nor the location of an enemy limited enough to be demolished in Vietnam but still powerful enough, if successful there, to threaten the freedom that remained in the world. But for much of the public such details seemed inconsequential. The central theme which underwrote the popular endorsement of the war emerged with absolute clarity. Whereas the nation's security demanded a victory over what one Louisiana congressman termed "a minor, backward, disorganized, fourth-rate dictatorship," the nation's power and resources—sufficient to place astronauts on the moon—seemed more than adequate to achieve it. If victory remained elusive, the answer lay not in Asia but in Washington.

The absence of conditions which demonstrated their own dangers and suggested their own responses, as did the inescapable realities of Hitler's power and ambitions after 1939, compelled Washington to invoke an elaborate rationale for United States military intervention in Southeast Asia. In Vietnam the United States and its allies faced no powerful, efficient, modern antagonist, organized for war and prepared to dispatch massive, trained, and magnificently equipped armies across the territories of its neighbors. To identify Ho Chi Minh with a global danger necessitating vast expenditure of American human and material resources to contain his influence required much persuasion of the public. Tangible and readily comprehensible evidence which might have rendered the rhetoric unnecessary did not exist. For that reason the perennial experience in Vietnam (which included the mounting death and destruction in that small country as well as the inflation and neglect of this nation's challenges at home) increasingly separated those Americans who took the words seriously from those who did not. With time the war in Vietnam divided the nation and embittered the minority which rejected its necessity and denied its "morality" as had no previous external issue in the nation's history. As J. William Fulbright of Arkansas, the leading senatorial critic, declared in May 1970, following the Cambodian venture: "It is what is going on in the United States that bothers me. It is terrible to allow a comparatively unimportant part of the world to put us in this condition." The physical and emotional demands which Vietnam has finally imposed on the American people should come as no surprise. Even in the more optimistic 1950s writers predicted such results with singular unanimity.

After seven years of American involvement, the war in Vietnam still posed two fundamental questions: Could the desired result be obtained at any cost? Was that result demanded by the security interests of the United States? There was always doubt after 1964 that the struggle for Vietnam could be resolved militarily. The firm American commitment to the defense of the seventeenth parallel had always denied the existence of strong revolutionary pressures below that parallel and the requirement that Saigon come to terms with those pressures through political rather than military means. For United States officials not even the struggle within South Vietnam itself represented a civil conflict. It was because the South Vietnamese insurgency comprised, in large measure, a powerful nationalistic impulse that its termination required the creation of a genuinely national government—something which Diem and his successors, understandably fearful of the Vietcong and assured of the almost limitless support of the United States, refused to grant.

Nor can the struggle be resolved automatically through the successful Vietnamization of the war, for Vietnamization is designed less to broaden the base of the Saigon regime than to enable that regime to impose its will on its enemies with its own military power. Whether Vietnamization alone can stop the death and destruction is doubtful, for Hanoi will scarcely accept defeat at the hands of Saigon when it has refused to compromise its purposes in its long war with the United States. Vietnamization, in short, promises a war without end. By fighting in South Vietnam, Laos, and Cambodia, the United States has reduced the level of resistance; it has not ended the war. Ultimately the war will be won in North Vietnam or not at all. This is the heart of the problem, and it has challenged from the beginning the long-range effectiveness of President Nixon's move into Cambodia late in April 1970. James Reston defined the nation's dilemma in the *New York Times* on May 3: "Geography, history and time are on the side of the enemy. It is a devilish problem. He can always retreat into other sanctuaries in Cambodia, Laos, North Vietnam or even China—and wait. The question is whether we are willing to fight and wait or whether we are merely determined to pretend." What has perpetuated the war, then, is not only the conflict of interest between Saigon and Hanoi, but also the Asian balance of power which includes China and the Soviet Union. If North Vietnam is the immediate problem, the danger of a wider war remains the second, and perhaps decisive, barrier to the successful termination of the war, with Hanoi recognizing at last the existing Saigon government.

The domino theory has bound United States security to a victory in Vietnam. Yet other nations have scarcely behaved as if they shared Washington's fears. Western governments have been generally reluctant to criticize American intervention; the Asian allies have lauded the intervention as the essential guarantee of their independence from Communist aggression. But beyond a network of intricate and costly special inducements from the United States, no government supposedly endangered by the domino theory has seen fit to support the American involvement in Vietnam at any level commensurate with its verbal acknowledgement of a global Communist menace. India, Indonesia, Pakistan, Burma, Laos, and Cambodia have sent no troops to Vietnam. Neither have Singapore or Malaysia. Thailand, the Philippines, Australia, and New Zealand have sent token forces. South Korea has committed larger numbers to the Vietnam war, but again in payment for massive United States aid and blanket security guarantees. Yet these nations are by definition the next alleged victims of aggression. Their rejection of a proportionate share of the defense burden suggests either gross irresponsibility or a conviction that the war in Vietnam is, after all, a unique episode, rising from peculiar conditions and not likely to recur elsewhere. Fighting in Vietnam, they understand, will not guarantee the peace of all Asia. Vietnam is not Armageddon.

Vietnam has acquired its strange importance simply because five successive Washington administrations have said it was important. Yet none of them has ever managed to demonstrate why this small jungle country has come to control the world's destiny. What has aggravated the problem of unwinding the long and costly involvement is the rhetorical escalation employed to cover the nation's elusive stakes in Vietnam. United States officials first courted disaster when they invariably assured Saigon that American support was limitless and everlasting. Such policy seldom encourages efficiency or realism in the recipient. But the ultimate failure has been in Washington's perennial refusal to recognize that Hanoi's strength lies in nationalism, not in visions of falling dominoes. Saigon may deny it, but for the vast majority of the Vietnamese people the conflict which has swept through their country year after year is in fact a civil war. Because they regard the challenges facing Saigon as basically internal rather than external, they have neither flocked to the support of the South Vietnamese government nor accepted the massive American forces as the saviors of their country. The challenge posed by Ho Chi Minh is concrete, not abstract; limited, not universal. This nation's costly experience in Vietnam does not deny that intervention conducted in a vacuum of nationalism may reap momentary, perhaps even permanent, political change. It reveals, however, that intervention, when made in opposition to the thrust of a nationalist movement, arouses such dogged resistance that the price of war eventually exceeds the anticipated gains.

Suggestions for Further Research

Obviously the need for further understanding of the long struggle for Vietnam can be measured by the continuing divisions which that struggle sustains among the American people. The fundamental issues in conflict are as elusive as they are troublesome. What is the nature of the struggle? It cannot at the same time be a civil war and a threat of global proportions. It must be one or the other. The war in Vietnam, as of 1970, has cost the United States 43,000 dead, over 300,000 wounded, and well over $100 billion, because five successive administrations have regarded the outcome of the struggle as vital to this nation's security. All five administrations have denied that the Vietnamese conflict is a civil war. Yet all of them have applied United States financial and manpower resources to the struggle as if it were indeed a local struggle to be resolved in Vietnam and not elsewhere. The ends of our policy—the containment of world communism—have had little relationship to the limited means that Washington has employed to resolve the conflict on American terms. Nowhere has the United States sought a direct confrontation with either Moscow or Peking over Vietnam; instead, it has done everything in its power to avoid such a confrontation. How the United States can terminate an expansionist movement that allegedly centers in Moscow and Peking by fighting North Vietnamese in the jungles of South Vietnam and Cambodia is not clear. Still, it was on the foundations of that theory that the United States became involved and remains involved in the struggle. What are the vital interests of the United States in Vietnam? On what evidence have they been based and how have they been sustained? From the viewpoint of the American commitment to Vietnam, these remain the critical and as yet unanswered questions.

VIII

PEACEKEEPING BY OUTSIDERS
The U. N. Congo Expeditionary Force

ERNEST W. LEFEVER

In its twenty-five year history the United Nations has authorized a dozen peace observation groups to monitor a truce or patrol a neutral zone. But only once did it dispatch an expeditionary force to restore and maintain peace in a theater of unresolved conflict. Ironically, this one exception, which involved a multinational army of division strength, was designed to deal with civil strife, not interstate conflict. The Congo crisis that erupted in 1960 was essentially a domestic civil disturbance that posed no serious threat to international peace. In fact, the very presence of the U.N. Force internationalized a local conflict and probably exacerbated and prolonged it.

The assertion by Soviet and Afro-Asian spokesmen that the modest Belgian police action, which in a few days had largely succeeded in restoring order with a loss of about twenty lives, was a threat to international peace cannot be sustained by evidence. Brussels never sought to reestablish political authority over Katanga or any other portion of the newly independent Congo. If there was a threat to peace, it was inherent in the attempted military intervention by the Soviet Union in behalf of the ousted prime minister, Patrice Lumumba, in September 1960—an effort frustrated by Andrew W. Cordier, the U.N. representative in Leopoldville (now Kinshasa). At no time did the Congo conflict threaten any neighboring state, much less disturb the balance of forces in the area. At no time did the Security Council label any government an "aggressor,"

Portions of this chapter have been drawn from the publications by Professor Lefever noted in the bibliography at the end of the book.

though Moscow sought to have Brussels so designated. Before assessing the legal basis of U.N. involvement in an internal conflict and the political consequence of the peacekeeping mission, the essential facts of the un-raveling crisis should be briefly noted.

Central to the drama was the charismatic Lumumba, who on independence day, June 30, 1960, declared, "We are going to show the world what the black man can do when he works in freedom, and we are going to make the Congo the center of radiance for the whole of Africa." In a matter of days Lumumba's radiant dream became a dark nightmare, and largely because of his own inexperience, ineptitude, and irrationality.

The continuous, though often low-level, conflict that engulfed this giant new state during its first seven years was not inevitable. The granting of instant independence to a handful of untrained leaders contained the seeds of chaos and the abrupt and premature transfer of authority was at best a perilous undertaking, but it might have succeeded if Lumumba had understood the substantial Belgian interest in successful decolonization and had had the wisdom to recognize that the Belgian officers of the Congolese army were essential allies in the task of maintaining the political and territorial integrity of a country almost as large as Western Europe. That was perhaps too much to expect of a former postal clerk afflicted by serious psychological problems, especially in view of the sustained pressure of foreign Communist agents to turn him against Brussels and the West.

Be that as it may, the Congo became within a week an off-center stage of confusion, chaos, and violence that drew the attention of the United States, the Soviet Union, and the world. Within a fortnight it attained the distinction of being the only state that ever became host to a large United Nations expeditionary force armed by the Security Council with a broad and uncertain mandate. The various Security Council resolutions identified five sweeping objectives for the U.N. mission, to be accomplished without intervening in or seeking to "influence the outcome of any internal conflict, constitutional or otherwise." The first three objectives were directed to the internal situation: 1) Restore and maintain law and order throughout the Congo. 2) Prevent civil war and curb tribal conflict. 3) Transform the Congolese army into a reliable internal security force. The latter two objectives were directed toward external problems: 4) Restore and maintain the territorial integrity and political independence of the Congo. 5) Eliminate outside interference in the Congo's internal affairs.

These far-reaching goals were set forth without reference to the enforcement provisions of Chapter VII of the U.N. Charter, which authorizes the Security Council to take military measures against a state persisting in peace-threatening behavior.

Why did the United Nations, with the sustained support of Washington and the initial support of Moscow, become involved so deeply and so long in an essentially internal conflict? In retrospect, it is clear that each member of the supporting coalition, led by the United States, perceived an external element in the situation that affected its interests. Washington and other Western states sought to arrest chaos, fearing it would be exploited by the Communist powers. Moscow apparently gave its early support to preempt direct U.S. military assistance, which President Eisenhower, despite a specific request from the Congo government, never seriously considered. In an effort to "radicalize" the situation and help Lumumba to become the preeminent revolutionary leader in black Africa, Moscow and some of the more militant Afro-Asian states were more interested in exorcizing Western political and economic influence than in restoring law and order. The battle cry of "decolonization" was a euphemism for expelling Belgian troops and overthrowing Tshombe's secessionist regime in Katanga. Afro-Asian support for U.N. peacekeeping dropped off sharply after the U.N. force ended Katanga's secession in January 1963. Neither the militant states nor Moscow showed the slightest interest in efforts to protect the central government against the growing rebel threat in 1963 and 1964, a much more serious challenge to the integrity of the Congo than Katanga's secession ever was.

Perhaps no state in recent times has been subjected to such a wide range of violence and conflict as the Congo. It has seen army mutinies, secessions, assassination plots, tribal war, religious uprisings, ritual cannibalism, anti-European attacks, regional conflict, provincial insurrection, and large-scale rebellion. The Congo has also experienced two coups led by General Joseph D. Mobutu, the first a five-month intervention undertaken in September 1960 to "neutralize" the conflict between President Joseph Kasavubu and Lumumba, and the second, five years later, to take over the country as self-proclaimed president in the wake of a Kasavubu-Tshombe stalemate. During its four-year mission, the U.N. force, which averaged about 15,000 men from two dozen states, became involved in a dozen small clashes with various Congolese armed units, three in Katanga with Tshombe's gendarmerie. The third Katanga clash ended the autonomy of the province.

In terms of bloodshed the totality of four years of Congolese strife, which sometimes involved externally recruited mercenaries, did not begin to match the magnitude of the eight-year conflict in Algeria or the subsequent tribal-civil war in Nigeria. Probably fewer than 100,000 Congolese were killed.

The present essay is concerned with politically significant violence in the 1960–64 period, especially that which subverted, detracted from, or sought to replace the authority of the central government, and with the effect of the U.N. peacekeeping mission on these largely internal challenges.

In the Congo drama there was no single and coherent civil war, but rather an assortment of confused and often unrelated challenges to central authority. The closest approximation of a civil war was the 1964 rebellion. The present analysis is addressed to four separate challenges, including the rebellion: 1) the mutiny and fragmentation of the Congolese army in July 1960; 2) Lumumba's confrontation with Kasavubu in September 1960; 3) Katanga's secession, 1960–63; and 4) the 1964 rebellion. After each is defined, the effect of the U.N. mission is assessed.

The immediate cause of the first Congo crisis was the timid and vacillating response of Belgian officers to a small, isolated, and unorganized mutiny at the Leopoldville army camp on July 4, 1960, and Lumumba's subsequent unprecedented dismissal of the entire Belgian officer corps four days later. On independence day it was assumed on all sides that the 1,100 Belgian officers and NCOs would continue serving the *Force Publique* (the name was changed to National Congolese Army on July 8) until qualified Congolese could replace them. The July 4 mutiny was caused by a handful of Congolese NCOs who wanted the promise of faster promotion. They directed their ire at Lumumba, who had publicly warned them that promotion could come only with training and experience.

When the unexpected protest broke out, the Belgian officers failed to assert normal disciplinary authority. Their equivocation stimulated the disaffection and prompted the intervention of Lumumba. He moved in with erratic and emotional outbursts and in panic on July 6 promoted every Congolese soldier one rank—thus creating the first army in history without privates. Instead of calming the situation, Lumumba's act of ap-

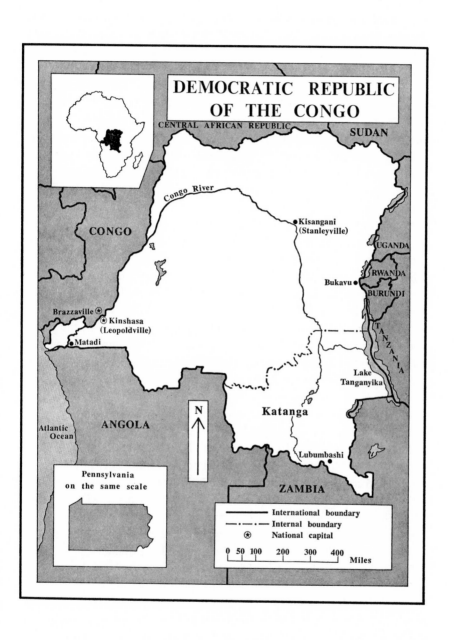

DEMOCRATIC REPUBLIC
OF THE CONGO

CENTRAL AFRICAN REPUBLIC   SUDAN

Congo River

CONGO   • Kisangani
                                           (Stanleyville)

                                                      UGANDA

                                                      RWANDA
                                    Bukavu •
                                                      BURUNDI

Brazzaville ⊛
         ⊛ Kinshasa   T
           (Leopoldville)   A
         • Matadi   N
                                                      Z
                                                      A
                                                      N
                                            Lake   I
                                            Tanganyika A

Atlantic   N   Katanga
Ocean   ANGOLA ↑

                                        • Lubumbashi

       Pennsylvania
    on the same scale   ZAMBIA

                              —————— International boundary
                              —·—·—· Internal boundary
                                ⊛   National capital

                              0 50 100 200 300 400
                                                        Miles

peasement poured oil on the fire. Some soldiers went on a rampage, and Belgian civilians began to flee across the Congo River to Brazzaville. General confusion, exacerbated by sensational press reporting, led to the most damaging and far-reaching of Lumumba's acts—on July 8 he dismissed the 1,100 Belgian officers and NCOs, making the Congolese Army the first army in history without either privates or officers.

This was followed by the abrupt Africanization of the officer corps, a disaster without parallel in military organization. The instant appointment and "election" of untrained Congolese soldiers as officers destroyed what was generally considered, a mere two weeks before, one of the best trained and most disciplined security forces in all of Africa. When the army fell apart, the country fell apart. The symbol of unity and the instrument of law and order was fragmented. With one stroke it was transformed into a centrifugal force of disunity and conflict. The army headquarters in Leopoldville, however, was kept intact by Colonel Mobutu, who was named chief of staff on July 8, and by his faithful Belgian military advisers, but the headquarters and Ministry of Defense had little real control beyond the capital city.

Two events followed hard upon Lumumba's destruction of the army, and together they created the swirling vortex which sucked in outside military force. The first event was Belgian intervention on July 10 to protect Congolese and European lives, and the second on the following day was Tshombe's declaration of independence in Katanga. It is likely that neither of these would have occurred had it not been for the fragmentation of the army.

Since the day Lumumba dismissed the Belgian officers, the chief preoccupation of Mobutu as chief of staff, later as commander in chief, and since 1965 as president, has been to rebuild a reliable, disciplined, and unified statewide army to guarantee the integrity of a sprawling country of 16,000,000 people divided into more than 200 tribal and linguistic groups. The considerable extent to which he has achieved this central objective is a tribute to his determination and the military and public safety assistance he has received from Belgium and the United States.

The U.N. mission was given the task of assisting the government in transforming the Congolese army into a reliable internal security force, but it failed completely, primarily because Secretary-General Hammarskjold ruled out the most obvious and immediate source of military assistance—Brussels. He regarded the former colonial power as morally disqualified. The effect of his anti-Belgian policy was to delay, perhaps by three years, bilateral aid which was desperately needed and sought by General Mobutu and President Kasavubu. The two U.N. efforts to provide the Congo with an Afro-Asian training staff were rebuffed by Mobutu, who insisted that an independent state had a right to select its own sources of external assistance.

To deal with the panic caused by the mutiny and Lumumba's dismissal of the Belgian officers, Brussels on July 10 sent paratroopers into the Congo to restore order and deter violence. Foreign Minister Bomboko said the Belgian troops moved in at his request. It was largely a successful mission. This humanitarian intervention was not the cause of civil strife but a response to it. There were never any clashes between Belgian and U.N. troops. The Belgians were frequently welcomed by local Congolese authorities, and troops were deployed peaceably in twenty-six places throughout the country. There was one important exception to peaceful deployment, a clash at the port city of Matadi, where about a dozen Congolese were killed and thirteen Belgians wounded, an incident that was blown all out of proportion and provided the occasion for Moscow and others to charge Brussels with "aggression." After restoring order, the Belgian paratroopers left within ten weeks, except for 231 officers and men of other ranks who remained to direct Katanga's gendarmerie and police; even these had gone by September 1961.

One of the most serious challenges to Leopoldville was Lumumba's direct attempt to eliminate President Kasavubu in a power play backed by Soviet diplomats, advisers, and military planes in the Congo. Kasavubu and Lumumba were natural rivals long before independence. Lumumba's conniving with the Soviet bloc, his lack of self-control, and his attempt to use the U.N. force for his own purposes led the more moderate Kasavubu to lose confidence in his prime minister. Charging that Lumumba was plunging the nation into "fratricidal war," Kasavubu dismissed him on September 5, 1960, and appointed Joseph Ileo to replace him.

In angry retaliation that same day, Lumumba in three fiery speeches over Radio Leopoldville denounced Kasavubu, "dismissed" him as president, and called upon the workers and the Congolese army to rally to his cause. The situation was tense. Charged with responsibility for maintaining order, the U.N. representative, Dr. Cordier, was confronted with the dual problem of forestalling civil war and preventing the collapse of the central government. He had to deal with mounting disorder without interfering illegally in Congolese internal affairs. He acted quickly. On the evening of September 5, he closed all major airports in the country to non-U.N. traffic "in the interests of the maintenance of peace." In a supporting move the following day, he closed temporarily the Leopoldville radio station. Five years after the event Cordier said:

> One move I made was to close the airports. Thus we checked the influx of reinforcements to those centers of gravest danger, particularly Leopoldville and South Kasai. It was also essential to turn off the transmitter of the Leopoldville radio station, since highly charged emotional appeals inciting the people were on the verge of producing a totally uncontrollable situation . . . these steps had to be taken as temporary measures to preserve law and order.
>
> The various actions taken did contain the conflict, and respect for the United Nations Force and its individual members was greatly increased.

Cordier's dramatic acts also had a significant impact on the struggle for control of the Leopoldville government. Closing the airports blocked unilateral Soviet military action on behalf of Lumumba which would have been a violation of the Council resolutions. Specifically, it prevented the ten Soviet IL-14 planes already in the Congo from transporting pro-Lumumba troops to Leopoldville and elsewhere.

The silencing of the radio transmitter was a more serious deprivation for Lumumba than for Kasavubu because Lumumba was the more persuasive orator and only Kasavubu had access to Radio Brazzaville. After vigorous protests from both men, the Leopoldville radio was returned to the central government on September 12. The airports were retained under U.N. control for four years.

The political effect of Cordier's actions, whatever their intention, was to frustrate the ambitions of Lumumba and his outside supporters and to advance the fortunes of Kasavubu and other moderate leaders. Was this a violation of the Security Council's nonintervention rule? Under the circumstances it was virtually impossible for U.N. representatives or the U.N. force to take any significant initiative in the Congo without affecting its internal affairs. Further, many domestic matters had such immediate international implications that the two could not be separated in the real world of political decision, even if they could be in the world of legal abstractions. Cordier's grounding of Soviet planes and his closing of the radio station can be justified under the law-and-order mandate, even though both actions substantially affected the internal political struggle. If Cordier had *not* acted he might have influenced the internal situation even more, and in quite another direction. If he had not acted as he did, the result might have been civil war with Soviet planes supporting Lumumba's insurrection.

Tshombe's creation of the "independent state of Katanga" never resulted in civil war between Katanga and the central government, though there were several inconsequential forays against the secessionist "state" by provincial military units. In the summer of 1960 Lumumba wanted to move militarily against Tshombe, but he was powerless to act without the help of either the Soviet Union or the U.N. force. Cordier frustrated the former and Hammarskjold rejected the latter. He insisted on establishing a peaceful U.N. military presence in Katanga because the Security Council gave him no mandate to fight his way in.

Though Katanga had the trappings of an independent state—a flag, a currency, and an army—it never succeeded in gaining diplomatic recognition from a single government. Contrary to a widespread view, Belgian policy did not back Katanga against Leopoldville, but supported both simultaneously. In the first turbulent months, Brussels wanted to cover all bets. A high priority was to isolate mineral-rich Katanga from the chaos in the rest of the Congo. If the other five provinces were engulfed in conflict, at least Katanga should be kept afloat and made safe for Europeans and European investments. At the same time, by diplomacy and technical assistance, Brussels was trying to help the central government succeed.

In terms of public attention and actual U.N. policy, the broad law-and-order mandate frequently was subordinated to what Hammarskjold once referred to as the "elimination of the Belgian factor," that is, forcing Belgian military and civilian officials supporting Tshombe to leave the country. It was widely believed that Tshombe was simply a tool of Belgian political or financial interests, but Jules Gerard-Libois in his book *Katanga Secession* demonstrates that this was not the case. A shrewd politician, Tshombe used external forces as much as or more than they used him. He was operating with a long tradition of Katangan autonomy, and it is likely that his insistence on juridical independence was essentially a bargaining strategem designed to achieve a loose Congolese federation in which Katanga could control its own revenue and operate its own internal security force.

Whatever the complex forces that produced the Katanga problem, the

Security Council called for the end of secession under the rubric of "eliminating the Belgian factor," though Washington emphasized the objective of maintaining the territorial integrity of the Congo. To carry out the Security Council's desires the U.N. force in Katanga became involved in three clashes with Tshombe's gendarmerie. The September and December 1961 confrontations were inconclusive, but the third operation (December 1962–January 1963) ended the secession when U.N. units established "freedom of movement" throughout Katanga. In military terms, the three rounds were modest police actions with light casualties and with some atrocities committed by both sides. The U.N. lost 42 men killed and suffered about 200 wounded. Approximately 300 Katanga gendarmes and 50 civilians were killed.

The ending of secession by force was the most controversial action of the U.N. force, damned by critics as the mission's greatest mistake and praised by supporters as its greatest accomplishment.

The closest approximation to a civil war between the central government and an organized military force occurred in 1964, after the last U.N. troops left on June 30 of that year. The rebels were not a unified movement, but a conglomeration of various dissenting troops located largely in the northeastern provinces. Endemic tribal, religious, and regional disaffection was rekindled by political turbulence and enflamed by Communist agitators. Stanleyville (now Kisangani) was the chief but not the only center of the rebel activity which had been building up since the formal integration of Katanga. By mid-1964, the rebel groups had controlled or harassed more than one-third of the country and constituted by far the most serious challenge the Congo government faced before or since. In fact, the Congo rebellion was independent Africa's largest uprising. Unlike the secessionist Katanga and Biafra, which sought only autonomy or independence, the Congolese rebels sought to replace the Leopoldville government.

By early 1964 the subversive involvement of Red Chinese agents in the Congo had become a significant factor. Operating out of Peking's embassies in Burundi and Brazzaville, Red agents provided Congolese rebel groups with political and technical advice, money, equipment, and weapons, though the Chinese never succeeded in controlling the disparate rebel elements. In June 1964, Peking's *Jenmin Jih Pao* welcomed the "excellent revolutionary situation" in the Congo.

The U.N. force did nothing to help General Mobutu defend the country against the growing rebel challenge, chiefly because there was little political support for such an effort. The Afro-Asian regimes which provided most of the U.N. troops were quite prepared to move against Tshombe, but they had no interest in helping to repel Communist-backed rebels. Their selective interest in maintaining the integrity of the Congo reflected both racial and ideological factors.

The end of the U.N. mission marked the beginning of the Congo as a normal state in at least one important respect—it was now free for the first time to deal with its security problem in its own way. The new prime minister, Tshombe, confronted with rampaging rebels, promptly requested increased military aid from Washington and Brussels under programs initiated by Prime Minister Adoula, and he started openly to recruit European mercenaries to spearhead the antirebel campaign.

Stanleyville fell to the rebels on August 4, 1964, and the plight of some 3,000 innocent foreign residents from nineteen countries who were held as hostages became desperate. When protracted diplomatic efforts failed to secure their release, the Americans and Belgians launched a joint rescue operation, "Dragon Rouge," on November 24 with the full consent of Leopoldville. Its five-day mission, using a dozen U.S. Air Force C-130E planes and 545 Belgian paratroopers, saved more than 2,000 persons of many nationalities in the Stanleyville and Paulis areas. Carried out for humanitarian reasons, it had the inescapable side effect of helping the government's offensive against the rebels. For this reason Washington and Brussels were accused of cynically supporting "imperialist Tshombe" against the "liberation fighters" under the cloak of a humanitarian mission. Charges of "wanton aggression," "deliberate genocide," and "massive cannibalism" were underscored by government-led or government-permitted demonstrations in a dozen countries, including violence against U.S. buildings in Moscow, Sofia, Prague, Cairo, Nairobi, Djakarta, and Peking.

The less-than-outstanding record of the United Nations in peacekeeping and crisis management in the Congo points to the severe limits of U.N. intervention in the Third World and underlines the substantial constraints confronting any external agency, state or interstate, seeking to deal with civil war inside the borders of a sovereign country. The very governments that most strongly supported U.N. involvement in the Congo did not advocate U.N. intervention in Nigeria. The Congo operation has become a warning rather than an example.

Of the four challenges to central authority discussed above, the U.N. mission dealt effectively with only one—liquidating Katanga's secession by force. It failed completely to transform the fragmented Congolese army into an effective and unified instrument of internal security. It did nothing to help the central government deal with its most serious challenge, the rising rebellion in 1963 and 1964. The mission did, however, effectively prevent the Soviet-backed Lumumba's causing more mischief in 1960 and perhaps starting a serious civil war. The bold action by the U.N. representative may have been due more to the particular man in Leopoldville than to U.N. policy as such. As an American citizen, Cordier was probably more willing to move against Lumumba and the Russians than would the various neutralist representatives, such as Dayal of India, who subsequently held the Leopoldville post.

In terms of the broader Security Council objectives, the U.N. mission performed somewhat better and, given the inherent constraints of a multistate operation, did reasonably well. During its first three years the U.N. force succeeded in maintaining minimal order and actually improved the situation somewhat, the improvement due in great measure to the political and economic efforts of friendly governments as well as the psychological impact of the U.N. presence. The U.N. force also helped deter tribal conflict and civil war by its very deployment and by several specific measures, such as establishing neutral zones between warring factions. Though there was sporadic tribal and factional fighting, no full-scale civil war erupted until after the U.N. troops departed. By liquidating Katangan secession and by frustrating Lumumba's military efforts, the mission helped preserve the territorial integrity of the Congo. Cordier's closing of the airports prevented the only external intervention that threatened the country.

This analysis makes it abundantly clear that the U.N. mission did not suspend internal or international politics. By internationalizing the Congo, the mission magnified the crisis and probably prolonged the conflict, while at the same time muting the violence of the adversaries. Designed to insulate the Congo from the Cold War, the mission insured that the Cold War would be waged there, but under constraints that furthered the interests of the United States and frustrated the objectives of the Soviet Union. The normal struggle of power and interest, pressure and persuasion, assistance and advice, persisted in the Congo and was only slightly inhibited by the legal constraints imposed by the Security Council and the actual presence of the large and obvious U.N. establishment.

The U.N. force was a marginal actor in the complex and essentially internal Congo drama. At best it served as a stopgap until the basic structure of central authority and internal security could be established. At worst the U.N. mission postponed effective assistance from Western states and complicated the resolution of major internal conflicts by internationalizing a largely local crisis. At the mission's end Secretary-General Thant soberly acknowledged its limited crisis-management capacity: "The United Nations cannot permanently protect the Congo, or any other country, from the internal tensions and disturbances created by its own organic growth toward unity and nationhood."

With the benefit of a decade of hindsight, it appears that the unfolding 1960 crisis could have been dealt with more efficiently and at less cost by conventional means. Since the initial army protest on July 4 was mild, local, unorganized, and largely unrelated to outside political interests, prompt and decisive disciplinary action against the mutinous soldiers by their Belgian officers might well have nipped the crisis in the bud and without bloodshed. The officers had the authority to discipline their troops without special permission from the government. Their indecisiveness encouraged the mutiny and prompted the instant Africanization of the officer corps.

Even at the second stage of the crisis, marked by panic in the European population, the Belgian intervention would probably have been entirely successful had it not been for the fateful Matadi incident on July 11 which sparked Tshombe's proclamation of independence. These two events transformed the crisis into its third and most critical stage. Decisive Belgian action at the first or second stage of the crisis, with the quiet diplomatic support of Britain, France, and the United States, as suggested by President de Gaulle, might have been the best and least costly alternative, politically and morally, for containing the original mutiny.

After the Matadi incident and Tshombe's secession, the only feasible immediate sources of external aid were Moscow, Washington, or the joint action of Britain, France, and the United States. The United States could have done the job, and was invited to do so on July 12, but refused, mainly because the political cost of direct U.S. aid was overestimated in Washington. This miscalculation resulted in part from exaggerated reports of the disorder and the State Department's oversensitivity to anticipated charges of "neocolonialism."

A quickly dispatched United States military presence in mid-July could probably have stopped the mutiny without killing a single Congolese. If this had been done, the political backlash against U.S. aid in 1960 would doubtless have been smaller and less intense than the criticisms of the Belgian-American mission to rescue foreign hostages in the Stanleyville area in November 1964. In the Stanleyville mission, Washington was accused of backing "reactionary" Tshombe as prime minister against the Communist-supported rebels. In 1960 Washington would have had the propaganda advantage of helping to protect the Congo's independence for the "great African nationalist," Prime Minister Lumumba. The Congo experience, illuminated by the Stanleyville rescue mission, reveals a great deal about the limits and possibilities of U.N. intervention.

In the management of a crisis between states that threatens the peace, the U.N. instrumentality can be effectively employed only at an early stage or after a settlement between the conflicting parties has been achieved. Under the "peaceful settlement" provisions of Chapter VI of the Charter, a U.N. mediation team can, given propitious circumstances, help two states to resolve a dispute peaceably if each prefers such a settlement to the risks of a violent resolution. Peacemaking is a dynamic political process involving threats, bargaining, adjustment, and compromise. A peaceful settlement can be achieved by the conflicting parties alone or can be imposed from without by a strong third party. A third party cannot force two adversaries to make peace against their will without violating the integrity of one or both.

The major mistake in the Congo case was to send a Chapter VI peacekeeping presence to a theater of unresolved conflict. The peacekeepers had no peace to keep. If the Congo crisis had been a threat to the peace, and if a truce between the adversaries had been established, with or without U.N. assistance, it would then have been appropriate to consider sending a U.N. observer group. But the essential prerequisites for effective peacekeeping were not present. The U.N. mission had the impossible job of trying to make and keep peace at the same time, with no clear political directives from the Security Council for either task. The fault rests mainly with the Council for authorizing the sweeping and contradictory objectives, though it must be said that Hammarskjold actively lobbied for a comprehensive peacekeeping, peacemaking, and state-building mandate. In this he had the general support of Washington and the moderate Afro-Asian states, the partial support of Britain, and the opposition of France and the Soviet Union.

The responsibility for the confused and unsatisfactory mandate rests squarely with the permanent members. As the chief proponent of the enabling resolutions, Washington must share the blame with London and Paris, whose leaders, in the face of Afro-Asian pressures, lacked the political courage to veto what they regarded as a fundamentally unwise course.

The Congo experience demonstrates that U.N. emergency intervention to shore up and rebuild a collapsing system of political and military authority in a fragmented state is almost bound to fail. Such emergency intervention, of which the Congo is the sole historical case, may be defined as the deployment of a sizable, multistate military force under the executive control of the secretary-general to deal with internal disorder and insecurity.

On the practical side, the requirements of efficiency, accountability, security, confidence, and mutuality virtually dictate that emergency military assistance to a state in trouble be provided by one or more friendly governments with parallel interests and under carefully drawn bilateral arrangements. It should have been clear from the outset that a multistate effort, serving as the instrument of a voluntary coalition of governments whose interests often clashed, was a singularly inappropriate agency for helping a weak and divided government to deal with the highly sensitive problem of rebuilding a shattered army. A multinational staff could hardly be expected to meet the minimal requirements of security and confidence, to say nothing of efficiency.

The very presence of the large and obtrusive U.N. multinational headquarters staff, civilian and military, was strongly resented by Congolese authorities. At best it was looked upon as a necessary evil. U.N. officials from many states with differing interests in the Congo tended to exacerbate existing internal conflicts by taking sides and confusing lines of authority. This problem was illustrated by the celebrated case of Ambassador Dayal of India, who served as the U.N. representative in Leopoldville from September 1960 to May 1961. President Kasavubu and General Mobutu were convinced he was siding with the Lumumba forces against the central government, but were unable to have him recalled. Hammarskjold finally yielded to the pressure of several Western governments and agreed to relieve Dayal, but only on condition that the U.S. ambassador, Clare H. Timberlake, and the British ambassador, Ian Smith, be transferred out of the Congo at approximately the same time. Leopoldville's great difficulty in getting rid of an undesirable U.N. mission head contrasted sharply with the ease with which it could expel the heads of normal diplomatic missions. On two occasions, for example, all members of the Soviet mission were declared persona non grata and expelled from the Congo within forty-eight hours.

Outside assistance for long-range, nation-building activities is entirely different from emergency intervention. Most forms of technical and economic aid are not as sensitive as military aid or political advice. Whether a state accepts bilateral or multilateral help should be determined by the circumstances on a case-by-case basis. This is not to make a political or moral presumption in favor of multilateral action over bilateral action. If a bilateral arrangement between a powerful state and a weak state is based upon mutual respect and compatible interests, what more can either party ask or expect?

In relation to the Congolese experience, the fundamental legal-political question is this: Does the Security Council have the right to intervene in any civil conflict situation, regardless of how bloody it may be, when the conflict does not endanger neighboring states or threaten the balance of forces in the area? To ask the question is to answer it. Attempts have been made to justify such interferences by appealing to the right of self-determination or human rights generally, but on this point the U.N. Charter is clear. Article 2, paragraph 7, reads: "Nothing contained in the present Charter shall authorize the United Nations to intervene in matters which are essentially within the domestic jurisdiction of any state or shall require the Members to submit such matters to settlement," unless the behavior of that state is a threat to the peace.

For this reason the Security Council action invoking economic sanctions against Rhodesia, in which the United States unwisely voted with Britain and the Soviet Union, was excused by calling peaceful Rhodesia a threat to the peace, a proposition far from self-evident. The neighboring states aiding the guerrilla fighters are the real threats to the peace.

Given a common-sense interpretation of the charter and the inherent limitations of multistate intervention, U.N. emergency action in Third World crises should be regarded not as a first option but as a last resort, to be undertaken only when the more traditional means of crisis management involve unacceptable costs or risks. The small army mutiny in Tanganyika (now Tanzania) in January 1964, which bore a striking resemblance to the pre-Matadi Congo crisis in 1960, was settled in a few hours at a cost of five lives by some 500 British marine commandos invited in to restore order by President Julius Nyerere. This suggests that the timely assistance of a friendly power is a more effective way of dealing with internal strife than the intervention of a large and intrusive multistate military force under the U.N. flag.

The U.N. Charter explicitly prohibits U.N. involvement in any civil war situation unless the crisis presents a clear and present danger to international peace. Politically, the Security Council has never invoked military sanctions against any state for threatening or breaking the peace, and is not likely to do so in the near future because of the persistent political differences in assessing Third-World conflict between the United States and the Soviet Union, either of whom can veto a proposed sanctions operation by the other. For these reasons, governments assailed by internal conflict would be well advised to turn to trusted friends for help rather than to the international community.

Suggestions for Further Research

A comparison of the 1960 Congo crisis with the 1964 Tanganyika crisis might be fruitful. Both crises were essentially internal and started with a localized army mutiny demanding more rapid Africanization of the officer corps. The Congo crisis was dealt with inconclusively by a four-year U.N. intervention. The Tanganyika problem was solved quickly and effectively by a disciplinary action of a British marine unit invited in by the president. Were there, then, essential political differences?

An analysis of the different responses of governments in Asia and Latin America which have had serious insurgent problems and have sought external military assistance might yield useful knowledge. Such questions might be asked as: Under what circumstances did a regime rely on one friendly power? When do governments seek the aid of two or more outside powers? Why have such governments never turned to the United Nations for help?

An attempt to assess the legal and political constraints on any external power attempting to assist a friendly state requesting aid in a serious civil war situation is another possibility.

Still another question to be examined is: Can the international community, specifically the U.N. system, do anything effective to prevent the flow of "freedom fighters" or "terrorists" across international frontiers? The Organization of African Unity openly encourages and finances such terrorist groups who illegally cross state borders to harass and overthrow governments in southern Africa.

IX

THE IMPACT OF EXTERNAL WAR
The Demise of Chiang's China

PAO-CHIN CHU

T HE JAPANESE INTERVENTION in China in 1937 not only destroyed the traditional institutions of local control but also removed the newly established local governments of the Nationalists from the urban areas. As a result, the vast areas behind the Japanese lines and the awakened millions left by the fleeing Nationalists offered the opportunity for the well disciplined and indoctrinated Communists to establish their border governments and grow their armies. By the time of the Japanese surrender in 1945, the Communists were strong enough to defeat the demoralized Nationalist army and drive Chiang's government to Taiwan.

Chiang's demise and the advent of Communist rule in China were the end product of one of the longest periods of civil warfare in modern history, dating back to the Anglo-French invasion of China and the Taiping Rebellion in the 1860s. There was no major civil warfare between 1895 and 1911. The 1895 Sino-Japanese War had the dual effect of creating both the Ch'ing reform movement within the Manchu government and the revolutionary Westernizing movement known as the Kuomintang. The latter, led by Dr. Sun Yat-sen, won out in the revolution of 1911–12, destroying the 268-year-old Manchu dynasty. With an intellectual legacy from the West, which included the English civil war and the American and French revolutions, Sun's revolutionism was a mixture of nationalism, democracy, and socialism. But Sun was an idealist and his revolution perished in the face of Chinese warlordism, a dominant political reality of his time.

President Yüan, a powerful northern warlord with monarchical ambitions who had helped destroy the Manchus, quickly quashed a revolt in the seven southern provinces in 1913. After he became emperor, however, his followers deserted him and he lost the next civil war, one in which Japan recognized the opponents. The years from Yüan's death in 1916 to 1927 were filled with more warlordism. Four major campaigns failed to settle the country, though Sun reached Peking in 1924, only to die. Meanwhile, in 1923 a young general named Chiang Kai-shek had been sent on a three-month visit to Russia from which he returned with new military ideas, one direct result of which was the founding of the Whampoa Military Academy, which began to provide a cadre of officers for the Nationalist armies. In 1926, Chiang led the "Northern Expedition" and finally, in nine victorious months, largely succeeded in putting down the warlords, but not before he had alarmed the Japanese.

In the meantime, Chinese intellectuals had been profoundly disturbed by the backwardness of the country and had by 1917 begun a cultural movement against Confucianism and the traditional ethics, customs, human relationships, and social conventions of China. The movement, as a part of its drive toward modernization, sought to promote the use of plain language and the vernacular to replace the classical literary tradition which had dominated Chinese culture. Directly connected with this movement was the 5,000-student demonstration in Peking against the Versailles settlement, in which Shantung was effectively given to Japan. This famous May 4 demonstration in 1919 was also opposed to warlordism in Peking. The ferment generated caused the Chinese delegation in Paris to reject the treaty. More importantly, May 4 showed that nationalism, public opinion, and mass demonstrations had surfaced in China. Henceforth, the Chinese Communists, who held their first congress in Shanghai in 1921, designated May 4 as the dividing line between the Old and the New Democracy.

Under Russian pressure, however, the Nationalists and the Chinese Communist Party (CCP) merged in 1922–23 by the simple process of the CCP members taking out individual memberships in the Nationalist Kuomintang (KMT). Thus in 1926 when Chiang marched north he was aided by CCP sabotage in the cities. But doubts and suspicions arose over CCP membership in the KMT, and in 1927 Chiang purged the KMT. With the CCP ousted, the left and right wings of the KMT were reconciled, and the Nationalist government was established at Nanking. Nevertheless, from 1928 to 1936 there were endless civil wars which were only

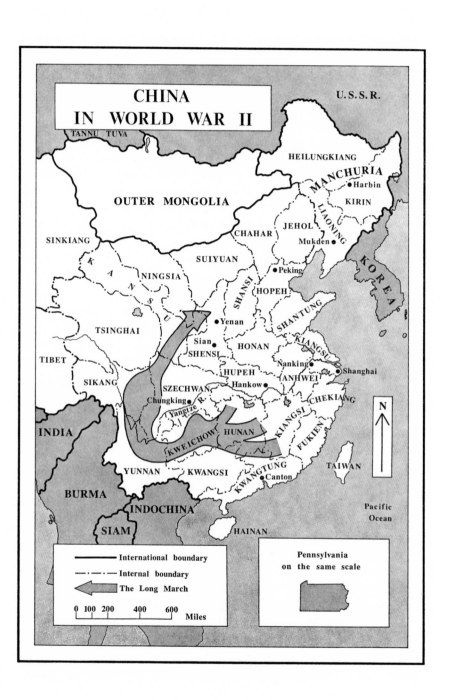

CHINA IN WORLD WAR II

U.S.S.R.

TANNU TUVA

HEILUNGKIANG

MANCHURIA

Harbin

KIRIN

OUTER MONGOLIA

LIAONING

SINKIANG

CHAHAR

JEHOL

Mukden

KOREA

K A N S U

NINGSIA

SUIYUAN

Peking

SHANSI

HOPEH

SHANTUNG

TSINGHAI

Yenan

KIANGSU

Sian

HONAN

SHENSI

TIBET

Nanking

Shanghai

SIKANG

HUPEH

ANHWEI

SZECHWAN

Hankow

CHEKIANG

Chungking

Yangtze R.

N

KWEICHOW

HUNAN

KIANGSI

FUKIEN

YUNNAN

KWANGSI

KWANGTUNG

TAIWAN

Canton

BURMA

INDIA

INDOCHINA

Pacific
Ocean

SIAM

HAINAN

———— International boundary

—·—·— Internal boundary

The Long March

0 100 200   400   600
                        Miles

Pennsylvania
on the same scale

temporarily brought under control when the Comintern in Moscow asked the Chinese Communists to form united fronts with their domestic opponents in order to make common cause against Japanese imperialist aggression.

Unification after the Northern Expedition was only nominal and was effective only in areas of the lower Yangtze River delta, then definitely under Chiang. Local and provincial warlordism was gradually weakened by the surge of nationalism against the common enemy and was finally destroyed either directly by the advancing Japanese invaders or indirectly by the retreating Nationalist government, forced out of East China into the semi-independent areas.

In 1929–30 the local warlords who had so recently been Chiang's allies in the Northern Expedition refused to accept Chiang's proposal that his Whampoa-trained army be the nucleus of a national force. The result was another series of civil wars in which the warlords Yen, Feng, and Li were defeated. Han Fu-Chü, who had been Feng's batman, became governor of Shantung after he defected to Chiang in 1929. He held Shantung until January 1938, when he disobeyed Chiang's orders and withdrew his troops without fighting the advancing Japanese army. He was at once arrested and sentenced to death. Shang Chen, long a lieutenant of Yen, held firm during the crucial battle between Chiang and the Northern Coalition of Feng-Yen in 1930, and was rewarded by Chiang with the governorship of Shansi. Yen, however, soon returned to his base in Shansi and ruled until the Japanese army drove him into the mountains of West Shansi. While the Japanese took over Taiyuan, capital of Shansi, and major cities along the Tientsin–Pukow railway, the countryside came to be ruled by the Communist border-region governments.

The situation in South and Southwest China was no better than that in North China and Manchuria. In Szechwan alone, between 1920 and 1937 sixteen major warlords waged ten major battles against one another in constantly changing combinations. Chiang could do nothing but grant certain appointments to the winning factions, a recognition of de facto strength, much as the Peking government did before 1928. The endless strife offered the Communists the opportunity to establish several large soviets in Kiangsi, Hupeh, Honan, Hunan, and Szechwan provinces.

From 1928 for a number of years Chiang had German military advisers, but although he conducted four campaigns against the Communists between 1930 and 1934, he was usually frustrated by internal or external circumstances. In 1933 he mobilized 700,000 men, struck down a revolt at Fukien and moved into Kiangsi. There the Bolsheviks had finally succeeded in taking over the powers of Mao Tse-tung, the leading advocate of guerrilla warfare, and themselves tried to organize a positional resistance to Chiang. This was a complete failure, and in October Mao was back to help lead the famous Long March from Southeast to North China via the west. In the course of this operation the Central Red Army invaded Szechwan, thus giving the Nationalists their first chance to influence its politics by offering their military support to the local warlords. But Szechwan was not finally "rehabilitated" into the Nationalist government until the Second Sino-Japanese War broke out in 1937. Liu Hsiang then took his forces out of his native province to defend Nanking while Chiang moved his capital to Chungking in eastern Szechwan.

Lung Yün, the feudalistic Governor of Yunnan, kept his province semi-independent until the end of the Second Sino-Japanese War. Chiang's coup to remove him in 1945 became possible because Yunnan's political mode was altered by the influx of refugee schools and universities and by the Burma Road, used for supporting the Sino-American military units during the war. Then, too, Lung's troops were sent to northern Indochina to accept the Japanese surrender.

In Kwangtung, the warlord Ch'en Chi-t'ang, in combination with the neighboring Kwangsi Clique, maintained the most formidable local government to challenge the power of the Nationalist government after the Northern Expedition. Only the sense of national emergency and unity due to Japanese aggression in Manchuria and North China made its leader send an Anti-Japanese National Salvation Force out of Kwangtung, thereby fundamentally weakening his position. When Ch'en's ranking subordinates defected in July 1936, Kwangtung ceased to be autonomous. At the same time, neighboring Kwangsi was also brought under Chiang's Nationalist government.

Japanese Imperialism in China

In the meantime, the Japanese, having at first been forced to relinquish part of the spoils of the Sino-Japanese War of 1895, had soundly thrashed Russia in 1904–05, annexed Korea in 1910, and seized Manchuria in 1931.

During World War I, Japan filled the vacuum in the Far East and on

January 18, 1915, forced the Twenty-one Demands on China, subordinating it to a nation determined to dominate the Far East. Japan emerged from the war stronger than most other powers and supported by the Anglo-Japanese Alliance. In addition, secret wartime agreements with France and Britain had granted her the right to station troops in Shantung and to control Kiaochow Bay in eastern Shantung and the Kiaochow–Tsinan Railway, as well as other privileges. In spite of great diplomatic efforts, China recovered only limited rights in Shantung after the 1922 Washington Conference.

The arrival of the victorious Chiang at Tsinan, the capital of Shantung, understandably upset the Japanese. A unified China would obstruct plans for Japanese expansion. However, to avoid an international confrontation before national unification had been achieved, Chiang ordered his troops to withdraw from Tsinan, though only after a bloody conflict between the two sides. The Northern Expedition was completed by Chiang's allies. Fearing Japan's further ambition in Manchuria and resentful of the murder of his father by the Japanese Kwantung Army, Young Marshal Chang Hsüeh-liang finally in 1928 raised the flag of the Nationalist government and brought Manchuria back to China against the repeated warnings and threats of Japan.

Diplomacy having failed to regain Manchuria, the Japanese Kwantung Army, a semiautonomous command, took direct action on September 18, 1931. Its well-planned operation was successfully concluded within a few days, and the Kwantung Army established its puppet "Manchukuo"—the Manchu state—with the abdicated Aisin-Gioro P'u-i of the late Ch'ing dynasty as its head. The next year, neighboring Jehol was also conquered.

Encouraged by the easy conquest of Manchuria without the military intervention of the European powers and stimulated by the success of Nazism and Fascism in Europe, the Japanese militarists were anxious to make further conquests before China became united. A series of "incidents" followed, and a number of "autonomous governments" were created in North China and Inner Mongolia before July 7, 1937, when nationwide resistance to the Japanese was touched off by the Marco Polo Bridge incident. To Japan's great surprise the Nationalists were able to trade space for time and eventually secured themselves behind the gorges of the Yangtze River.

When the Japanese attack on China opened in 1937, in spite of a stubborn resistance by the Nationalist Twenty-ninth Army, the motorized

Japanese divisions with their tanks and aircraft moved rapidly ahead. Chinese resistance along the railways and in the cities collapsed rapidly. By November, Shanghai had fallen, to be followed in December by Nanking, the Nationalist capital. By the end of 1938 the Japanese had captured Hankow and Canton, but progress became slower, and from 1941 to 1944 a stalemate existed. This the Japanese decided finally to break by opening a through route from Manchuria to Canton and thence to Indochina, thus cutting Nationalist China into two parts. This campaign saw Changsha and Hengyang in Hunan seized, with thrusts also at Kweichow and Yunnan.

The young officers of the Kwantung Army had precipitated the Marco Polo Bridge incident in order to gain a quick victory over China before it could gain strength through unification. Instead, they mired Japan in an eight-year war of attrition against outwardly united Chinese forces. Though the Japanese set up puppet governments, they never controlled more than a network of corridors and key cities. On the Chinese side, both the CCP and the KMT fought the external enemy, but both were also concerned with their own political future. For most of the war, Chiang was as much concerned to blockade the Communists in the northwest as to fight the Japanese. His aim was to be in a good position to strike the Communists when the Japanese withdrew. What saved him from defeat by the Japanese was the pressure exerted upon the latter by the Americans and their British allies in the Pacific. Chiang's attitudes complicated his relations with the American General Stilwell, who demanded that Chiang stop blockading the Communists and use the Communist Eighteenth Army Group, or Eighth Route Army, to fight the Japanese. Chiang, in turn, demanded that President Roosevelt recall Stilwell and replace him with the more suave General Patrick Hurley. To further his own strategy, Chiang made a treaty with Moscow in which Russia agreed not to help the Chinese Communists in the struggle and was rewarded with rights in Manchuria and the "independence" of Outer Mongolia from China. At Yalta the British and Americans persuaded the Russians to enter the war against Japan. No sooner had the Japanese collapsed in 1945 than Mao with his 900,000-man army proceeded to challenge Chiang for control of China.

The Nationalists and the Communists

During the protracted struggle of the Chinese people for liberation from Japanese imperialism, Chinese nationalism reached its greatest pitch. The need for national salvation and unification against external enemies profoundly touched every corner of the country.

A by-product of Chinese nationalism and the modern mass movement was the rise of political societies, most of which were Western-oriented. Of all of these, the Communist party was the most indoctrinated and best organized. The imperialist threat from outside and the warlordism in various provinces made the first Kuomintang-Communist United Front of 1923 an uneasy but practical union. The alliance eventually ended in 1927 when Chiang was able to replace once indispensable Soviet assistance with Anglo-American support after the Northern Expeditionary Forces reached the Western-dominated Yangtze River delta. Membership in the CCP dropped to only 10 percent of its previous strength. Most of the stalwarts turned to underground activities or secluded themselves in the South China mountains after abortive uprisings. Chiang's Fifth Campaign of Encirclement and Termination of 1934 forced the Communists out of their Kiangsi soviet in the south. After the Long March, they eventually ended up in North Shensi near the Russian border.

In many ways the Long March was a triumph for the Communists, who remained undefeated by Chiang. The last (1936) Nationalist campaign, in fact, fizzled out both because of low morale and because of public demand for a united front against the Japanese. To try to overcome these difficulties, Chiang flew to Northwestern Pacification Headquarters at Sian, where two of his generals, opposed to his policy of "pacifying the internal before resisting the external," had him arrested. However, at this point the CCP saw the elimination of Chiang as an open invitation to the Japanese and sent Chou En-lai as an impartial mediator. They succeeded in obtaining Chiang's release on condition that a national army would be formed as part of a united front against the Japanese.

In September of 1937, two months after the outbreak of the Second Sino-Japanese War, the 30,000-man Red Army was reorganized into the Eighth Route Army and was formally integrated into Chiang's Nationalist Army. Three of the divisions of this army later established governments and operated along the northern borders of China. Lin Piao headed the 115th Division, which eventually established the Shansi-Chahar-Hopeh Border Region government behind enemy lines. Liu Po-ch'eng headed the 129th Division and created the Shansi-Hopeh-Shantung-Honan Border Region government, also behind enemy lines. And Ho Lung headed the 120th Division, which established the Shansi-Suiyuan Border Region government to guard the security of the home base (the Shensi-Kansu-Ningsia Border Region government) and to maintain communications with the two pincerlike border regions.

The occasional pacification operations conducted by the Japanese army were generally limited to the countryside near major cities or railways, but even then they usually could not stay away from their key points and lines more than a few days. Many areas were thus frequently visited in turn by the Japanese army, Communist guerrillas, and Nationalist forces. The army of the puppet Wang Ching-wei's government, established on March 30, 1940, in Nanking, consisting mainly of reorganized bandit troops or released prisoners of war, was reluctant to be involved in any fighting. Consequently, great areas behind the Japanese lines were a power vacuum only waiting to be filled.

Much more than the Nationalists with their landowner backgrounds, the CCP was successful in building up in the countryside political and military systems which had not only the immediate goal of defeating the Japanese, but the eventual one of controlling all of China. To the CCP leaders such as Mao, the war against Japan was another stage of the ultimate struggle. Communist political workers were so effective that in many areas almost everyone was a Communist at night. CCP administrative and military forces even covertly coexisted with the Japanese in many cities.

The Communists penetrated everywhere, and their capital at Yenan in Shensi provided the guidelines for progressive intellectuals and students. Many of these took great risks to get through Japanese and Nationalist blockades to study at the Anti-Japanese Military and Political University of Yenan. Here propaganda textbooks were devised which could be readily applied in daily activities, which were easily comprehended by parents and children, and which emphasized Chinese unity and hatred of the Japanese imperialists.

The Economic Collapse of the Nationalist Government

Sun Yat-sen's Three Principles of the People—nationalism, democracy, and the people's livelihood (sometimes called socialism), were the philosophical foundation of the Nationalists much as Marxism-Leninism was for the Communists. The principle of the people's livelihood consisted of two ideas: equalization of land ownership and state control of capital. Chiang's Nationalist followers were mainly from landlord and merchant families. Thus Chiang's purge of the Communists in 1927 was due in part to pressure from his officers, whose parents or close relatives in their rural homes had often become the victims of the Communist-directed peasant struggle. Chiang's training both in China and in Japan and his early experience as a career soldier convinced him that military power was the decisive factor, so he neglected the economic and social aspects of society. Consequently, the Nationalist government from the days of unification in 1928 lived on customs-house revenues and contributions from financiers of the lower Yangtze River delta and coastal cities rather than by taxing inland villages.

Arthur N. Young, financial adviser to China from 1929 to 1947, has estimated that at the beginning of the nationwide war in 1937 the financial position of the Chinese government was much stronger than at any previous time. It had such reserves of gold, silver, U.S. dollars, and pounds sterling that the total note issue was about two-thirds solidly backed.

During the 1937–45 war, however, inflation rose without pause. If average retail market prices in the first half of 1937 are considered as a base of one, then by the end of the war in August 1945 retail prices in Free China were 2,647, while in Shanghai, the financial capital, they were 85,200. The granting of credit also exploded, rising from 1.2 million Chinese dollars in 1937 to 1,175.3 million by 1945. Paper currency in circulation rose about 1,000-fold in face value over the same period.

Inflation was caused by disruption of trade and communications, destruction both of goods and of the means of production, reduction of imports, the influx of refugees (including this author) into Free China, and the reduction in the number of workers by military and other wartime demands as well as by the uncertainties of doing business. After Pearl Harbor inflation worsened. The loss of the Burma Road in 1942, early Allied defeats, the cost of construction of American B-29 bomber bases, which were shortly afterwards overrun by the enemy, the increased demand for *fapi* (legal paper money) for American military personnel in China, liberal credit policies to industry, the U.S. Treasury's refusal to sell gold to China in 1944–45, and hoarding and speculation—all contributed to the excessive issue of notes and eventual hyperinflation. Adding to these woes were the puppet currencies starting in 1935 in Hopeh, the Japanese flooding of the market with both yen and Korean currency, as well as military yen, or *gunpyo*, used by the Japanese army to pay for goods and labor in occupied places; and Chinese provincial currencies issued in the various isolated areas.

From 1937 to 1941 China received foreign aid in varying amounts from the United States, the Soviet Union, Great Britain, and France. Most of it was in purchase credits, but some of it was for monetary stabilization. After Pearl Harbor the United States provided US$500 million for financial measures and US$440 million in payment for American activities in China, as well as US$800 million in lend-lease. British support included training Chinese troops in India. This financial aid was helpful for the support of morale but was insufficient in itself to hold back inflation. Material aid, because of the Allied "Europe first" policy, was inadequate, and the limited and expensive air route over the Hump was simply incapable of supplying what was needed. At its peak in 1944, China's share in American lend-lease was only 4 percent.

It is impossible to estimate accurately how much of all Nationalist resources were used against the Japanese and how much went into the continuing civil war. Chiang never clearly selected the most dangerous enemy.

Not only did the national economy collapse, but the already unbelievably low standard of living for the majority of the salaried classes, both military and civil, was severely depressed. Military demoralization and civil inefficiency were becoming more common in the Nationalist-held areas. Nevertheless, patriotism against the Japanese aggressor and the increased hope of final victory stayed the collapsing Nationalist regime for a time.

The Demise of Chiang

By 1945, shortly before the Japanese surrender, the Chinese Communists had engaged in over 115,000 large and small battles and had established nineteen large bases in nineteen provinces from Manchuria to the South China Sea. They had a regular army of over 900,000 and a militia of some 2,200,000, and controlled a populace of 95,500,000. Closer to the immense plains of North China and Manchuria, they rapidly pushed into the huge areas formerly occupied by Japan when victory suddenly arrived. They were already in control of the cities as well as the countryside when the Nationalist forces from West and Southeast China were either airlifted to North China or convoyed to Manchuria by the Americans. The Nationalist army, replacing the Japanese occupation authorities, was eager to compensate itself for its long, hard struggle. Military officers and civil officials were more interested in enjoying the properties left by the Japanese than in the welfare of their newly liberated fellow countrymen. Corruption alienated the soldiers from their officers. The uprooted landlords and students (again including this author) from combat zones in North China and Manchuria swarmed into large cities such as Mukden and Peking and increased the threat of a food shortage and the insecurity of the Nationalist authorities. With the gradual demise of Chungking's popularity and with the increasing hostility of the intellectuals and the students toward the Nationalist authorities, Chiang was well on his way to losing his mandate in China before he actually lost the struggle with the Communists.

In the years 1945–49, as war between the CCP and the KMT went on, the decline of Chiang's popularity was aggravated by increasing strikes and demonstrations by students, and by military mutinies. These demonstrations were usually touched off by cases of individual misconduct, such as the famous Shen Ch'ung incident when a college girl was allegedly raped by an American soldier in Peking. This eventually led to a nationwide student movement against starvation and against the United States for its continuous assistance to the Nationalists in waging the civil war. The great majority of intellectuals and civil servants, including police, whose fixed salaries were shrinking with an unbelievable rapidity, was generally sympathetic with the student strikes. The eight years of the anti-Japanese war had already reduced the savings of every intellectual and middle-class family to nothing. The continuing civil war in effect made every honest man a beggar. Thus all were extremely anxious for a change in order to save themselves from starvation, and peace of any kind was their only hope for survival. The generally demoralized troops were also greatly dissatisfied, as their condition changed from bad to worse within the besieged cities or tight areas. "Rising up for righteousness" (defection) became a popular outlet for military men of the Nationalist government. On August 3, 1949, General Ch'eng Ch'ien, who had been a Kuomintang general since 1910, "liberated" Hunan before the Red Army came. Liu Wen-hui, the warlord governor of Sikang province since 1934, declared his allegiance to the Communists even before Chiang abandoned neighboring Szechwan province.

While Chiang was convening his constituent National Assembly at Nanking, he was losing battles from north to south. The Liao-Shen operation in which Chiang lost both Manchuria and half a million men trained and equipped by America, ended in victory for Lin Piao at the end of 1948. This was followed by the battle of Hwai-Hai, which also ended in a crushing defeat of the Nationalists on January 10, 1949. Lin Piao then moved on Peking and its satellite cities, and the Nationalist supreme commander in North China, aware of the complete hopelessness of the Nationalist cause, surrendered Peking at the end of January. Because of the defections of Nationalist garrison commanders fed up with the war, the Communists were across the Yangtze by the end of April and had mopped up the rest of the Nationalists within a few more months. Chiang evacuated to Taiwan, but not before moving the gold reserves and other essential supplies there. The People's Republic of China was formally established on October 1, 1949, at Peking.

The experience in China shows that an external threat can be a unifying influence, especially if slogans can be developed to accentuate this message. But at the same time, provincialism was very evident, and neither the Nationalists nor the Communists could forget their distrust of each other. Both were, in fact, justified in their suspicions. The Nationalists suffered from the fact that their leadership came from the propertied classes such as landowners and merchants; thus they never grasped the possibilities at the grassroots as did the Communists. And while Chiang claimed to be the Nationalist leader, he often seemed more interested in defeating the Communists than the Japanese. Mao's guerrilla activities before the Second Sino-Japanese War gave him the necessary training, and the Long March placed him in the physical and political position to exploit his Russian links. Mao believed, correctly as it turned out, that he would win the final victory.

The Japanese aggression was, of course, not in aid of either party, but purely selfish. What the Japanese did was to facilitate the transformation of China from its provincialism and warlordism to a centralized national state. During the protracted armed struggle, the Communists, more conscious than the Nationalists of the need for social reforms, commanded the great majority of the rural areas through excellent organization and indoctrination.

The Chinese Civil War also showed that traditional underdeveloped countries, at least in Asia, cannot succeed until led by a Western-oriented elite capable of creating mass support in the awakened rural millions.

X

TRIBALISM AND HUMANITARIANISM
The Nigerian-Biafran Civil War

CLARENCE C. CLENDENEN

IN JANUARY 1970, the war in Nigeria came to an end. Biafra's effort to break away from the federation had failed, after an agony lasting two and a half years. It was a strange war that offered nothing new in tactics or other military matters. It was fought by relatively undeveloped peoples using modern weapons and techniques. It was a civil war, fought within the boundaries of a recognized sovereign state, and at the same time it was an intertribal war such as Africa has known for hundreds of years.

Nigeria is an almost accidental product of the heyday of the British Empire. In the early half of the nineteenth century British traders established themselves in the region of the "Oil Rivers" (actually the mouths of the Niger) to trade for palm oil, needed by the machinery of the Industrial Revolution. British interest and influence expanded northward from the Niger delta, and by the time the European powers carved Africa into colonies for themselves, the area now known as Nigeria was a recognized British "sphere of influence." It was not until 1914, however, that any sort of centralized government was established for the region.

When British sovereignty was established over Nigeria, there was neither ethnic nor cultural unity among the varied and various peoples of the country. In the north there were old, established Moslem monarchies, which were frequently at war with each other. Among the more primitive tribes of the south and east, intertribal and even intervillage warfare was

The writer wishes to acknowledge his deep indebtedness to Dr. Louis Gann, of the Hoover Institution on War, Revolution, and Peace, Stanford University, for making the extensive collection of material on Biafra available to him.

164

a normal condition. There were (and are) some 400 tribal and linguistic groups in Nigeria, most of which have been suspicious of each other for centuries, usually with ample reason. But in these hundreds, there are five language and cultural groups that are predominant—the Hausa, the Fulani, the Gwari, the Yoruba, and the Ibo, the latter being the majority of the present-day Biafrans.

At the turn of the century, as British authority was being extended over Nigeria, the Ibos were the most primitive of these tribes. They lived in the country south of the Benue and east of the Niger rivers and were unified only by a common language and cultural tradition. There was no system of tribal chiefs, no hierarchy of officials, no common priesthood or any kind of tribal control. Their villages were fiercely independent and the Ibo tribesmen were passionately individualistic. They recognized no higher authority than their village elders, and often refused to respect even them. A pioneer missionary among them said, "The Ibos, prior to the British occupation of the country, occupied their spare time fighting. . . . It led to the isolation and independence of each town through the perpetual fear which existed." The virtual anarchy in the Ibo country was further aggravated by the existence of secret societies which were formed for plunder and whose members were more than willing to do a bit of murder if they were paid for it. War, robbery, and murder were not the only Ibo customs upon which the British frowned. Cannibalism and human sacrifice were commonplace occurrences.

It took several years and numerous small military expeditions before the Pax Britannica was firmly established over Nigeria, and during those years the Ibos were among the most troublesome of the tribes. But at last, in the early years of the twentieth century, British control became firm. Slave raiding was sternly suppressed, cannibalism, human sacrifice, and intertribal warfare were banned, and the vast region known as Nigeria enjoyed internal peace for the first time in either recorded or traditional history.

British rule was strict, sometimes stern, but always fair, and within a few years the tribes of Nigeria came to have confidence in it, no matter how much they might resent the loss of their previous independence. In both of the great wars of this century the Nigerians rallied loyally to the British crown and flag. In World War I, Nigerian troops were the backbone of the Allied forces that conquered German Cameroon after a campaign that lasted two years, and also fought in East Africa. In World War

II, they made up two-thirds of the two African divisions deployed in Burma against the Japanese.

Once internal peace was firmly established and maintained, the people of Nigeria developed rapidly. In only a few decades the Ibos, from being the most primitive peoples of Nigeria, became the most advanced. Largely because of their strong individualism and their freedom from feudal restraints or a restrictive religion, they quickly adapted themselves to new ideas and new ways. The efforts of numerous missionaries, both Protestant and Catholic, converted masses of them, possibly the majority, to Christianity. Ibo students thronged the schools and in due time the newly established universities. Large numbers of Ibo students who either had the means or obtained scholarships, studied in America and Europe. The Ibo population increased by leaps and bounds, and early in the century their own home region could no longer support the population. They began spreading into other parts of Nigeria to settle, often using means that did not endear them to other tribes; if a place pleased them they simply moved in and took possession. Another source of irritation grew from the fact that the Ibos did not assimilate themselves into the tribes into whose territories they moved. They remained Ibos, keeping to themselves and apparently feeling greatly superior to other peoples.

As great numbers of Ibos spread to other parts of Nigeria and their educational standards and energy put them ahead, they attained a position in the economy and organization of the country that was not reached by any other tribe. From small shopkeepers to big businessmen, the majority finally were Ibos. Most of the professional men, physicians and lawyers, were Ibos. Ibos were railway station agents, locomotive drivers, section foremen. As the road network of the country was expanded and motor vehicles replaced human carriers, the truck drivers were likely to be Ibos, as were the mechanics and maintenance men. And after World War II, when the British government began placing more and more responsibility and authority upon Nigerians, Ibos swarmed into government offices until the number of Ibos holding official positions was disproportionate to their numbers as compared with other tribes. There is evidence that the Ibos regarded their role in the country as being only their due, and that they did not hesitate to favor their own tribesmen when in positions of power.

After World War II it appeared that Nigeria was the most stable and advanced country of Black Africa. Step by step the British prepared the country for eventual independence. There were several successive changes in the constitutional structure of Nigeria, each change being designed to bring independence closer. One of the last measures was to divide the country into four almost autonomous regions, under a federal government with clearly defined and limited powers. This measure was designed to minimize tribal differences and the different economic conditions imposed by accidents of geography and climate. Under this arrangement the Ibos occupied the Eastern Region, where they also constituted the majority of the population. In 1958, control over the army passed from the British to the Nigerian federal government, and a Nigerian navy was created. In 1960 the federal government formally requested independence; an Independence Act passed both houses of Parliament and received Queen Elizabeth's assent on July 29, 1960. At midnight on September 30, in an impressive ceremony, the British flag was lowered, and the new Nigerian national flag, three vertical stripes, green, white, green, was raised slowly in its place. Three days later the Duchess of Kent, a member of the Royal Family and personal representative of Her Majesty the Queen, opened the first Parliament of the new commonwealth, with all of the traditional British pomp and pageantry. A few weeks later the last British governor general left Nigeria; he was replaced by Dr. Nnamdu Azikiwe, former president of the Senate and a member of the Ibo tribe. A year later, in October 1961, the Republic of Nigeria was proclaimed, with Dr. Azikiwe as its first president.

For several years Nigeria seemed completely stable and appeared to be making both social and economic progress. Oil was discovered in the area around the Niger delta and just north of the Gulf of Biafra, giving employment to large numbers of people and adding to the government's income through the royalties paid. Nevertheless, there were internal tensions in Nigeria that were not apparent to the outside world. After World War II there had been labor troubles in the country, with disorders in which the antagonists split largely along tribal lines. After independence, in spite of the positions held by Ibos in the government, the Northern Region held a majority of the seats in the Parliament because of its greater population. (The population of the Northern Region was estimated at about 27,000,000.) The Northerners are largely Moslem, a fact that added a religious factor to the rapidly developing friction. In various parts of the country there were sporadic riots in which numbers of Ibos were killed; the Ibos responded in kind, killing members of other tribes. There were charges of all sorts of malfeasance and corruption in politics, probably correct. In October 1965, for example, there was a regional election in the Western Region, whose Chief Akintola was allied politically with the North. Election officials vanished, voters were openly intimidated by Akintola's henchmen, and the ballots were counted by his officers. Quite naturally, his candidates were elected by huge majorities. In the resulting riots, over a hundred people were killed and many more were injured.

The situation and discontent became more tense. In January 1966, a small group of junior officers of the army, mostly Ibos, attempted a coup d'etat. The coup failed, but before it was suppressed the federal premier, Sir Abubakar, Chief Akintola, and the sardauna (or emir) of Sokoto were all killed. The sardauna was both premier of the Northern Region and the spiritual head of the millions of Moslems of Nigeria. A group of moderate senior officers, led by Major General Johnson Aguiyi-Ironsi, an Ibo, took control and proclaimed the establishment of a military government with Ironsi at the head. Ironsi appointed a military governor for each of the four regions, designating Lieutenant Colonel Odumegwu Ojukwu as governor of the Eastern Region. At the same time he named Lieutenant Colonel Yakubu Gowon to be chief of staff of the army.

But in July 1966, during a second attempted coup, Ironsi was killed and Gowon assumed leadership of the military government. During the early part of 1966 there were widespread disorders throughout the whole country in which hundreds of people, mostly Ibos, were killed. On September 29, anti-Ibo riots broke out in the city of Kano in the Moslem north. Mobs of hoodlums raged through the Ibo quarter of the city, looting, murdering, and burning. Estimates as to the number of Ibo tribesmen killed vary widely, but 30,000 is a conservative figure. There was an immediate exodus of terrified Ibos from all parts of Nigeria, fleeing for their tribal homeland. Colin Legum, a correspondent for the *London Observer*, described the arrival of some of the refugees at Enugu, the capital of the Eastern Region:

> Hacked, slashed, mangled, stripped naked and robbed of all their possessions, the orphans, the widows, the traumatized. A woman, mute and dazed, arrived back at her village after traveling for five days with only a bowl in her lap. It held the head of her child, severed before her eyes.

It was reported that the Ibos were not hesitant in taking revenge upon the non-Ibo people in their region. At Port Harcourt, for example, it was claimed that hundreds were killed in a few days and that several hundred trying to escape by rail were slaughtered without mercy and their bodies dumped into the river.

In the midst of the tension, fear, and distrust, Gowon announced a plan for reorganization of the country. The autonomous regions would be abolished and the country divided into twelve states, all together constituting a federal union. The Ibo country would become the East-Central State, with its capital at Enugu. The Niger delta area, which was part of the Eastern Region, and which included the producing oil fields, would become the Rivers State, cutting the proposed East-Central State off from direct access to the sea. Military Governor Ojukwu immediately protested, saying that the intended reorganization of Nigeria was arbitrary, high-handed, and undemocratic. He demanded also the immediate withdrawal of all federal troops from the Eastern Region.

The controversy quickly became so bitter a quarrel that the two leaders could not meet on Nigerian soil. Neither trusted the other. They agreed to confer on neutral ground and accordingly met in January 1967 at Aburi, Ghana. The conference accomplished nothing; no real agreement was possible. In a short time Ojukwu asserted that Gowon had failed to keep promises made at the conference and began a series of steps that led to secession and civil war. He seized all federal funds in the Eastern Region, decreed that all revenues must be paid into the regional treasury instead of the federal, and pressed the oil companies to pay their royalties to the regional government. On May 6, 1967, he boasted to a National Reconciliation Committee, "I started off this struggle in July [1966] with 120 rifles to defend the entirety of the East. . . . Quietly I built. If you do not know it, I am proud, and my officers are proud that here in the East we possess the biggest army in Black Africa. I am no longer speaking as an under-dog, I am speaking from a position of power."

On May 30, 1967, in defiance of Gowon's announcement of the forthcoming reorganization of Nigeria, Ojukwu formally proclaimed the independence of "The Republic of Biafra." "The territory and region known as and called Eastern Nigeria together with her continental shelf and territorial waters shall henceforth be an independent and sovereign state of the name and title of 'The Republic of Biafra.' "

Revolutions almost always polarize about leaders, and the revolt of Biafra was no exception to this general rule. Biafran will was personified in Ojukwu; Nigerian determination to crush the revolt was centered in Gowon. The two men were strikingly similar in many respects. They were both relatively young, being in their thirties when the trouble started.

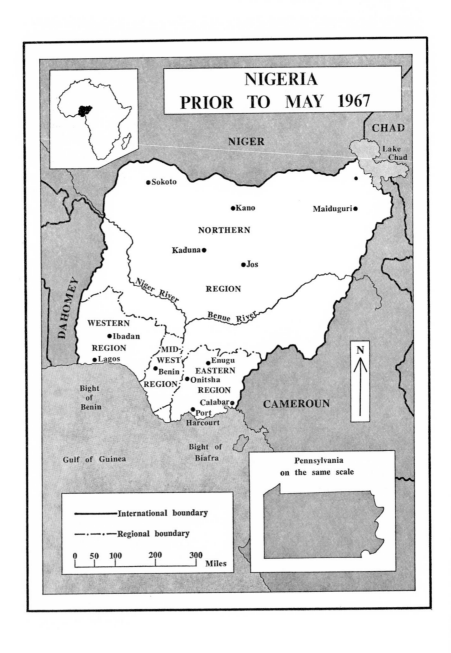

NIGERIA
PRIOR TO MAY 1967

CHAD

NIGER
Lake Chad

•Sokoto

•Kano   Maiduguri•

NORTHERN

Kaduna•

•Jos

DAHOMEY

Niger River

REGION

Benue River

WESTERN
•Ibadan
REGION
•Lagos

MID-
WEST
•Benin
REGION

•Enugu
EASTERN
•Onitsha
REGION

Calabar•

•Port
Harcourt

CAMEROUN

N

Bight
of
Benin

Gulf of Guinea

Bight of
Biafra

Pennsylvania
on the same scale

International boundary

Regional boundary

0   50   100   200   300
                              Miles

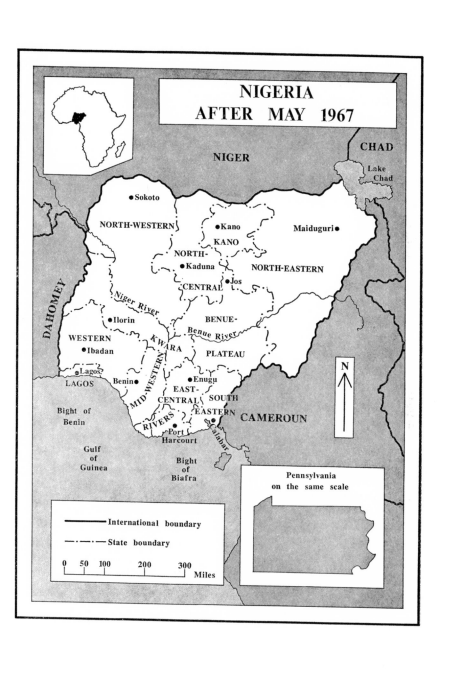

**NIGERIA
AFTER MAY 1967**

CHAD

NIGER

Lake
Chad

•Sokoto

NORTH-WESTERN

•Kano

Maiduguri•

KANO

NORTH-

•Kaduna

NORTH-EASTERN

CENTRAL

•Jos

Niger River

BENUE-

•Ilorin

Benue River

WESTERN

KWARA

PLATEAU

•Ibadan

•Lagos?

Benin•

•Enugu

LAGOS

EAST-

MID-WESTERN

CENTRAL

SOUTH

Bight of

EASTERN

CAMEROUN

Benin

RIVERS

Port

Calabar

Harcourt

Gulf

of

Guinea

Bight

of

Biafra

DAHOMEY

N

Pennsylvania
on the same scale

International boundary

State boundary

0   50   100   200   300
                              Miles

Gowon came from what can be described as a upper-middle-class family. He was born in Northern Nigeria, a member of a minor tribe. He was educated in mission schools and professed the Christian religion. He has been described as "small, dapper and handsome, always beautifully groomed and with a dazzling, boyish smile." At the age of nineteen he enrolled in the army (then the Royal Nigeria Regiment) and soon after was sent to England for officer's training, first at Eaton Hall, then at Sandhurst. He was in the Nigerian contingent of the United Nations force sent to the Congo to restore peace in that troubled region and, as already mentioned, was made chief of staff of the Nigerian army by General Ironsi.

Odumegwu Ojukwu was a son of Sir Louis Ojukwu, one of the wealthiest men in Nigeria. He was educated at the best and most expensive schools of Nigeria (modeled after the famous English public schools) and at Epsom College in England. At the age of eighteen he matriculated at Oxford and obtained his degree without difficulty, but also without any special distinction. His father wanted him to study law, but instead he specialized in modern history. When he returned to Nigeria he was noted at first, according to his own statement, only for "the impeccable cut of my English clothes." Instead of entering one of the numerous family firms, as Sir Louis had hoped, he went into the Nigerian civil service and threw himself energetically into building roads, digging canals, and constructing culverts. After three years of this he decided upon the army as his career. He was trained at Eaton Hall and received further training at Hythe and Warminster. Like Gowon, he served in the Congo, and in 1962 he returned to England for the course at the Joint Services Staff College. Upon completion he was promoted to lieutenant colonel and made quartermaster general of the Nigerian army. In that office, in which he was responsible for all procurement for the army, he established a new policy. It had been the practice, holding over from before independence, to obtain all military supplies and equipment from Great Britain. Ojukwu purchased wherever he could get the best prices—in the Netherlands, Belgium, West Germany, Italy, and Israel.

Ojukwu's declaration of Biafran independence made war unavoidable. Initially all advantages seemed to be with Biafra. For months Ojukwu had been building up his forces and accumulating munitions and supplies. The first pitched battle, on July 6, 1967, was a draw, with neither side able to advance. On July 25 the Federals seized the island of Bonny, which commanded the channel from the sea to Port Harcourt, but beyond that they were unable to exploit the success. Early in August a Biafran column swept across the Niger at Onitsha and sliced deep into federal territory. The Biafran advance was helped by the defection of some officers of the federal garrisons who were members of the Ica-Ibo tribe. Within a few days the Biafrans were less than a hundred miles from Lagos, the capital of the country. With the Biafrans in possession of the area, officials of the Mid-West Region proclaimed the formation of the State of Benin and its adherence to Biafra, but the State of Benin lasted just one day. The Federals were able to assemble forces and counterattack; the Biafrans were driven back across the Niger almost as fast as they had advanced beyond it. The Federals successfully occupied Enugu, the capital of the Eastern Region, and in fear of an attack from Federal-held Bonny, the Biafrans started to fortify Port Harcourt. They were able to reinforce and supply the city by using speedboats commandeered from the yacht club.

Before the end of 1967 the Federals had Biafra completely surrounded, and through the latter months of the year and the early part of 1968 they slowly and inexorably increased their pressure. Optimistic hopes expressed at the beginning of the war that it would be short proved illusory. Federal attacks in the Calabar region were sharply repulsed. Three Federal attempts to capture Onitsha were driven back with heavy casualties, but in March 1968 they succeeded in crossing the river, capturing the city and thus establishing a bridgehead on the Biafran side of the Niger. In May, a Federal amphibious assault against Port Harcourt carried that city; thus Biafra was cut off from any possibility of access to the city and at the same time lost its major airport. By the end of 1968 continuous Federal pressure had reduced the Biafran territory to a mere enclave of some 5,000 square miles, a very small space for the original population plus the hundreds of thousands of refugees who had poured into it.

During 1969 sporadic fighting continued, although no major battles were reported. Biafra was completely surrounded by a cordon of hostile forces. Steady Federal squeezing reduced further the size of the enclave. From the scanty information available it seems probable that the Federals adopted a deliberate strategy of attrition, based on their superiority in numbers and the knowledge that time was on their side.

The question naturally arises as to why the Biafrans continued to fight, knowing as they must have that the enemy had vastly greater numbers and free access to the munitions makers and arms dealers of the world. The answer seems to be that the Ibos and their allied tribes remembered the massacres of 1966 and fully believed that their enemies intended to exterminate them. They believed in their own superiority over the other peoples of Nigeria and knew that they were heartily disliked by other tribes. They had had plenty of evidence of that dislike and were terrorized by the possibility of defeat. *Biafra News Letter*, a publication of Ojukwu's government, carried as a part of its caption, "Ours is a Fight for Survival." The lead article in the issue for July 12, 1969, was entitled, "Save Biafra from Genocide."

Where and how did the Biafrans obtain the munitions and weapons that enabled them to hold out as long and as stubbornly as they did? To this question only a tentative answer can be given. Ojukwu was able to amass considerable quantities of arms and munitions during the months when he was preparing for secession. The raid of August 1967 into Federal territory resulted in the capture of arms and vehicles, possibly the only tangible result of the raid for Biafra. Following the massacres of 1966, hundreds of Ibo truckers fled into the Eastern Region with their vehicles, which were thus available to Biafra after the war started, also making spare parts available by the cannibalizing of worn-out trucks and cars. Fuel of a sort was obtained by improvising crude refineries hidden in the brush and villages. There is ample evidence of a steady inflow of small arms and ammunition by airlift from Portugal, from the former French colonies close to Biafra, and even from China via Tanzania. Biafra never seemed to suffer from any shortage of weapons or munitions.

A civil war is always the most viciously fought of all wars. Everything is pure white or dead black, with no grays or neutral shades. There are "good guys" and "bad guys," with nothing intermediate. The enemy commits unspeakable atrocities; the conduct of one's own side is above reproach. On no battle front was the fighting more deadly than on the paper front—the battle of propaganda in newspapers, books, on the radio and television. Neither side in the Biafran war was at all hesitant in charging the enemy with committing unspeakable horrors. Speaking somewhat cynically, it is not at all unlikely that all such charges were true, and that "the pot was calling the kettle black."

A Biafran, presumably an Ibo, said that "In areas that have fallen to the Nigerians, towns and houses were pillaged and what could not be stolen was destroyed. Men were tortured and shot and women defiled." On the other side, an Ibo tribesman who remained with the Federals and who was identified as the "provincial secretary of Calabar," was quoted as saying that at the village of Ikot Ekpenyong, "three miles from my home town," Ibo soldiers lured some 300 people into the church on a Sunday morning, then surrounded the church and set fire to it, murdering everyone, men, women, and children alike. Such allegations were made so freely by both sides that additional examples would be simply cumulative, and specific documentation seems unnecessary.

The Biafrans must be awarded the laurels for success in the paper war and in arousing worldwide sympathy for their side. Biafran propaganda was skillfully conducted and so telling in its emphasis upon sick and starving children that it made a deep impression on the outside world, especially in the United States. In the face of the almost universal sympathy for Biafra in the United States, and in Canada as well, a statement by Dr. Ralph Hendricke, a professor of pediatrics at the University of Idaban who visited Toronto while en route to a pediatric conference in Mexico, struck an almost discordant note:

> The results of Ojukwu's international propaganda based on "genocide" and "starvation" have become painfully apparent. The righteous indignation of decent citizens the world over, which had been kept at fever heat by the public relations organizations, has provided the cloak which Ojukwu needed to his military objectives and has forced certain governments to step up their support for his regime.

The effectiveness of Biafran propaganda in the United States may be measured by a glance at some of the various organizations which were set up for Biafran relief, and by considering the articles, books, and pamphlets that were published depicting the horrors of the war. A list of fifty-eight relief organizations shows thirty-five that, from their titles, were devoted to Biafra alone. A glance at the literature put out by organizations that include "Nigeria/Biafra" in their titles indicates that all of them were purely pro-Biafra. Inclusion of the word "Nigeria" was pure camouflage. Incidentally, the American Red Cross Society does *not* appear in this list. The numerous "ad hoc committees" included such organizations as "The American Committee to Keep Biafra Alive," with headquarters in New York City and branches in several other cities. Then there was "BROTHER" (Biafra Rescue Organization to Hasten Emergency Relief), also with several branches. There were detached, independent organizations in such remote places as Blair, Nebraska, where a "Student Council Committee to Save Biafra" was formed at a small college. It should be noted, too, that virtually all Americans who visited and wrote on the war in Nigeria went to Biafra and wrote from the Biafran point of view. The Biafran propaganda was not only skillfully conducted, but bore unmistakable professional touches, as indicated by Dr. Hendricke. The Nigerian commissioner for labour and information, in an address at the San Francisco Commonwealth Club on March 19, 1969, charged that Biafra had employed well-known public relations firms in the United States to conduct propaganda. This charge is partially corroborated by the fact that press releases from Aggrey K. Oji, who was described as "the representative of Biafra in the United States," were registered with the Department of Justice by a New York public relations company.

But regardless of propaganda exaggerations, there is no doubt that the suffering and starvation in Biafra, particularly among young children, were appalling. Even before the war the food resources of the Ibo country were inadequate for the needs of the people. That was the basic reason for Ibo emigration to other parts of Nigeria. At the outbreak of the war the Ibo country probably produced enough, but barely enough, of the basic agricultural products for the needs of the people remaining there, but they were almost completely dependent upon other sources for most of their meat and other proteins. After the 1966 massacres and after the start of the war, an enormous mass of fugitives crowded into the already thickly populated country. Some estimates place the number of refugees as high as three million or more. The ever-tightening cordon of federal armies made it impossible for food or anything else to come into Biafra by road or rail.

Early in 1968 the International Red Cross attempted to ship in small amounts of food and medicines on airplanes that were owned by a freelance American pilot who made semiweekly flights from Lisbon with arms and ammunition, but he was primarily a munitions runner who was after a quick profit. The amounts shipped in by this means were negligible. The federal government refused to permit daylight flights by Red Cross airplanes on the ground that such flights could be easily made into munitions flights and would afford Biafran observers an opportunity to see Federal concentrations and installations. Proposals by the Red Cross and others for a neutral corridor through which relief supplies could be sent into Biafra after inspection by and under the supervision of Nigerian officials were refused flatly by Ojukwu because Biafrans feared that the Federals would poison such supplies.

Meanwhile the suffering in the ever-narrowing Biafra enclave intensified and became known to the world. In an editorial in November 1968, the *New York Times* predicted grimly that three-quarters of a million people would perish in Biafra during the next month. The Biafrans, it added, had had to harvest their yam crop early and had already eaten their seed yams. In Biafra, Father Anthony Byrne, the representative of Caritas Internationale, told an interviewer, "The truth is that we don't know—and can't know how many people are starving or might starve." Dr. Herman Middlekoop, a Dutch physician who headed the work of the World Council of Churches in Biafra, predicted that the deaths in the winter of 1968–69 would reach 25,000 a day, while Father Donal O'Sullivan, the superior of the Holy Ghost Fathers in Biafra, said simply, "This could be a ghastly winter." Glen Haydon, an American Red Cross worker who spent several months in the war zone, upon his return to the United States said, "We never asked if anyone had died during the night, but how many."

When the terrible plight of Biafra became known, the response on behalf of the pitiful children of the country was spontaneous and massive, especially in the United States. At least a score of relief organizations, in addition to those already mentioned, sprang into being. Catholics, Protestants, and Jews together formed "Joint Church Aid—U.S.A." Individuals, their hearts touched by the pictures and stories of starving children in Biafra, came forward by hundreds, giving food, money, time, and labor. A salesman returning to his home in New Jersey after his day's work in New York City heard over his car radio that volunteers were needed. He was so moved that he turned around and spent the whole night packaging food to be shipped to Biafra. A housewife in Westport, Connecticut, made her home a headquarters to collect contributions for "Food for Biafra, Inc." In a supermarket in New York City a young woman with two small children "buttonholed" other customers for packages of rice and cans of tuna and all sorts of food that could be sent to Biafra, saying, "We're all mothers and we don't like kids starving." A wealthy citizen of Israel, with some associates, chartered a ship which was sent on a voyage to various ports of Europe and America to collect a cargo of food to be sent to São Tomé, and from there, it was hoped, into Biafra. The public response to appeals for Biafra was so enormous that a veteran worker for National Catholic Relief Services said, "I have seen nothing comparable in my twenty-three years in the field." Figures that are admittedly fragmentary (and may represent a certain amount of wishful thinking) indicate that between January 1 and November 1, 1968, more than 9,000 tons of relief supplies were shipped to Biafra from the United States and various countries of Europe.

A rather curious by-product of the Biafran conflict was the overt sympathy of the Jewish people of the United States for Biafra, and the converse, the open cultivation of the Moslem countries by Nigeria. Rabbi Marc H. Tannenbaum, one of the promoters of Joint Church Aid—U.S.A., believes that Jewish compassion was deeply aroused because Jews saw a close parallel between the starving people of Biafra and the plight of the Jews under Hitler. The rather frequent references to the Ibos as the "Jews of Africa," because of their business acumen, may have helped this image. On the other side of the panel lay the facts that a large part of the population of Northern Nigeria is Moslem. In the Israeli-Arab troubles the sympathies of the Northerners naturally are anti-Israel. In January 1969, there was a Nigerian delegation at the Second International Conference of Solidarity with the Arab Peoples, at Cairo. At a press conference a Nigerian delegate said, "Long before secession the Ibo leaders had entered into a league with Zionists and the financiers of French imperialism. . . . There is a Zionist organization in the United States called the Jewish Association for Solidarity with 'Biafra.' "

It was not lack of food or any failure by donors to contribute that made the problem of getting relief into Biafra so difficult. Biafra was cut off from the outside world by land and sea; the only possible access was by air. After the capture of Port Harcourt by the Federals the only airport in Biafra where heavily loaded cargo planes could land and take off was a narrow runway improvised from the remains of a paved road. Trees and brush on both sides made night landing a tricky and dangerous business. Daylight flights were impossible because of Federal antiaircraft fire and fighter planes—fast Russian MIGs, manned by Egyptian pilots trained by the Russians. Not the least of the problems faced by relief organizations was that of obtaining suitable aircraft. Over the months an air fleet that was almost weird in its composition made flights into Biafra. The planes varied from light craft piloted by adventurous philanthropists, through war-weary relics of World War II, held together by baling wire and prayers, to powerful jets. After some hesitation the United States government sold four obsolescent but still serviceable C-97 Stratofreighters to Joint Church Aid—U.S.A. for a nominal sum. They were ferried from

Long Beach, California, to São Tomé. From the Portuguese base they took off into the African darkness for a landing field where none of the pilots had ever been before. The first one to make the flight into the unknown was delayed for several hours because several flights earlier in the night were turned back by Federal fighters and ground fire. There was one particular Federal fighter pilot who spoke English and who announced over his radio that he was going "to get the Yanks." His specialty was to bomb the runway just before a landing, and then machine-gun it after. However, "Genocide," as the pilot proudly called himself, did not interfere, and the American plane landed successfully, although it broke a propeller in landing. Quickly unloaded, it took to the air in the pitch blackness and arrived safely back at São Tomé just after daybreak.

And so for week after week and month after month a succession of airplanes lifted supplies to the stricken people of Biafra. There was a continual turnover of pilots and air crews. Night flights over unknown and unmarked country, with all of the hazards of war flying included but without the stimulating excitement of combat missions, were too much for human nerves to stand over a long period of time. Volunteer pilots and crews, however, never seem to have been lacking. The mercy flights continued until the very end of the war. In spite of the hazards only three planes and two flight crews were lost, and a total of over 5,000 flights delivered more than 30,000 tons of relief supplies. Eleven planes belonging to or chartered by Joint Church Aid—U.S.A. delivered more than 200 tons each night during the latter months of the war. In spite of the Federal blockade of Biafra and in spite of the terrific difficulty, the humanity of the Western world, particularly of the people of the United States, did much to alleviate suffering in the war zone. Available statistical tables indicate that relief shipments going into Federal Nigeria were as large as those into Biafra, but that part of the war has received no publicity.

In September 1968, to offset the widespread allegations of deliberate genocide, the Federal government invited Great Britain, Canada, Sweden, Poland, the United Nations, and the Organization of African Unity to send observers to the war zone to report on the conduct of the Federal forces. The observers arrived in Nigeria late in September and by mutual agreement split themselves into two teams, so as to be able to cover the largest possible territory. They submitted an interim report on October 2, saying, "Each team visited front line positions, military units and headquarters, villages, market places, medical and food distributing stations, refugee camps and major cities and towns. The Observers talked to officers, soldiers, local inhabitants, refugees, members of the Civil Administration, Police, Red Cross officials and missionaries." Early in October the observers again divided themselves into two teams and visited other parts of the fighting front. They were originally scheduled to leave Nigeria in December, but at the special request of the Nigerian government they remained until January 1969. At the conclusion of their stay the representatives of the United Nations and the Organization of African Unity submitted separate reports, while the other delegates rendered a common report. The three reports, however, were virtually unanimous in their recorded observations and conclusions. They agreed that there was no destruction of property beyond what was to be expected in war, that the Federal soldiers showed strict discipline and firm control by the officers, and that there was no evidence whatever of deliberate genocide. The observers unanimously stated that no restrictions were placed on their movements or their freedom to interview anyone to whom they might want to talk, except that they were not allowed to enter the camps where civilian internees were detained. The only times when Nigerian officers or officials were present were when they were specially requested to act as interpreters. The delegates of the Organization of African Unity, voicing the unanimous opinion of all of the observers, said in their report, "The discipline and good behaviour of the Federal troops are commendable."

The war dragged on through 1969, with the Federals continuously tightening their grip on the Biafran enclave and slowly reducing its size. It was apparent that without some miracle Biafra's days were numbered, but the Biafrans hung on doggedly. Appeals for aid continued to go out to the world, and the world continued to respond. Television late in December 1969 and early January 1970 showed pictures of pitiful Biafran children, emaciated and covered with sores from a nutritional disease. On Christmas Day, 1969, a press item stated that a check for $100,000 had just been presented to Joint Church Aid—U.S.A. for food for Biafra.

Biafra was doomed, but fighting continued. Three days after Christmas a Biafran communiqué said that during the past week more than 2,000 Federal and Biafran soldiers had been killed in battle. But Biafra was weakening. Early in January 1970, the Federals captured Owerri, which had been Ojukwu's capital since the fall of Enugu, and were able to move powerful, long-range 122 mm artillery to within shelling range of the Uli airstrip, severing Biafra's last link with the world and sealing its fate. On

January 10, Ojukwu, whose iron will and unquestionable military ability had created Biafra and kept it alive, announced that he was leaving "to explore possibilities for peace."

Ojukwu's flight left the responsibility for Biafra in the hands of Major General Philip Effiong. Three days later he broadcast an order to the Biafran troops to stop fighting, and offered to return Biafra to allegiance to Nigeria. Gowon ordered a cease-fire and amnesty for secessionists who surrendered. After thirty terrible months the war was over.

The open fighting was over, except for scattered pockets of Biafrans who had not received word of the surrender, but the aftermath of war remained. During the last few days of the fighting the roads were again choked with refugees flying for safety. There were still myriads of hungry people to be fed, hundreds of thousands to be repatriated, and sick and injured to be treated. The relief problem was complicated by the announcement by the Federal government that relief was a Nigerian problem only, and that persons and organizations that had disregarded Nigerian sovereignty during the war and aided the rebels would not be permitted to remain in the country. No aid would be accepted from any organization that had helped Biafra during the war, a pronouncement that put Joint Church Aid—U.S.A., Caritas Internationale, and similar organizations out of business.

The good citizens of the Western countries, especially the United States, whose hearts had been wrung by the stories and pictures of diseased and starving children, felt that the devil had triumphed when the news of Biafra's surrender came out. Gowon's announced policy of reconciliation was regarded skeptically, and it was remarked that there is often a gap between a leader's orders and the acts of his subordinates. The first newsmen and observers who entered Biafra after the surrender found the conditions were not as bad as had been pictured or anticipated but were worse than the Nigerian government, in its moment of triumph, had announced. They found that people were hungry and that children were undernourished, that women had been raped, and that wounded men were not receiving the care that the wounded receive in the armies of European countries and America. They found that Nigerian soldiers were doing some looting and seemed to be indifferent to the suffering about them. At that, the Nigerians were no more callous than some television cameramen who tossed handfuls of good Nigerian currency in the air so that they could film the destitute Biafrans scrambling and struggling for it.

And so Biafra continued to appeal to the benevolent people whose sympathies had been aroused. The stories in the daily press after the surrender stressed the horrors. An Irish missionary, Father Eamon Macmahon, "surrounded by hundreds of refugees . . . in the main square of the shell-pocked Owerri," said, "They have no food, their money [Biafran] is useless and we have no way of getting anything to them." A Swiss woman relief worker "had tears in her eyes as she pulled and tugged at a pileup of old men and women over a sack of wheat that had fallen and burst open."

The refusal of the victorious Federals to sanction any of the agencies that had provided relief for Biafra during the war virtually cut off any private aid from the outside for the Biafrans, for practically all relief organizations, at least in the United States, had openly devoted themselves to Biafra alone. This placed the burden of relief upon governments and into official and diplomatic channels, and upon the Red Cross, which was required to work through the Nigerian Red Cross. It appeared from the first reports that the basic trouble was not so much a shortage of food in Nigeria as a lack of transportation to carry food where it was most needed. Some persons, with the best intentions but unable to take their vision from the trees immediately in front of them and see the forest behind, were bitterly critical of the Federals for not using their military transportation for relief purposes. Unnamed members of an "observer team" from an unspecified source told newsmen that Federal units inside Biafra had less than one hundred vehicles, but a training division in Lagos had five times as many—the inference being clear. An anonymous "Scottish doctor" complained that the Nigerian army "is never short of beer and their whores get transported everywhere, but they can't get a truck to take my nurses out to the clinic. Where are all the trucks that kept Biafra going for 2½ years?" Well-meaning people also complained, within ten days after the surrender, that Nigeria was too slow in getting relief organized and operating. It was unfortunately true that food and medicines did not pour into the country within hours after the surrender, but the failure was not due to indifference on the part of Gowon's government so much as to the inescapable confusion that follows closely after any war. As for the inference that the Nigerian army should have used its own motor transportation at once for relief, any soldier realizes that in a doubtful, confused situation, an army's first concern must be to preserve its own mobility and integrity. No army has ever yet had all the transportation it needs.

Considering the delays that are usually concomitant with diplomatic and governmental operations, the Western countries acted with praiseworthy promptitude. Great Britain airlifted numbers of motor vehicles and sent heavy vehicles by sea. Articulate opinion in the United States was so thoroughly committed to Biafra that the government would not have dared to fail to contribute. A 200-bed field hospital was flown by chartered commercial airplane, with the promise of two more hospitals and more motor vehicles to follow. Soviet Russia sent a medical team of specialists on child care. Relief efforts by several countries continued, and a year after the fighting was over the most immediate necessities of the war-torn region had been satisfied.

The gloomy predictions that the Nigerians would embark upon a wholesale slaughter of the Ibos were happily untrue. Within a year the Ibos were again returning to their prewar homes and occupations. Ibo officials were again holding important government positions. The fusing of the disparate tribes of Nigeria into a unified nation of sorts seems possible. Gowon has unquestionably shown a statesmanlike restraint that few observers expected. Yet the war's effects will be felt for a long time. The mutilated will continue to limp on amputated stubs and suffer agony long after those who died in battle have been forgotten. For years to come people will show the effects of childhod malnutrition. That prediction is a safe one. Otherwise, as for the future of Nigeria, who can tell?

XI

ECONOMIC ASPECTS
OF THE NIGERIAN CIVIL WAR

E. Wayne Nafziger

Although social scientists are interested in the integration and disintegration of nation-states, there has been little study of the economic aspects of civil wars in developing countries. Few events alter the economic structure as radically as the convulsions and displacements concomitant with war and political upheaval. In Nigeria, the coups d'etat of 1966 and the civil war of 1967–70 have had a profound effect on economic activity, and in turn have been affected by economic variables.

Nigeria ranks among the bottom one-fourth of the countries of the world in income per capita. Over three-fourths of all persons gainfully occupied in the country are engaged in the agricultural sector; most of these are employed in small-scale peasant farming. With an official population of fifty-six million in 1963, it is the country in Africa with the largest number of persons and perhaps the greatest degree of ethnic and cultural diversity. Its political, social, and economic problems are in many ways a microcosm of those of the African continent. An understanding of the vital economic interests and factors in the war can provide insights into the problems of postwar reconstruction.

Several questions are important when examining the economic variable in an internal political conflict such as that in Nigeria. How do the dynamics of economic growth and accompanying structural change affect the relative political strength of regions in the country? How do economic factors affect the costs and benefits of continued preservation of the

The author has based his study on sources to which he had access while in Nigeria and which are cited in his other scholarly publications.

nation-state from the standpoint of the center and the various regions? What is the nature of the relationship between tendencies toward political disunity and economic disintegration? How are the structure of the economy and the level of economic activity affected by the war? Specifically, how does the disruption of interregional trade flows resulting from the conflict affect the level of living of the belligerents? Because of space limitations only a part of the scope indicated by these questions can be discussed in this chapter: the economic factors contributing to the war, and the economic impact of the war.

Economic Factors Contributing to the War

Economic aspects of the war can be understood more clearly with some knowledge of the political milieu. Clarence C. Clendenen discusses the political background to the conflict in the preceding chapter of this volume.

It is useful here to treat the economic variable as independent and the political variable as dependent, while in the next section to reverse the relationships between the variables. Even though the causes of the Eastern (or Biafran) secession and the subsequent war, or the motivations of principal actors in the conflict cannot be pinpointed, another approach to factors contributing to the civil war can be used. The probability of secession of a regional unit from a nation-state is dependent upon the expected costs and benefits to the region from the maintenance of the national unit and those of secession from it. It is possible to ascertain how economic factors affect the costs and benefits of continued preservation of the nation-state from the standpoint of the federation and the various regions.

The expansion of petroleum output, with its implication for a strong Eastern economic position, was a major factor contributing to the civil war. The benefits of regional autonomy for the East increased relative to the benefits of continued membership in the federation as a result of the discovery and commercial exploitation of crude oil centered in the region in the late 1950s. The growth of petroleum production enhanced the prospective international balance-of-payments position, domestic budgetary position, and level of living of the political unit controlling the area.

The dominant structural change in the Nigerian economy in the decade before the civil war was the very high rate of growth in the output of crude oil, centered primarily in the East. In 1966, 7 percent of the total domestic production of goods and services was contributed by the mining sector, compared to only 1 percent in 1958—an increase due almost entirely to the substantial increase in petroleum output. Production of crude oil averaged 415,000 barrels per day in 1966 as a result of a growth rate of 76 percent per annum in the previous three years.

The rapid increase in oil exports had very favorable implications for the international economic position of the political unit controlling the oil-producing areas. The value of crude oil exports increased from a negligible percentage of total export value in 1958 to 10 percent in 1962 to 33 percent in 1966, the year before the beginning of the civil war. In 1966–67, the oil sector made an average annual net positive contribution of N£39.5 million (or $110.6 million) to the balance on current and capital account, to counter an average yearly deficit balance of N£43.8 million in the other sectors. This surplus is a significant contribution to an economy which had an average export value of N£272.2 million for the same period.

Despite the significance of oil as a leading growth sector in the Nigerian economy before the war, it promised to be even more significant in the future. Scott R. Pearson, who assumed only that Biafran-controlled territory would not increase after April 1969, projected Nigeria's crude oil production at 1.8 million barrels per day in 1973, an output more than four times that in 1966, despite decreases in production in 1967 and 1968.

A major source of interregional conflict has been the determination of a formula for revenue allocation to the regions. The share of revenue accruing to the East from the expansion of its petroleum industry became a point of friction between the East and the other three regions. Before 1959, all the revenue from mineral and agricultural products (that is, export duties) was retained by the region of production. However, after 1959, the East was dissatisfied that it received only a fraction of the revenue from petroleum (that is, none of the profits tax and only 50 percent of the rents and royalties) in contrast to all the revenue from agricultural exports.

It is unlikely that the East, a food-deficit area, would have seriously considered moving toward greater autonomy and eventual secession without a rapidly expanding petroleum industry and the implications of this for growth in income, foreign exchange position, and government finance, and further, for the relative international politico-economic power of Nigeria and an independent East. Because of oil, an independent East would be very viable economically, as long as it could prevent an effective embargo on its territory.

The immediate triggering factor for the declaration of independence by Biafra was the politico-economic impact of the creation of twelve states from the previous four regions and federal territory in May 1967. (See maps, pp. 170–71.) Although before the July 1966 mutiny the East had strongly favored the break-up of the North—the region with over half the population—its division into six states in 1967 was accompanied by the creation of new states in the East which effectively cut down the politico-economic position of that region's majority and politically-dominant group, the Ibos. Under the new state system, the Ibos would control only the East-Central state, with only about one-sixth of Nigeria's petroleum output in the previous year. Almost half of the oil output was in the two other eastern states. In addition, the Ibo-dominated city of Port Harcourt, a manufacturing center, an oil refining center, and the second most important seaport in the country, was divided from the new East-Central state. Finally, the division into states left the East-Central state landlocked. The new state system was considered by the Ibo political leadership in the Eastern Region to be a deliberate attempt at severing the seaports and the oil areas from Iboland, in violation of the understanding by the East in January 1967 that Nigeria would move towards a confederation of four regions.

An alternative interpretation is that the creation of the twelve states was undertaken in anticipation of secession by the East. For a number of years certain factions of the minority ethnic groups in the East had clamored for the creation of separate states. The new state structure, through providing greater autonomy for Eastern minorities, gave the non-Ibo peoples of the East an additional reason for supporting the federation.

The low degree of economic integration between regions and ethnic group areas, exacerbated by further economic disintegration in 1966–67, contributed to the civil war by making the cost of secession and the benefit of unity low. Political cohesion is partly a function of the extent of interregional trade flows, the extent of interregional migration, and the relative power of the various groups perceiving benefits and losses from greater economic integration.

The value of interregional trade as a percentage of the value of merchandise imports is lower in Nigeria than in other African economies with the same number of "regions." Furthermore, indigenous economic interests, with more political influence than foreign interests, were especially unlikely to be involved in production for interregional trade and thus benefited less economically from national integration. For example, in 1966 indigenous firms, which accounted for only 30 percent of paid-up capital in manufacturing firms with ten or more employees, and a lower percent of larger firms, sold primarily to a local market.

Because of language barriers and credit difficulties, most of the interregional trade was confined to that between members of the same ethnic group. Although credit was crucial to a large proportion of the transactions between small businessmen, there was a dearth of credit facilities between persons from different tribal groups as a result of the lack of a common language, customary law and cultural traits, and a lack of access to kinship arrangements for checking creditworthiness and guaranteeing against default.

Interregional migration in Nigeria does not seem unusually low for a developing country. However, because of economic restriction, language and cultural barriers, or the potential direct physical threat from intertribal conflict or a political crisis, virtually no capital and entrepreneurship moved between regions and ethnic group areas in order to establish firms with large amounts of fixed capital.

The events of 1966–67, with the forced return of a large number of persons to their region of origin, could only have reinforced the attitudes that the most prudent course for the businessman was to remain in his own region, and that the risk of default was smaller when persons from the same tribal group were recipients of credit.

Economists in both Nigeria and Biafra have stressed the significance of the high rate of urban unemployment in Nigeria and its relationship to regional discrimination in employment opportunities as factors contributing to and influenced by the socio-politico-economic disintegration of the Federation. In response to the dissatisfaction of the large army of the unemployed—especially among primary and secondary graduates— policies of regionalization were instituted in all regions after independence (1960), in which "persons of regional origin" were given preference in filling job vacancies in the public and private sectors. These policies were merely expressions of autarkic attitudes in economic activity from the level of the family to the nation-state—power was obtained by and used for the securing of jobs for relatives and clients. Policies of regionalism, which were intensified as a result of the events in 1966, discouraged emigration to other ethnic group areas and instigated emigration by minority groups to their ethnic homelands.

The most vigorous policy of regionalization in the 1960s was pursued in the Northern Region, especially in Hausaland. Prior to the civil war, the modern sector of the Northern economy was dominated by Levantines, Europeans, and southern Nigerians, who were, in general, sending their earnings out of the North. In addition, the socio-politico-economic power of these groups was posing a threat to the Hausa-Muslim way of life and social structure.

Northernization was especially directed against the Ibos and other southerners, who dominated a large part of trade and transport in Hausaland before 1966. The resentment against Ibo migrants reached a peak in the weeks following May 23, 1966, when the Ibo-led regime of Major General J.T. Aguiyi-Ironsi announced a unitary state, with nationwide integration of the government service. The greater educational achievement in the South than in the North engendered fear in the North that government integration would lead to greater dominance by southerners in the Northern economy. One element of the North's uneasiness, leading to the revolts and disorders in 1966, was the increased fear of control by another group which would lead to a lack of economic opportunity and a threat to the Northern culture.

Important factors decreasing the cost of secession by the East in 1966 were the exodus of Eastern refugees to their homelands and the closing of opportunities for emigration from the East to other regions. Even before the exodus, the East had a population density of 420 persons per square mile compared to 156 in Nigeria as a whole. Although the East had poor agricultural land, 70 percent of its population was employed in agriculture. The overpopulation was especially acute in Ibo-speaking areas, which had been characterized by high rates of emigration before 1966.

In the twelve months prior to April 1967, interregional migration in Nigeria was close to two million. Most of the migrants, according to Professor Aluko, could be classified as refugees since they moved because of fear, force, or edict. About 98 percent of migrants were Ibos and other Easterners returning to their ethnic homelands. Violence and disorders directed against Easterners in May, July, and September–October 1966 resulted in several thousand deaths. The East, previously overpopulated with about 12 million inhabitants, increased its population by about 15 to 20 percent in the year before the civil war, while losing its transfer income from other regions.

In the period prior to early 1966, the migration of labor from the overpopulated East to other areas of the Federation had been a powerful factor drawing the East to the Federation. However, the exodus of large numbers of Easterners from other parts of Nigeria and the closing of employment and investment opportunities outside the East, decreased substantially the attractiveness of the Federation from the standpoint of the East.

The problem of unemployment helped create pressures for new states or secession. In Nigeria it was generally assumed that job opportunities and political power went together. Jobs in the public sector, the chief sources of employment in the modern sector and for the highly educated, were more likely to go to the majority tribe of a political unit, less likely to minorities within the unit, and rarely to a member of an ethnic group with an origin in a different political unit. Much of the pressure for additional states and for secession was aimed at solving the unemployment problem for the group clamoring for the new political unit.

The lack of employment opportunities in the East might have had some impact on its decision to secede. Easterners were afraid that the North, which used its political power to realign economic power through Northernization, could do the same in the federation as a whole. In early 1967, the surplus population in the East, consisting in part of displaced and destitute persons, constituted a combustible and manipulatable group for the pursuit of military mobilization, secession, and conquest.

The East may have been encouraged to take an independent course because of the potential economic vulnerability of the landlocked North in the event of secession by the southern states. In May 1967, the Western Regional consultative assembly indicated that if the East seceded the West should also become a sovereign state. Three months later, after the declaration of independence by Biafra, its head of state, Lieutenant Colonel Odumegwu Ojukwu, embarked on a strategy of conquest of southern Nigeria. Biafran leaders may have reasoned that the invasion of the Mid-West and West would have the effect of encouraging tendencies toward their secession from the North. If the whole south had seceded, it would have had a strong bargaining position, since the North depends on it for an outlet to the sea and a market for its agricultural products. Among other things, the Federal military government's appointment of the most prominent Western leader, Chief Obafemi Awolowo, to be vice-chairman of the Federal Executive Council and federal commissioner for finance, may have helped thwart the forces for Western secession and formed a basis for Northern-Western cooperation against the East.

Another factor contributing to the political conflict was the disproportionate number of army officers from the East. At independence, three-fourths of the Nigerian army officers were Ibo. Even though regional quotas for recruitment into the armed forces were instituted in 1962, the earlier start of Ibos in pursuing careers in the army gave them a majority in the senior ranks in 1966. The large representation of Ibos in high positions in the army was partially a result of limited home employment opportunities, the rapid development of secondary education in the East, the lack of socio-political impediments to positions in the armed forces, and the encouragement of army careers by the Ibo political elite. It was primarily the experience and skills of Eastern army officers that led Ojukwu to boast that, at the beginning of the war, Biafra had the best army in Black Africa.

The Economic Impact of the Civil War

The consumption of civilian goods per capita declined slightly in Nigeria during the war as a result of the rapid expansion in the production of military goods during a period of slow overall economic growth. Nevertheless, the majority of the population, living in villages and rural areas, found that the war had virtually no impact on their way of life. However, traders, transporters, and wage laborers in urban areas suffered from a decline in business activity, especially in the first year of the war. In addition, the Nigerian elite had to sacrifice some luxury import items and a few other conveniences.

The adverse impact of the war on the level of living in Biafra was greater than in Nigeria and reached all segments of the population. In July 1967, after over two months of a limited embargo, Nigeria imposed a total blockade on Biafra, which was effectively enforced by Nigeria's small navy. By the middle of 1968, food and other essentials were scarce in a number of Biafran areas as a result of the embargo and the general disruption and destruction in the war zone. The Biafran economy was geared almost entirely to mobilization for the war and the production of bare essentials. Biafra received virtually no civilian goods from overseas except food and other necessities from relief organizations, and badly-needed capital goods.

Data from official Nigerian sources indicate that the growth in real gross domestic product (where capital destruction is not subtracted) decreased from 6 percent per annum in the fiscal years 1958–65 to 2 to 3 percent in 1966, 1967, and probably 1968. Part of the deceleration in growth can be explained by a weakening in private investment as a result of increased anxieties about the strength of the economy following the political crises of 1965–67, the administrative difficulties in submitting and implementing viable and well-planned government investment projects with the instability and government turnover, the drop in oil output and manufacturing production in the secessionist East as a result of the embargo, the disruption in the transportation and domestic trade sectors stemming from the forced exodus of skilled personnel to ethnic homelands in 1966–67 and the breakdown of economic relations with the East, and the direct cost of loss of human lives and damage to capital assets.

Nigeria avoided much of the severe inflationary pressure usually accompanying wartime. The stable prices characteristic of the period before 1966 continued throughout the crisis, except in 1966 among lower-income groups, and in 1969. Low-income classes were especially affected in 1966 because of food shortages resulting largely from the departure of traders from their customary markets during the political disturbances. Food prices decreased, however, for one and one-half years after the beginning of the civil war, since a large part of the food supply was diverted from the blockaded East, a food-deficit area, to other parts of the country. Restrictive financial policies, which curbed expenditures in the civilian sector, added to the restraint on the general price level in 1967 and 1968. However, the demand for food and sustenance and their high distribution costs in war-damaged areas regained from Biafra, and the rising government spending financed by the banking system put pressure on prices, so that the consumer price index increased by 7 percent in 1969 and by 23 percent in 1970.

Agricultural consultants to the Comité International de la Croix-Rouge reported that prices of basic items of food, clothing, and tools in Biafra increased by 5 to 50 times between the immediate prewar period and

May 1969, although wages remained relatively constant. Gari, a staple food item, rose in price by 18 to 36 times during the period, banana prices increased by 40 times, and salt prices by over 1,000 times. The scarcity of food, which approached famine conditions, resulted largely from war damage and the lack of trade with the outside world.

The direct cost of the war, which comprises only a part of its total cost, was rather substantial. A. Akene Ayida, permanent secretary in the Federal Ministry of Economic Development, estimated that the total cost of military expenditures to the Nigerian government from the war was N£300 million from September 1967 through May 1969, a cost N£270 million above "normal peace-time" expenditures and equal to about one-tenth of gross domestic product for the period. About one-third of the military expenditure consisted of direct and indirect foreign exchange expenditures.

Ayida estimated the replacement cost of physical assets damaged and destroyed by the war to be N£250 million by the end of the second year of the conflict. The economic loss as a result of deaths to persons is incalculable. UNICEF estimated that at least two million persons on the two sides died of starvation alone between the beginning of the war and early 1969.

Current government expenditures on general administration, social and community services, and economic services declined from N£44 million per annum in 1965–66 to N£36 million per annum in 1968–69, while capital expenditures were reduced from N£52 million in 1966 to N£35 million in 1968. A number of measures were used to expand revenue sources, including a compulsory savings scheme, a reconstruction levy, an excess-profits tax, a levy on pioneer companies, and increased import and excise duties. However, despite the overall increase in the tax rate, current government revenue, which averaged over N£160 million per annum in 1964–67, dropped to N£142.4 million in 1968, partly because of the dampening of demand as a result of restrictive measures in the civilian goods sector, the destruction and dislocation of economic activities, and the loss of revenue in the East, especially from the crude oil industry. The government budget deficit rose from N£48.3 million in 1966 to N£141.7 million in 1968, in spite of the attempt by the fiscal authorities to curb the expansionary effect of the budget.

Nigeria's balance-of-payments and foreign exchange position deteriorated substantially as a result of the war. The value of the country's foreign exchange assets was slashed from N£84.4 million at the end of 1966 to N£38.9 million at the end of 1967. By the middle of 1968, external reserves had been drawn below a point sometimes considered the critical minimum by international bankers—an equivalent of the value of imports for four months. An external liquidity crisis was averted only by the use of stringent trade barriers and exchange controls.

A major cause of the declining external economic position was the primary and secondary effects of military expenditures abroad, which equalled one-fourth to one-fifth the total value of exports throughout the war. In addition, the value of exports dropped by 14 percent in 1967 and an additional 13 percent in 1968 because of disruptions in production, transportation bottlenecks, and the loss of exports from secessionist areas. As a result of the Eastern secession and the Federal embargo, the value of petroleum exports dropped from N£92.0 million in 1966 to N£72.1 million in 1967 to N£37.0 million in 1968. The drop in foreign aid and private capital inflows, and in 1967 the increase in repatriation of earnings, contributed to the country's balance-of-payments deficit. These developments stemmed primarily from the growing anxieties about Nigeria's political instability and the impact of this on its domestic and international economic position.

A number of measures, in addition to the restrictive domestic financial policies discussed above, were undertaken to improve the country's international payments position. At the time of Biafran secession, Nigeria instituted a requirement that official permission be received for all foreign payments—a measure that also tended to reduce the international use of Nigerian currency by the Biafrans. Import duties and other trade restrictions were also increased in 1967.

In 1968, after these changes proved inadequate, more severe controls were placed on international trade and payments. Even so, in 1968–69, the Nigerian government was able to prevent a balance-of-payments crisis only by suspending the authorization of a number of payments to foreigners—an amount totalling N£60 million (or about $168 million) by the end of the war. Finally, in May 1969, the federal government required importers to obtain specific licenses on virtually all goods brought into the country.

The restrictions, together with the loss of import demand from the East, resulted in substantial decreases in imports in both 1967 and 1968, especially in consumer goods. In 1969, the balance-of-trade surplus increased by N£56.9 million, largely due to the increase in petroleum exports by N£99 million to the highest total in Nigeria's history, N£136 million. The increase stemmed primarily from the resumption of oil production in areas regained in the fighting in 1968.

Although some industrialists gained from the opportunities from import substitution with the increased tariffs, businessmen were generally dissatisfied with the increased restrictions on trade and payments. Foreign firms were prevented from repatriating earnings, and in some cases lacked funds for routine expenditures in offices overseas. Furthermore, a number of factories were forced to cut back on production and employment substantially as a result of delays and rejections in obtaining the import licenses needed for equipment, repairs, inventories, raw materials, or other inputs.

The little published data available indicates that Biafra had relatively substantial financial reserves at the time of secession, May 30, 1967. The reserves were obtained by converting funds from taxes and other revenues collected in the East, the reserves of the African Continental bank, and the money of an Eastern-based political party, into foreign exchange deposited in foreign banks. Biafra was able to finance the purchase of equipment to fight the early campaigns of what it expected to be a short war of independence.

By April 1968, Biafra's foreign exchange reserves were virtually exhausted. Because of the Federal blockade, oil revenues did not materialize. Before September 1968, foreign assistance was limited primarily to Portugal, which made available supply stations for planes flying into Biafra.

However, Kennedy Lindsay estimates that in 1968 Biafra may have obtained as much as $17–19 million worth of foreign exchange. France supplied an estimated $5 million worth of arms and related assistance beginning in September 1968. Other major sources of foreign currency were the expenditures by relief and mission organizations in obtaining Biafran currency needed for the local costs of the programs, the donations by overseas Ibos and Western private groups, and the contribution of Nigerian currency by Ibos in the Federation for the covert purchase of goods from Nigeria. It is estimated that in 1969 the amount of foreign exchange available to Biafra from these sources increased.

Although Nigeria tried to make its local currency component of military expenditures as large as possible, it probably spent five to ten times as much foreign exchange for defense in 1968 as Biafra. Yet Biafra did not collapse for some time, because after 1968 it was fighting primarily a defensive war using small infantry formations. In such a war, it was possible to rely mainly on small-arms ammunition together with mortar and anti-aircraft ammunition. Old but usable small-arms ammunition was obtained cheaply from Europe. Except for defense expenditures, most of Biafra's foreign exchange was spent for essential equipment, intelligence requirements, supply planes, ocean shipping, overseas missions, and propaganda.

Petroleum production and exports declined for two consecutive years, 1967–68, because the secessionist areas, which were the major oil-producing regions, were blockaded by the federal government. After Nigeria instituted a blockade on oil tankers in July 1967, Biafra's crude oil output, produced only for internal consumption, dropped to less than 1 percent of its prewar rate. Petroleum output in Nigeria, confined to offshore wells in the Mid-West Region, dropped 86.7 percent from the first half to the second half of 1967. Production leveled off in the first quarter of 1968, swung upward in the middle of the year, and increased abruptly in the last quarter to a rate almost six times as high as in the same period in the previous year. The sharp rise resulted from the resumption of production on a limited scale in the Rivers area. Restoration of output lagged about one-half year behind the regaining of the territory, since it was necessary to repair and replace pumping and transport facilities damaged in the fighting.

In the first half of 1969 the rate of petroleum output increased 64 percent over that in the last quarter of 1968. Crude oil production dropped 7 percent in the second half of the year following disruptions to production from a series of attacks by Biafra on Nigerian oil installations. Although production in 1969 exceeded the previous yearly peak in 1966 by 26 percent, no quarterly output attained the level reached in either of the first two quarters in 1967.

The rate of growth in manufacturing output decreased from 21.2 percent per annum in 1964–65 to 12.9 percent in 1966, 5.3 in 1967, and —1.5 percent in 1968. The slowdown in growth began in the last half of 1966, as a result of lower profit expectations and reduced investment outlays following the political crises of 1964–65, the loss of skilled labor as a result of population movements, and the increased cost of distribution because of disruptions in the trade and transport sectors. Industrial output picked up rapidly between the last quarter of 1966 and the first quarter of 1967, but decreased by 36 percent between the second and third quarter. The problems of 1966 were compounded by the secession of the East and its blockade in the middle of 1967. Manufacturing output in the East, which had previously accounted for about 30 percent of total output, was virtually at a standstill. Output in the Federal areas decreased because of the further disruption of established trading networks and the loss of Eastern markets.

Quarterly manufacturing output grew steadily from the third quarter of 1967 through 1968, with output in the fourth quarter of 1968 at 28 percent higher than in the same quarter in 1967. In part, this large increase reflects the growth of import substitution in response to the tightening of trade restrictions.

Few Eastern factories resumed operation in 1968 and 1969 after they were regained by Federal forces. Even though physical installations were largely intact, production was not possible because of the looting of storage facilities, the dispersion of high-level manpower, the unavailability of finance, the disruption of normal trade flows, and the small size of the Eastern market.

Disruption of railway and road traffic as a result of the political disturbances and civil war had an adverse impact on domestic trade and international exports, and created shortages and price increases in parts of the country. The first major bottleneck in transportation occurred from September to December 1966, during the return of southerners to their ethnic homelands. The North was especially hurt by the loss of transport labor, as its economy depended on railroads to bring gasoline from the south and to take groundnuts and groundnut oil to the seaports.

In 1967–68, transport problems were exacerbated by the loss of locomotives and rolling stock to Biafra, the closing of railroad transportation via the eastern route to Port Harcourt, the destruction of strategic roads and bridges in the Biafran retreat, and the severe cut in funds for road maintenance. Both passengers and goods carried declined by 30 to 40 percent in 1967, after decreases of about 15 percent in 1966. The disruption in domestic transportation caused shipping activity to decrease about 50 percent in 1967 and to rise only slightly in 1968.

The cutback in transportation volume, combined with the uncertainties from the political upheavals, the departure of traders to their regions of origin, and restrictionary policies toward the private sector, created depressed conditions in internal trade in the last part of 1966, which continued until the end of the war. Political disturbances and the accompanying breakdown in interregional trade and transportation necessitated the pursuit of economic activity closer to the ethnic group area, and a greater emphasis on regional self-sufficiency in production.

Biafran secession further severed the nationwide trading system. Onitsha, an Eastern city whose physical capital was almost completely destroyed when it was captured by Federal forces in March 1968, had been the hub of a vast trading network extending throughout Nigeria and much of West Africa. The city, however, could not be restored as an integral part of the trading system because of the destruction of its facilities, the closeness of the war zone, the dislocation of traders, and the major structural changes taking place in an economy which had partially adjusted to the severance of a region.

Benue-Plateau and Kwara states, which exported food to the East before the war, suffered the most from the secession of the East. Some illegal trade occured between these states and Biafra, but the volume of transactions was only a trickle compared to trade prior to June 1967. The volume of trade did grow, however, as a result of the retaking of Eastern areas by the Federals.

The war, together with the effective blockade of Biafra by Nigeria, was instrumental in creating a food crisis in Biafra. The availability of food in Biafra was linked to domestic military strength and the international propaganda battle, which was in turn related to the problem of obtaining international recognition, foreign currency, and most importantly, military armaments.

The embargo on Biafran ports from near the beginning of the war prevented trade of any significance with a region that was overpopulated and plagued by a refugee problem, and which had long been a food-deficit area. Since Biafra could not export its petroleum and palm products, it lacked the foreign currency to obtain essential consumer goods while prosecuting a war.

Food shortages reached a crisis in mid-1968, when Biafra was a shrinking enclave completely surrounded by Nigerian territory. Gradually, beginning in the last two months of 1967, Nigeria retook the outlying areas of the East, areas which constituted the most fertile agricultural land in the region. Large segments of the rural economy were destroyed and disrupted; at the same time the internal system of transportation and distribution became dislocated and refugees fled from areas captured by Nigeria into a contracting territory. In the area remaining, Biafran farmers attempted to use more intensive methods of production and to expand the cultivated acreage. By late 1968, Biafra, one-fifth its original size, was supporting a population of seven million, of which about three million were refugees from Eastern territory regained by the Nigerians.

After the middle of 1968, food, medical supplies, and other forms of relief were flown into Biafra by church and other humanitarian organizations. To arrange relief flights not subject to attack was difficult, since both Biafra and Nigeria refused to allow entry of relief which would cast doubt on their claims of sovereignty or which would interfere with their military plans.

Hunger was widespread throughout the Biafran population in 1969. Agricultural consultants to the Comité International de la Croix-Rouge estimated that about one and one-half million Biafrans died from hunger from the beginning of the war to May 1969. The cutback in relief flights in the latter half of 1969 led to a rapidly deteriorating medical and health situation in Biafra just before the end of the war. The relationship between the curtailment of relief efforts and the collapse of the Biafran military position seems to support the Nigerian charge that relief flights prolonged the war. After the end of the war, food shortages continued for a few months because of the lack of indigenous resources to organize the relief arrangements that the political elite insisted should be a Nigerian effort, and because of the length of time before Nigerian currency was issued to holders of Biafran currency.

Major Postwar Economic Problems

Despite the end of the war, a number of basic economic problems remain. Let us briefly consider the prospects for amelioration of some of Nigeria's major postwar economic problems, especially those which were at the root of the conflict.

The immediate priority is the reconstruction of wartime damage to the economy. This implies more than relief for the destitute or the replacement or repair of destroyed equipment; it involves the restoration of production and trade flows disrupted by the war, and the reinstatement of basic social and economic services. The recovery of areas in the war zone in southeastern Nigeria does not entail a return to its prewar configuration, but a readjustment toward a Nigerian economy which has experienced widespread structural change as a result of the war.

A primary part of reconstruction is the reintegration of the East into the economy. Despite the decrease in population during the war, the East is still overpopulated. During the political conflict, a number of Easterners employed in the Nigerian civil service were replaced. In addition, much of the gap from the exodus of self-employed Easterners in trade and transport to their ethnic homeland was filled by other Nigerians during the war. Furthermore, barriers to the migration of Easterners will be lifted slowly; Ibo emigration from the East-Central State has been limited, especially to the neighboring Rivers State. Finally, a decree of August 1970 gives governmental units the power to dismiss civil servants who participated in the Biafran rebellion. The unemployment rate in Iboland can hardly fail to increase in comparison to the prewar period.

There are important political constraints on the provision of opportunities for emigration from Iboland and on the use of resources for reconstruction of this overpopulated area. In the allocation of resources and development of policy in the postwar era, Nigerian leaders are sensitive to charges from loyal elements in other war-affected areas that a major focus on the needs of the East-Central State can be interpreted as a reward for secession.

The politics of oil will probably still be important in the reconstruction period. The Rivers, East-Central, and Mid-Western states will want to retain or increase the share of producing states in oil revenues. However, the problem of petroleum revenue will be less significant to Ibo politicians than it was before the war. The Biafran surrender implies the acceptance of the twelve-state system, in which boundaries are drawn so that the East-Central State includes only about one-sixth of the oil output.

Some of the major economic tasks facing Nigeria after the war are restoration of production and trade flows in the war-affected areas, provision of employment opportunities in the civilian economy, and determination of a formula for revenue allocation. The carrying out of these tasks needs to be viewed in the context of the effort to reintegrate former Biafrans into the federation without alienating loyalist groups. The crucial factors in the process of postwar reconstruction are not so much physical resources as planning ability, organizational manpower, and, most importantly, the skill of the national leadership in the attempt to create a political accord between the various states and ethnic groups.

Concluding Remarks

The Nigerian experience suggests some possible generalizations which can serve as hypotheses to be tested in the discussion of other civil wars.

Secession and civil war are more likely to be used for settling the grievances of a region when it lacks domestic political power commensurate with its international economic power. In the decade before their secessions, both Eastern Nigeria and Katanga experienced a rapid economic growth in export-oriented mineral production, a growth that gave them international economic significance which appeared capable of being translated into foreign support and international political power.

The lack of foreign exchange may place a constraint on the ability of an economy to mobilize goods and services for the prosecution of a civil war. Biafra, like the American South in 1861–65, experienced a substantial drop in the value of its exports as a result of an effective blockade by the Federal government. Like the Confederacy, Biafra had to try to divert scarce resources to the production of essential items previously imported in which it had a substantial comparative disadvantage. The Confederacy was forced to try to expand its output of manufactured goods, and Biafra its production of food. Biafra miscalculated the international support it would receive to continue its vital oil flows, just as the American South underestimated the significance of its cotton exports to England and continental Europe.

Economic factors have played an important part in contributing to Nigerian political disintegration; in turn, the political conflict has had a substantial influence on the structure and growth of the Nigerian economy. More studies on the Nigerian economy during this period are needed to analyze these relationships in greater depth, and further economic research on other civil wars is essential before a general theory of the economic aspects of civil wars can be developed.

Suggestions for Further Research

1) A comparison between economic aspects of the Nigerian and American civil wars.

2) A comparison between economic aspects of the Biafran and Katangan secessions.

3) A study of factors influencing the decision of Shell-BP and the British government as to whether to pay oil rents and royalties to Nigeria or to Biafra.

4) A more detailed picture of Biafran acquisition of arms from European sources.

5) Studies of interregional migration and trade flows in Nigeria and their relationships to political cohesion.

6) The role of credit in interregional trade in Nigeria.

7) The impact of regional discrimination in Nigeria on unemployment.

8) A history of economic penetration by southern Nigerians into northern Nigeria.

9) The effect of the Nigerian war on the ethnic composition of traders and other entrepreneurs in the various states.

10) The effect of the Nigerian war on the ethnic composition of the civil service and industrial employment in the various states.

11) Estimates of national income in Nigeria during the war.

12) The adjustment of Nigerian trading networks to the war.

13) Food and relief in Biafra during the war.

14) The plan for postwar reconstruction and development in Nigeria.

15) Structural changes in manufacturing resulting from the Nigerian civil war.

16) The process of reintegration of the war-affected areas into the Nigerian economy.

XII

CIVIL WAR AND ARMS SALES
The Nigerian-Biafran War and Other Cases

MARTIN EDMONDS

A CLEAR DEFINITION of terms is essential to the study of civil war and its associated phenomena. Civil war is a form of armed violence within a nation state. It may be a war between the government forces and a secessionist group seeking either political autonomy within the state or a separate state, or a war between two elements of the armed forces, with civilian involvement, over the composition and form of the government. The number of countries experiencing civil wars on this basis since 1945 is limited to nine: India, 1945–64; Burma, 1948–54; the Congo, 1960–64; Laos, 1960–62; Yemen, 1962–64; Kenya, 1963–67; the Sudan, 1964—; Iraq, 1966–70; and Nigeria, 1967–70.

The term "arms sales," for all its apparent simplicity, assumes some complexity in relation to civil war. In relation to a number of civil wars, such sales may vary considerably as to source, volume, time scale, and impact.

Arms sales to parties engaged in civil wars come in many forms with many variables. The principal distinction is whether military support in this form is active or passive. Active support requires the direct involvement of the supplier, as in the case of the Egyptians in Yemen. Passive support is merely the provision or sale of materiel or facilities to either side to enable it to continue the war, as in the controversial case of British and Russian support for Nigeria, which provoked controversy in both Britain and Sweden.

Although these active and passive categories appear to be discrete, there is an ill-defined area between them. This is where external states

203

provide men and materiel to enable a party to a civil war to continue the struggle, and yet at the same time are immediately involved in the struggle, sometimes by accident, because the war is brought to them. Thus the Soviet engineers who maintained and flew the MIG fighters sold to Nigeria were at different times both active and passive. The determining factor might well be whether the provision of military materiel and logistic support is considered to be directly or indirectly involved in the conflict. Another blurred area is where mercenaries are involved; these private individuals may be there as "volunteers" with the sanction of their government. A further interesting example, though in the context of a different category of civil war, is the military adviser in Vietnam.

Whatever the form of arms sales, it has to be remembered that civil wars are not short-term, unique events. They usually develop over some period of time. Discussion of arms sales must, therefore, be qualified with reference to the pattern of events preceding the outbreak of hostilities and the pattern of events during the war itself. The form of arms sales, for instance, can be changed dramatically during the war either quantitatively, qualitatively, or both; the terms of arms transactions can be drastically altered, and new sources may unexpectedly emerge or old ones dry up. Britain, a traditional source of military support and supply to Nigeria, failed to meet certain of the demands for arms when war with Biafra broke out. The Soviet Union, somewhat unexpectedly, filled the gap. Likewise in the Sudan, the Russians replaced the British and West Germans as the principal source after the 1967 Arab-Israeli War, and by the 1970s this Soviet materiel was being used against the southern Sudanese provinces.

The situation becomes increasingly confused when the scale of a civil war and the sophistication of the weapons employed are considered. In civil wars since 1945 the weapons used have not been sophisticated and, although in most cases a high proportion of the population has been involved, the number of fatalities has not been considerable. The possible exceptions are Biafra and the Sudan, in which figures are sometimes guesses which do not distinguish necessarily between battle and starvation as causes of death. The explanation for the low battle casualties is that weapons of mass destruction, notably aircraft, have not been used; for the most part the weapons have been those which have withstood considerable periods of storage. In the civil wars noted above, some of the weapons were found to be over fifty years old, some were improvised and others home-made, and some were third- and fourth-hand castoffs from more militarily advanced states. (The Kurdish forces used an odd assortment against the Iraqis with outstanding effect.) Many of these weapons have come from arms sales and trafficking over the years.

It is therefore debatable whether these sorts of weapons should be included in the analysis of arms sales and civil wars. For the purposes here, such pre-civil war external provision of armaments are excluded. It is simply impractical to trace these weapons, just as it is to assess the availability of homemade pieces. The point is that civil wars are often fought successfully by nongovernmental forces with a weird variety of weapons from innumerable sources gathered over a long period.

On this practical point, a further qualification must be made. Experience has shown that antigovernment or rebel forces, especially in guerrilla and unconventional warfare situations as well as in civil wars, can have considerable success with obsolete and unsophisticated weapons. This is so because of the nature of the war and the way in which it influences tactics, and also because of the level of technical knowledge within the state as a whole. One lesson from this experience has been that as governments become sensitive to the success with which poorly armed dissidents defy their forces, they heighten their demand for more sophisticated custom-built counterinsurgency weapons from outside sources. Not only have the traditional arms suppliers responded to this demand, but more tailor-made weapons are being introduced. Both major powers have become involved—the United States, capitalizing on its Vietnam experience, and Russia, making available more of its first-generation equipment at an earlier date. Thus more civil and other internal wars of the future are likely to be fought with weapons bought with future intrastate wars in mind. The Nigerian civil war suitably illustrates this point. The Nigerian government demanded sophisticated weapons which were beyond the technical competence of its military personnel; consequently foreign personnel were required to maintain these weapon systems. Military contingency planning, even in anticipation of internal conflict, seems to have permeated even the "Third World," especially Latin America, where the demand for counterinsurgency weapons is high.

The Impact of External Sources for Arms

If, however, the focus of concern is the impact of external military materiel support upon the conduct, duration, and outcome of civil wars, once they have broken out, then three factors have to be considered: first, the specific contextual features of civil wars and the sort of military materiel demands that are generated by the parties involved; second, the question of the sources of arms; and lastly, the types of weapons that can be and are forthcoming.

The two principal forms of civil war noted in chapter 1 generate different demands. The secessionist war involves two opposing sides. The governmental side is equipped with systems acquired and maintained at public expense and possesses its own arsenals and, most likely, a regular external source of arms, usually through an intergovernmental agreement. The opposition has neither international recognition nor the legal right to bear arms. Thus the official forces clearly have an advantage. This is mitigated, however, by two major considerations: Firstly, the secessionist group may gain international recognition, as the Biafrans did; this was particularly significant in their case because they had access to seaborne supplies during the early part of the war. Secondly, on a practical level, the secessionists enjoy the initiative and a stronger commitment to the struggle than their professional opponents. The important question is, however, whether the early advantages can be sustained. The answer may well determine not only the extent of international recognition, but also continued arms supply. The Nigerian war was an extremely costly one in terms of consumption of weapons and ammunition as compared to other post-1945 civil wars; the length of time in which the Biafrans were able to sustain the conflict was directly related to the external supply of arms.

Secessionist forces generally draw heavily from the military, which may explain the conventional nature of civil wars. The Karens in Burma, the Kurds in Iraq, the Katanganese in the Congo—all had a high proportion of their respective national armies. In Nigeria the Ibos had been important in the officer corps, and this military leadership and expertise was lost to the Nigerians. Though the Nagas of the Indo-Burma border are peaceful, it is significant that they demonstrated military abilities in opposition to the Japanese in World War II and drew upon this experience in their war with Indian forces. In many cases the difference between two sides in a civil war is really determined by who holds what at the start. This may be a matter of coincidence or circumstance. In Yemen the loyalties of the armed forces in the tribal state were unaffected by the 1962 coup. The opposition forces came largely from the United Arab Republic.

Because civil wars take place within autonomous states, the level, duration, and intensity of such a war reflects the basic characteristics of the nation-state itself. Most civil wars have taken place in countries where the level of industrialization has been low, and this immediately places a limitation on the weapons systems that can be afforded, produced, maintained, and employed. These limitations will differ between the two sides. In one sense, the nine civil wars fought since 1945 (note that Vietnam is excluded from the list) have been largely byproducts of the external provision of arms. Of the cases mentioned, only India had an armaments industry of any significance at the outbreak of civil war, though by 1964 Nigeria could manufacture a limited range of small arms and ammunition. Neither example had any influence on either the outcome or the conduct of the war.

If the level of military technology and production has been low, there remains the important question of who has responded to requests for weapons from either or both sides. Clearly, as demonstrated by the British response to the Nigerian request, the source and type of arms are interrelated. The source of weapons is three-fold, however, and all three categories can apply to either side. The first source is traditional external arms suppliers to the government who continue in that role after the outbreak of civil war or who emerge to fill it, usually under bilateral trade agreements. A foreign state which sends arms to the rebels accords them a form of de facto recognition. French recognition of Biafra came on July 31, 1968, some time after the sale of arms had begun. Frequently governments avoid the overt provision of arms to secessionists by disguising the transaction through the use of third or fourth parties. France used not only private arms suppliers to help Biafra, but also worked through other states such as Gabon and the Ivory Coast. Clearly such action avoided diplomatic complications, made the sources hard to trace, and obscured the degree of involvement from domestic opponents.

The second source of arms supply is nongovernmental agencies. These private sources deal mainly in the surplus from advanced industrial states, including former colonial powers, though they can also arrange the bilateral transfer of weapons to the government or independent groups. Although in principle they purport to operate only with the knowledge and sanction of the governments concerned, the complex movement of arms throughout the world makes this an extremely difficult principle to uphold. The arms trade, indeed, is one that seems to function without regard for political boundaries, either between nations of between East and West. Because civil wars in the "Third World" tend to be fought with small, unsophisticated arms, private dealers can and have on occasion played significant roles as suppliers. In addition, they can deal with antigovernmental forces unhampered by diplomatic and political considerations. Thus private dealers have served as a cover for supplies from governmental sources. In addition, many mercenaries bring their own equipment with them and have their own logistic support.

Perhaps the Nigeria-Biafra civil war provides one of the best illustrations of the importance of external sources of arms supply, though the demand was exceptional. Even though atypical, it illustrates some of the motives behind private provision of arms in civil wars. Broadly speaking, the motives fall into two categories: straightforward commercial profit, and a material or political stake in the outcome. The latter helps explain much of the French private as well as governmental interest in Biafran success. For example, a £6 million loan was raised through the Rothschild Bank in France by Colonel Ojukwu, the Biafran leader, in return for exclusive mineral (including oil) rights over the ten years following the establishment of an independent Biafra. A "French exploration company" provided Biafra with a B-26 bomber, probably for similar reasons. Such motives were not, however, confined to the French; in Britain industrialists were reported to have engaged a Major Wicks to recruit mercenaries for Biafra, despite British government policy. It is hard to distinguish fact from rumor with regard to both these arms deals and the provision of capital with which to make purchases. Belgian sources rumored that Shell-BP raised capital for Biafra, and there were similar reports about the trading firm of A.G. Leventis and "other United Kingdom sources." On the other hand, private arms dealers only interested in profits are more clearly identifiable, though in their turn they are as likely as not to have been engaged by external parties to supply weapons and military materiel rather than by either side directly engaged. Significantly, in the Nigerian civil war private arms dealers became more prominent after the war had been going for some time than at the start. The names that figured most prominently were Swedish, American, and French; they were linked mainly with recruiting mercenaries, though they probably had some hand in arms supply as well. A number of dealers from France, Switzerland, Spain, Britain, Belgium, Holland, Czechoslovakia, and Portugal are also reported to have supplied Biafra.

The last source of supply, especially for secessionists, has been arms captured from the enemy or from any other expedient source. This was less evident in Nigeria, perhaps because of the more conventional nature of the fighting and the context within which it took place. In the Karen war in Burma it seems that many defecting military men, even of high rank, took their arms with them. The Kurds certainly managed to fight on with weapons captured from the Iraqi army. But the most colorful example comes from the Sudan, which had provided landing facilities for aircraft carrying arms to Katanga. After the war, these same weapons found their way back to the southern Sudanese provinces. This provided the incentive for the founding of the Anzanian Liberation Front.

The weapons best suited for civil wars have not been those of a sophisticated kind. Neither the finances nor the technical resources have been available. Only when arms suppliers have been prepared to give favorable credit, or have subsidized the sale, as in the case of the Soviet Union, has this been remotely possible. Where there have been instances of advanced weapons, they have been maintained or used with outside or mercenary assistance. The important question here, however, is to determine what constitutes military as opposed to nonmilitary support. It is hard to draw a line between warlike and nonwarlike stores, as the Biafran case showed. Here the Nigerian government, using the old precedent of blockade, consistently antagonized public opinion, especially in Britain and Sweden, by its refusal to allow food for the starving to be sent into the Biafran enclave. Its argument was that arms and ammunition were being flown in as well as food and medicines, and that the food itself was being diverted to the war effort. In Yemen, most of the financial support for the royalists came from Saudi Arabia.

Where the line is to be drawn is open to question. Rather than exclude everything but "defensive" articles—a term closely associated with the international arms trade—the line is drawn loosely here to include military and nonmilitary support which is provided either side to enable it effectively to continue the war. In this context financial assistance to both the Biafrans and the Yemeni would be included. The supply of food and medicine would not be included, for it was evident quite early in the Biafran war that such aid was necessary more for the survival of a civilian population, the majority of which was not engaged in the fighting, than for the effective maintenance of the war effort. That such aid was diverted to military or related ends does not come within this distinction, however significant it may have been at specific points in time.

The Nigerian civil war well illustrated the problem of what is and what is not an arms sale. Especially for Biafra, financial aid came from a wide variety of sources, and these sources as often as not decided what the Biafrans should get. Communist China was reported to have given them a "blank check" to draw on Chinese arsenals and to buy French and Czech equipment. Conversely, the Nigerians received an offer of financial aid from the Soviet Union. Examples of nongovernmental fiscal aid have been noted above.

There are other forms of external support which are not specifically a trade in arms, but which had some bearing upon the Nigerian-Biafran war. Facilities for Chinese training of Biafran soldiers were provided by Tanzania. More marginal were public relations work by a Hollywood agency, airlift assistance by airlines, and newsprint, all of which contributed toward the war. Whether or not these are considered arms sales, they serve to illustrate how complex involvement in civil wars has become and how tenuous is the distinction between support and the provision of arms.

In relation to arms sales in the post-1945 civil wars, several variables must be considered. First, there is the situation at the outbreak of hostilities. This usually reflects the degree of prewar preparation and governs the level of arms sophistication, at least in the early stages. Second, there are the external suppliers of arms and military materiel. It is important here to determine at what stage they become involved and whether the involvement is active or passive. Further investigation of this area might reveal not only which states appear interested in other's civil wars, but also how far they are prepared to go in support of one side or the other. In the latter context, the ideological, political, commercial, and traditional relationships between the warring parties and external states and groups may prove to be a useful indicator for future patterns of external involvement. Finally, there is the military materiel itself: what is the quantitative and qualitative flow? This includes not only what and how much help is given, but also from where, and how it reaches the recipient. These variables can be examined comparatively by focusing on the Nigerian-Biafran case.

Although it is sometimes difficult to give an accurate assessment of how the arms are divided between the opposing sides, and of the number in civilian hands, the assumption here is that by looking at the size, composition, and structure of the armed forces, a rough indicator of the character of the civil war can be made. Much information will, of course, be hidden—as for instance the clandestine importation of arms into Biafra before overt action—and cannot be included in these figures. The time factor also makes comparative analysis slightly misleading in the post-1945 period, owing to the increasing sophistication of weapons. But as far as references are made here to broad categories of arms, such as "armored vehicles" and "small arms," the time factor can largely be discounted, for the small arms with which civil wars are largely fought have developed least.

Military Results

Given these assumptions and qualifications, what were the general levels of military capability, expressed in terms of weapons systems, in the civil wars in question? In 1966 the Nigerian armed forces numbered about 9,000, with a gendarmerie of approximately 13,500 in a population of 56,000,000. The only advanced equipment in the military was two squadrons of Ferret armored cars, one field battery of artillery, and a few Dornier Do 27 light aircraft. An additional forty Do 27s were on order from West Germany. When the Eastern Region broke away on May 30, 1967, the army lost most of its trained officers as well as its Ibo soldiers. Ever since the massacre of the Ibo in the North in September 1966, the Biafrans had been smuggling in arms. Given the small size of the Nigerian forces, it is reasonable to suggest the two sides were evenly matched; indeed, Biafra may well have had the advantage. External supplies of arms and speed of recruitment and training would probably become the determining factors, given that both sides had the financial strength.

The situation in Iraq was markedly different. As in Nigeria, the immediate cause was again governmental discrimination against a minority with a significant number of men in the armed forces. In 1960 about one-seventh of the Iraqi troops were Kurds. The army had two infantry and one mechanized division in the plains, and a fourth mountain division, which contained most of the Kurds. When the Kurdish Democratic Party rebelled in protest against the anti-Kurdish policy, the mountain division effectively went over to its side. Though the more sophisticated mechanized division remained loyal, it was of marginal use in mountainous Kurdistan, while the IAF, equipped with Hunter and Venom jets, was also limited by the nature of the terrain.

Yemen in 1962 had about 2,000 troops left after the defection of some

8,000 Zaydi royalists following the 1962 coup and the declaration of the republic. The army had been reequipped with Soviet weapons in 1957, the bulk of which were Czech small arms. Though the Yemen Republic had UAR aid, the Zaydi in their mountain fastnesses successfully withstood what appeared on paper to be a more formidable army.

Only in Yemen and Iraq are there examples of advanced weapons systems at the outbreak of war, and in both these cases the terrain limited their use. The Nigerian war was exceptional in that, although the level of arms sophistication was relatively low at the beginning, it progressively improved throughout the war. This favored the government forces for two reasons: Nigeria could better afford such weapons, and the terrain did not restrict the use or limit the effectiveness of such weapons systems. The other instances of civil war have in common a low level of weapons sophistication at the start of hostilities. In the Sudan there was little except a few Land Rovers and some field artillery; in the Congo, which had one of the largest armies in Africa in 1960, neither organization nor equipment was of a high order, as the success of the Katangan mercenaries proved. In India there was clearly a marked disparity between the Indian army's equipment and that of the Nagas, but as in Iraq and Yemen, it was vitiated by terrain.

The Variables

A comparative study of civil wars since 1945 reveals a number of important variables that keep reappearing, and the combinations of these variables go some way toward explaining the character and proportions of each war. The impact of external supplies of arms has to be seen in relation to these recurring variables. The most significant of these would appear to be, first, the military expertise of the rebel forces; second, the level of weapons technology existing in the state at the time; and third, the region from which the rebels are fighting and the military advantages it affords them. Only lastly in importance is the nature of external support. Numbers of people actively engaged in fighting do not appear to be of particular signifiance. In cases where rebels lacked military experience, the terrain balanced this out; certainly this was the case with the Nagas. With the Karens in Burma, the Somalis in Kenya, and the Katanganese in the Congo, where terrain was perhaps not relevant, other factors redressed any imbalance. In Kenya, for example, the war was complicated by border disputes between Somaliland and Kenya; in the Congo the Belgian mercenaries and the financial assistance of the Union Minière was fundamental; and in Burma the Karens drew strength from troubles throughout the state and the complication of Chinese intervention. Generally speaking, however, the broad pattern remains.

Once hostilities have broken out in a civil war, analysis of the patterns of external involvement through arms sales becomes highly complex. First, there is the number of third parties involved. Second, there is the problem that the place of manufacture of a weapon may not be its immediate source. Czech arms may have reached both Nigeria and Biafra from private sources. Thus the distinction again has to be made between those states directly involved and those that are only indirectly implicated. The general impression is that the governments of relatively few states are themselves suppliers. The clearest cases are those of the British and the Soviet governments selling arms to Nigeria, of Egypt to Yemen, and of the Soviets to Iraq. The distinction must be noted that military materiel is often supplied in accordance with long-term agreements signed before, and not related to, the civil war.

The number of indirect sources of supply in civil wars is considerably larger. In the Nigerian war, France, for example, permitted private suppliers to send arms to Biafra a long time before the French government itself became overtly involved. Dahomey, Gabon, Portugal, Spain, South Africa, Rhodesia, São Tomé, Fernando Po, the Ivory Coast, Zambia, and Equatorial Guinea were all vital links in the supply chain to Biafra, and were all thus indirectly involved. Some of these states also themselves supplied arms. For the Nigerian government, Malta, Egypt, Algeria, Libya, the Sudan, and Ghana were likewise involved. Tanzania allowed Biafran troops to train on its soil under Chinese instruction.

In those cases where it appears that direct arms sales to either Nigeria or Biafra took place, one further qualification must be made. This is that the supply of arms to Biafra in particular was diffuse, sporadic, and covered a wide range of weapons. This was in spite of reports that supplies of the order of fifty tons a night were passing through Gabon or the Ivory Coast for Biafra. As an example of diffuseness, the French supplied arms from Bulgarian, Czech, American, Soviet (ex-Algerian FLN), and Swedish sources as well as their own. The arms supplied to Nigeria were, on the other hand, almost exclusively British or Russian. While Britain supplied about 15 percent in value, in terms of usage it was nearer

50 percent, for British contributions were mainly in small arms and ground equipment. The Soviet Union provided aircraft, which Britain had refused to make available. Only toward the end was there overlap, when the USSR also began to supply small arms. Other sources were, significantly, compatible with the two principal suppliers. Algeria, Egypt, and Ghana also provided ex-Soviet aircraft, which were flown by experienced East German and Egyptian pilots. This was not the case with the Biafrans, for though France was the principal supplier, the equipment was as varied as the states giving support. Israel sent ex-Soviet equipment captured in the 1967 Egyptian war, and private suppliers reportedly sold American equipment stolen in West Germany.

Compared with the Nigerian civil war, external involvement in the form of arms sales in all the other cases of civil war since 1945 was not extensive. In Yemen only Egypt and Saudi Arabia were active. The war was virtually supplied and financed by these two external states, though there was a peripheral involvement by Britain, Jordan, Iran, Czechoslovakia, and the Soviet Union. The situation in Iraq was much the same, though the main source for the Kurds was Iran, with the Iraqis getting their arms from the USSR. The examples of private sources for weapons in any substantial number are few and far between and were nowhere else as significant as in the Biafran case. This may well suggest that the participation of private arms dealers in the international arms trade is a relatively new phenomenon, at least on a substantial scale. The only known report of private arms dealing in any large quantity is that in which Roman Catholic organizations were reputed to have supplied the southern Sudanese provinces.

Conclusions

From all the cases studied, no really consistent pattern of external arms supply in civil wars can be said to emerge. The general impression is that government forces have continued to be supplied by traditional sources, while their opponents, the rebels, have sought aid wherever it was expedient. Most significantly, it would appear that the Nigerian-Biafran case, apart from being the most recent (as of 1970) example, differed from the other cases in four important respects. First, the war was shorter than almost all the others, lasting little over two years. Second, the weapons used, and used effectively by both sides, were comparatively more sophisticated and more expensive than in other cases. Third, the consumption of weapons was higher, as was the number of casualties. And lastly, the range of external support for the two sides, whether direct or indirect, active or passive, sophisticated or unsophisticated, from government or from private sources, or as arms or as finance, was considerably more extensive. For this reason, the Nigerian civil war is important, for one wonders whether it points to a new development, or whether its features suggest that it was an exceptional event, unlikely to be repeated again.

The answer probably lies somewhere between these two extremes. The Nigerian war demonstrated that civil wars could be sustained, if the antagonists were willing, for long periods of time with small quantities of arms, equipment, finance, and intangible support. Certainly it demonstrated the potential of the international trade in arms, whether governmental or private; and a capacity of this scale should not be underestimated. On the other hand, the war was distinctive in that its location, the history of the Nigerian federation, and the tribal overtones of the conflict all contributed to the conduct and bitterness of the struggle. But if any general proposition can be made as to how the Nigerian civil war differed from the other case studies, especially in regard to the provision of external support, it is that the significance of external sources of weapons is related to the marginal utility of advanced weapons systems. In the Nigerian civil war, the marginal utility was evidently high and was a function of the nature of the terrain. With external suppliers prepared to sell advanced weapons to both sides and with these weapons proving significant in the conduct of the war, many of the distinctive characteristics of the war can be explained. For the obverse reason, the other civil wars assumed their common characteristics whether substantial external arms support was available or not.

Civil wars are distinctive because of the conventional nature of the conflict and the scale that it involves in men and materiel. Just as the less conventional forms of internal warfare are likely to fall within the ambit of the international arms traffic, so is this especially true of civil wars where the marginal utility of advanced weapons is low. Pointers to future possibilities have already been made in Nigeria. Though it is hard to envisage a civil war on a greater scale than that in Nigeria, or one that could generate a comparable demand for arms and equipment, one question can hardly be avoided—how significant will external arms suppliers become in civil wars of the future, let alone in other forms of internal conflict, assuming that they are permitted to expand their participation and remain unchecked.

Suggestions for Further Research

Only one major examination in depth of the international arms trade has so far emerged. This is George Thayer's *War Business*. At the formal level, studies of arms sales and shipments cover fairly comprehensively the movement of major weapons systems. SIPRI and the U.S. Arms Control and Disarmament Agency, for example, have produced some valuable work, but one suspects that this is only scratching the surface. The informal movement of weapons is an area to be researched, though the reliability of the information, if it could be obtained, is highly suspect. An unresearched field is the movement of arms to nation-states during internal conflicts other than "civil wars." The impact of Communist Chinese aid in arming small states might well be a fruitful area for research. The Nigerian-Biafran war has attracted much comment; now that the dust is settling, it might repay further research. Of some interest, perhaps, would be the role of the military adviser, and the capacity of small states to master complex weapons systems and other advanced methods of war.

XIII

SOCIETAL PATTERNS AND LESSONS
The Irish Case

J. Bowyer Bell

A PROLONGED CIVIL WAR is the most overt indication of an attenuated societal schism. In the preliminary civil discord—no matter how divisive and mutually contradictory are the elements involved, no matter how long-standing the opposing values or how deep-seated the distrust—a society, however strained or artificial, continues to exist. Once civil strife has passed the point of no return into civil war, however, the prewar society has, for better or worse, committed suicide. There can be no restoration of the uncomfortable but familiar past, for civil war can lead only to the ultimate triumph and imposition of a new society, cherished by the victors, inconceivable to the vanquished. Thus every civil war ends with the effect of a revolution: the construction of a society with institutions and values that create an intolerable life for a substantial portion of the defeated, whose very identities had been first transformed by the polarization and then shattered. The vicious, almost permanent psychic wounds of civil war are less a result of the cruelty of the contest, the extensive violence, battles of vengeance, judicial murder, and wanton destruction, than of the "intolerable" terms of defeat, which must be "tolerated" by one side and imposed, year after year, by the other. There remain two societies: one hopelessly excluded from the reality of the old dreams and full participation in a new and abhorrent world; the other, arrogant in triumph, secretly insecure, twisted by constant coercion, grasping for the future. To sew up the raveled ends of these two societies into a single, even if patched, garment requires decades, often generations.

217

Most advanced societies, organized politically into nation-states, have serious or at least recognizable differences. Many new nations, particularly in the Third World, can scarcely be considered societies organized as states at all, but rather highly artificial umbrella structures tying together a clump of divergent societies with fragile and alien institutions. While the tensions of diversity may give an advanced, pluralistic society flexibility or creativity or stimulating variety, they may also impose strains so severe that two societies emerge. Thus there were two Englands in the nineteenth century, the rich and the poor; two Americas, the North and the South; two Frances, the Monarchist and the Republican. Around some nodal point of difference, such as Catholicism or poverty, a variety of values, customs, habits, and attitudes may accumulate, engendering a subsociety still not politically visible but having less and less in common with the rest of the country. Such a society under special circumstances may either seek to impose its particular values or secede. Either undertaking polarizes the previously "united" society; if either pole has or develops the military capacity to oppose and thus to postpone an ultimate decision, then civil war becomes likely.

Many deeply divided societies are commonly wracked with violence or near-violence; some nations have endemic fighting or habitual coups or massive disorders but lack the combined polarization of society and reciprocal military capacity to prevent integration. The capacity of both societies to wage war, but without the power to secure swift victory, means a struggle within the old society's husk for the future. The civil war that ensues will be a violent military struggle between two societies so committed that victory for one means extinction for the other. Thus a society organized as either envisions would be incompatible with the continued existence of the other: the alternative becomes Victory or Death, God or the Devil, Freedom or Slavery. Once the battle has been joined, the war is total and the outcome is seen only as total victory or total defeat. Neither side at any stage can seriously contemplate any alternative to victory except death—if not of the body then of the soul.

One of the most bitter and complicated of these civil wars took place in Ireland between 1916 and 1923, encompassing coups and pogroms, a war of national liberation, terror, communal violence, and ultimately a variety of imposed and contrived solutions which still haunt the island. On Easter Monday, April 24, 1916, a small band of Irish conspirators attempted a rising against the British, then otherwise occupied in France.

Planned as a national insurrection, a variety of ill-favored accidents largely limited action to Dublin, where a few hundred men siezed and held the city for a week. In Irish terms these men were nationalists, intent on establishing the Irish Republic and defending their country by force of arms. For them Ireland, though organized openly as a republic, had long existed as a submerged and occupied nation. The long procession of previous risings, nearly one a generation, were an outward sign of the peculiar integrity of an Ireland held in alien domination. Knowing that the Dublin rising would be crushed, they hoped that their blood sacrifice would awaken another generation, would water the roots of the "real" Ireland, would strip away the shell of assimilation, would in fact inspire a more successful war of national liberation. The British in turn were appalled at the senselessness of the rising, the pointless destruction of Dublin, the lost lives, the cost of fanaticism inflicted on Britain at a crucial moment by a tiny, unrepresentative band of rebels. For the British, the men of the Easter Rising *were* rebels. Britain had century after century absorbed diverse races into a single body politic and largely a single society. Ireland was an integral part of the United Kingdom, not a potential and distant dominion, like Canada or Australia. The Scots could be Scots, the Welsh, Welsh, but all were British, all were citizens of the United Kingdom. The king, the parliament, the army, and all enlightened opinion accepted the indivisibility of British society. The Easter Rising was rebellion; the rebels had sought to instigate a fratricidal civil war.

Momentarily it seemed that all decent people, the Irish included, would agree. Ireland had been promised home rule. There had been no violence for a generation and in the spring of 1916 no indication of sudden mass support for further "rebel" adventures. Vast numbers of Irishmen were fighting in France alongside the Welsh and the Scots and the English— no greater proof was needed of the loyalty and unity of Britain. The leaders of the Easter Rising were executed as traitors and the rebels interned. As usual, the British had misjudged the Irish—in fact the Irish had misjudged themselves. Under the superficial accommodation with Britain, behind the seemingly irreversible assimilation into Britain, the Irish found all their old values, their ancestorial aspirations. Within a year, Irish society changed utterly, transformed allegiances, and opened the door to civil war. The irresponsible rebels became martyred patriots, the released internees heroes. After the December 1918 elections for the Westminster Parliament, 73 of the 105 Irish winners agreed to form their own Irish Parliament, the Dáil, which met on January 21, 1919, with by then 36 members in British jails. The threads of conspiracy and resistance had been gathered by the survivors, joined by eager new recruits to the cause of the Irish Republic. The "Troubles" came to Ireland, years of bitter irregular war, assassination, and violent repression, guerrillas in the hills, shadow governments, religious pogroms, executions, and arson. The British were determined to restore order, maintain the authority of the crown, protect the security of the realm, and defend the loyal Irish unionists, largely Protestants. Either there was a united kingdom or there was not—and the Irish Republicans with their recourse to arms insisted there was not.

The seemingly insurmountable obstacle facing the Irish Republicans was the overwhelming military superiority of the newly victorious British Empire. The means available to the Irish Republican Army (IRA) to wage open war were limited indeed. The futility of seizing and holding part of the island had been underscored by the failure of the Easter Rising and a long series of earlier, abortive risings. Simple terror, bombs in the night, and murder from the ditch seemed unlikely means to coerce the British Empire. If the Irish Republic was to become a reality, the IRA had to discover an effective means of waging a war.

Pragmatically, with little recourse to theory, the Irish evolved a form of internal war that in time would be the archetype for national liberation movements. First, the structure of British control and intelligence was hit repeatedly: the Royal Irish Constabulary, the paramilitary police, became prime targets, as did British secret service agents. As British knowledge of the countryside declined, it became increasingly easier to maintain small guerrilla columns in the hills, men who struck at barracks and transport and disappeared when pursued. The more British troops moved into the island, the more the targets available for ambush. Within the cities, terrorist operations were carried out with sufficient frequency to force the British into increasingly repressive measures. The more stringent British regulations became, the more brutal the searches and seizures, the more harsh the restrictions, the more "immoral" the British presence became, first to the Irish and gradually to international opinion. And while the IRA sought to accelerate the "military" campaign, an effort was made to create parallel governmental structures—Irish courts instead of British, Irish tax collectors, Irish diplomats. Abroad, Irish representatives poured out their story and churned out endless papers, pamphlets, and manifestos. Despite their ingenuity, however, and despite the British inability to restore order, after nearly three years the Irish were still no closer to expelling the British by force of arms. The Irish had discovered only how to evade defeat, not how to impose victory.

Increasingly the British public appeared to have doubts about the repressive policies of the government, particularly since they had so far been ineffective. Cork city had been burned and young Irish lads hanged, while the struggle between Irish Catholic "rebels" and Irish Protestant "loyalists" in Northern Ireland resembled medieval religious massacres. Most of all, the "moral" right of Britain to impose order through brutality began to be questioned. The difficulty for the British government remained not so much the distaste of yielding to rebel violence and opening negotiations, as belief in the indivisibility of the United Kingdom. There seemed no common ground between an Irish Republic and a British crown: local autonomy, home rule, even federalism might yield a formula but either there was an Irish Republic or there was not. Still, the British cabinet decided to explore the prospects of diplomacy, hopeful that some of the more responsible rebels would accept less than a whole loaf. In Ireland, some of the leaders of the IRA and the shadow government increasingly felt that with victory as illusive as ever, a British initiative for a compromise solution would not be unwelcome. Beginning in October 1920, even while the war continued, negotiations were opened by a variety of agents and agencies. These eventually led first to a truce, July 11, 1921, and then to the arrival in October of an Irish delegation in London.

Under the shrewd and cunning leadership of Prime Minister David Lloyd George, the experienced and talented British delegation, which included among others Winston Churchill, managed to produce a solution which not only satisfied London's minimal demands, now far, far less than they had been a few years before, but also might not necessarily deny the basic Irish aspirations. A complicated, hybrid institution named the Irish Free State was proposed, which would be outside the United Kingdom but inside the British Empire. The government in Dublin would have to take an oath of allegiance to the crown but would have almost all the other attributes of an independent nation, as much as, if not more than, other British dominions. For some of the Irish delegation, the Free State seemed not to be the Republic or Freedom but a necessary means to achieve both in time. The responsibility for the loyal unionists, adamant to the point of rebellion in their refusal to accept absorption into a Catholic Irish Ireland, was accepted by London with the creation in six Ulster provinces of Northern Ireland—home rule within the United Kingdom for a majority of the unionists. Finally, the acquisition of military bases in the Free State satisfied British security requirements. Essentially the British had recognized the existence of an Irish society, organized as the Irish Free State in twenty-six of the thirty-two counties, but by a variety of legal and strategic ties retained that "society" within the British Empire if not the United Kingdom.

For a great many men who had spent years living on their nerves, seen their friends executed, and fought a long and bitter war, the legal ties that satisfied the British and some of their colleagues were chains. For them the sacrifices had been for recognition of the Republic, proclaimed Easter Monday, 1916, not a slick British formula called the Free State, which was not free as long as an oath to an alien crown was included and not a state as long as six counties were annexed and foreign bases imposed. During the bitter debates on the treaty, tensions grew within Irish society and the IRA. On January 7, 1922, when the treaty scraped through the new Dáil, 64 votes to 57, the Republican purists felt betrayed. Although they refused to recognize the existence of the "Treaty State," the advocates of compromise went right ahead organizing the new Free State. The British army evacuated the south, and a Northern Ireland government was set up in the north. The Troubles, however, were not at an end.

The Republicans, not unexpectedly, could not give up the Republic so easily. The IRA remained in existence. The old Republican government refused to fade away. Reluctantly, despairingly, two Irelands began to emerge. Through months of failed compromises, plots, meetings, and endless informal discussions, a middle way could not be found. Once more it proved a case of either/or: a Republic or the Free State, an oath or not. The breaking point came largely because the new government in Dublin could no longer tolerate the independent, potentially rebellious IRA. Either the Free State government was master of Ireland, or at least of twenty-six counties thereof, or it was not.

The Free State army, with artillery borrowed from the British, opened fire on the IRA headquarters at Four Courts in Dublin on June 28, 1922, and the last act of the Troubles began. While many of the most brilliant guerrilla leaders and articulate spokesmen had remained loyal to the

Easter Republic, the Free State—recognized as the legal government, possessed of the assets of the state, and directed by solid, efficient men—proved the stronger. Aided by a series of IRA strategic blunders, the Free State army first broke the IRA's thin, linear defenses and then forced the Republicans into guerrilla warfare. Whatever their sympathies, most of the Irish people were exhausted, felt they had sacrificed sufficiently, and were unwilling or unable to support the IRA's desperate struggle. By use of judicial executions and massive detentions, the IRA was intimidated, reduced to arson and ambush. Free State repression became sufficiently efficient that the IRA became little bands of armed men on the run. Finally the IRA chief of staff was forced on May 24, 1923, to issue an order not to surrender but to dump arms and disband. The shattered remains of the IRA were hunted down by the Free Staters. The jails were filled with internees, the emigrant ships with a new generation of exiles. The practical men of the Free State had crushed the pure of heart. There was to be no republic.

On the morning after final victory, the triumphant are faced with the task of securing that victory. Since few defeated societies have been totally annihilated on the field of battle, victors have to face the problem of assimilating or eliminating the remnants. The Irish situation was particularly complicated because of the variety of victories and defeats. First, when a war of national liberation is successful, then it is clear to the victors that no civil war took place. If Ireland had been intimidated by the British army, resistance ended, and order restored, then the civil war would have been won and the national liberation struggle denied. Normally, even logically, these alternatives are mutually exclusive—except in Ireland. In twenty-six counties the Irish forced a solution which largely recognized the independent existence of Ireland, that is, that the war had not been a civil war and that neither the new government in Dublin nor the old in London had to assimilate a defeated society. In Ulster, however, the loyalists emerged triumphantly dominating the new Northern Ireland government with their two-to-one majority, discriminating against their potentially disloyal Irish-Catholic neighbors, imposing, as one indiscreet spokesman noted, a Protestant parliament on a Protestant people. In the North the civil war had been won in the name of unity with Britain, and so the "rebels," doubly dangerous, for they could look south for aid and comfort, had to be closely controlled. Since assimilation was impossible without wholesale conversion to Protestantism, rather unlikely, the Northern Ireland government and the loyalist society by a tangle of legal and extralegal restrictions and practices set up a machine of domination, determined that their society would be safe by isolating and restricting the "other" minority society. With no other choice, the Catholics of Northern Ireland were forced to endure sullenly, too weak to rebel and too devout to convert.

In the Irish Free State, the victorious government after the real but brief civil war felt far less threatened than its Northern counterpart. The war had been vicious but not exceedingly bloody, with less than 700 killed. The irreconcilables of the IRA could in time be absorbed, once they recognized the futility of continued armed resistance. The hatred was deep and likely to be long lasting, but it was Irish hatred between Irishmen. The detention camps remained but for a year. The Republicans were permitted back into political competition. After various evasions and rationalizations the more practical Republican wing under Eamon De Valera entered the Dáil, and after their party's 1931 election victory formed the new government.

The die-hard Republicans, however, refused to recognize the Free State or to participate in parliamentary politics. The IRA remained in existence as a secret army but not only declined as a threat to the security of the state but also showed very considerable reluctance to reintroduce the gun into Irish politics. Thus despite the old and very real grievances, the Republicans were largely absorbed into the new Free State, and so successfully that in less than a decade they had taken over the government. The hard-core Republicans, who remained outside the governmental system, did not become a dissident society, but only a dissenting current within Irish society. The unreconstructed IRA did carry out a bombing campaign in England in 1939 and 1940, forcing not only the British and Northern Ireland governments to institute harsh repressive measures but also the government of De Valera in Dublin, fearful of the IRA's jeopardizing Irish neutrality. In 1956, after a series of spectacular arms raids, the IRA opened a six-year guerrilla campaign in Northern Ireland, again resulting in repressive measures north and south of the border, but again failing to seriously disrupt society. The hard core did and does exist, but without sufficient support to impose its solution on Britain or polarize Irish society.

Not all victors in civil wars select toleration as a method to secure a stable society; in fact, very, very few do, although a system foreseeing permanent repression is not necessarily a favored option. In point of fact, the most efficacious solution to disposing of a subsociety is genocide. At one level of efficiency or another, this has not always been discarded: Cromwell almost "solved" the Irish problem once before, and in more recent times the Soviet regime eliminated two classes, the nobles and the bourgeoisie, who were without function or place in their new society, relegating them to the garbage heap of history. A somewhat less severe policy is the transfer of the potentially dissident population, as occured between Turkey and Greece after World War I, or their expulsion, such as that of the Germans in East Prussia. A discreet balance between terror and expulsions may either completely eliminate the undesirable society or so bleed off the bold and daring as to emasculate the remainder. In both cases, however, moral considerations aside, the victors may not wish to eliminate the defeated society entirely, thereby also eliminating the possibility of exploiting the losers. After the long, bitter Spanish Civil War of 1936–39, Franco and the Nationalists could hardly eliminate or expel well over half the Spanish population. They could and did follow a policy of harsh repression, but the suspect classes and sections within Spain, if not reconciled to the victorious society, at least became resigned to the futility of opposition.

In some cases, once purged of active dissidence, the old society is simply ignored, feeble, and frustrated, while the new society is created around them or, as the case may be, on top of them. Thus in America the "rebels" were largely ignored and excluded during the post-Civil War reconstruction period. When the reconstructed society proved too feeble and too expensive for the victors, increasingly involved in the expansion of the new postwar industrial society of the North and West, the former rebels were allowed limited control over the devastated South. In the fullness of time, the Southern "society" evolved into Southern sectionalism and was gradually absorbed into the mainstream of America. No matter whether the relatively magnanimous policies of the Irish Free State or the United States, or the harsh repression of Spain or Northern Ireland are followed, the residue of a defeated society remains well into the following generations.

Although recourse to rebellion no longer holds any lures for most of the defeated (civil war inoculates a nation against a second attack), a not-always-conscious attempt is made to discover alternatives to defeat. In America, with the Confederacy crushed and the South devastated,

General Robert E. Lee could only offer acceptance. The South had fought the good fight and far longer than reasonable because there seemed no alternative. Said he, "We have fought this fight as long as, and as well as we know how. We have been defeated. For us, as a Christian people, there is now but one course to pursue. We must accept this situation." Understandably, to most shattered societies without hope in the future, simple acceptance proves scant comfort. The Lost Cause is enshrined in myths, becomes pure, a bold act of the spirit smashed by overwhelming, materialistic force. These legends of the past—dashing cavaliers, brave grand dukes, kings across the waters, peasants on the Madrid barricades—often provide fertile ground for subsequent generations' creativity, producing a rich artistic lode, rather the case of the sand transformed into the pearl. Even a "mild" civil war with relatively rapid reintegration will produce a society wedded to the issues of the past long after there is any viability in the old arguments. Men not yet born at the crucial moment of battle will in Ireland or Alabama vote basically for vengeance, rallying behind political symbols irrelevant to the issues of the day.

In summary, then, in social terms civil war is a struggle between two societies incapable of coexisting in the husk of previously unified institutions. Essentially the struggle is over either the purity or the unity of society, a battle for a Communist Russia or a free Ireland. With neither side militarily capable of enforcing a swift decision, the confrontation between totally contradictory aspirations must be fought to the bitter end. Such a war inevitably means total denial for the most cherished goals of one side. The process of accommodation for the defeated under even favorable circumstances almost always requires sufficient time for a generation no longer committed to the past to mature. In some cases, because of the adamancy of the differences, accommodation is not really possible, and the unreconstructed rebels are relegated to an almost permanent subcaste. New options or the decline of former advocacies may in the fullness of time mute the old bitterness, and exhaustion, or sudden wealth, or an external threat may bring toleration and then integration.

Suggestions for Further Research

Although all of the modern civil wars have yet to be chronicled definitively, a more promising avenue of approach might be concentration on framing a specific question about a special case. The most important aspect of scholarly investigation at any level, one which may carry the end product beyond a heavy compilation of readily available sources to a level of general interest, is the construction of the question. The most interesting question is always why. Why did Nigeria collapse and not Kenya? Why could not the Irish avoid civil war in 1922 or the Americans in 1861? Why did the Russian Communists win and the Chinese Nationalists lose? Why is—or is not—Vietnam a civil war? Then, too, defining what can be asked is vital. What are the preconditions for civil war, and are they present in Brazil or India or were they in Greece and Spain? Why, with so many desperately divided national societies, have relatively few civil wars occurred?

To pose the proper question is perhaps more important than to find a ready answer. In the study of civil war from any angle, sociological or historical or psychological, there are a great many unasked as well as unanswered questions. Some of the answers given in this chapter may, in fact, be invalid: civil wars are fought to unify or purify a society, or civil war is societal suicide. The real excitement of investigation is, of course, to find satisfactory answers. For to ignore the question and depend on accumulation of "research" material is at best to present a tale, perhaps "filled with sound and fury," but "signifying nothing."

Selected Bibliography

In THE voluminous literature of war and society, there is not a single volume dedicated to the general area of the impact of civil war on society. Sociologists have produced extensive works on conflict, on social tension, and on the strategy of conflict resolution. There is even a *Journal of Conflict Resolution*. Much the same is true of anthropologists and psychologists. There is substantial literature on minorities, on communal tensions, on national identities, but again, seldom within the context of civil war. There are, however, a substantial number of books concerned with specific cases of civil war, although largely from political or military viewpoints.

This bibliography represents a melding of the bibliographies supplied by each contributor together with the general bibliography collected by the editor. The footnotes in chapter 1 provide additional specialized materials. No item has been duplicated, even if it is applicable to more than one section. Where a field is already well covered by standard texts with adequate bibliographies, few references have been given.

Since the aim of the book is to introduce readers to the problem of civil war in the modern world, the items listed here are a rather random selection designed to suggest approaches as much as to provide factual material. In view of the fact that Arthur Larson's bibliography (see below) has now appeared, this list has been shortened. His work contains much useful material.

General Sources

BIBLIOGRAPHIES

Brassey's Armed Forces Yearbook.
Choice.
Great Britain. *Ministry of Defense Library Accessions Lists* [monthly].
Journal of Conflict Resolution.
Journal of the Royal United Service Institution.
Journal of the United Service Institution of India.

Larsen, Arthur. *Civil-Military Relations: An Annotated Bibliography.* Biblio-
    graphical Series, No. 9. Manhattan: Kansas State University Library,
    1971.
United States Air Force. *Air University Review.*
————, Maxwell Air Force Base. *Air University Library Accessions Lists*
    [occasional].
————. *Air University Periodicals Guide.*
United States Army Command and General Staff College. *Military Review.*
United States Naval Institute Proceedings.

NEWSPAPERS AND PERIODICALS

Economist.
Financial Times [London].
Foreign Affairs [New York].
International Defence Review.
Keesing's Contemporary Archives.

BOOKS AND ARTICLES

Acheson, Dean. *Present at the Creation: My Years in the State Department.*
    New York: W.W. Norton, 1969.
Alexander, Major-General H. T. *African Tightrope: My Two Years as Nkru-
    mah's Chief of Staff.* London: Pall Mall Press, 1965.
AlRoy, Gil Carl. *The Involvement of Peasants in Internal Wars.* Princeton:
    Center of International Studies, Woodrow Wilson School of Public
    and International Affairs, Princeton University, 1966.
Amann, P. "Revolution: A Redefinition." *Political Science Quarterly* 77
    (March 1962): 36–53.
Ambler, John S. *The French Army in Politics, 1945–1962.* Columbus: Ohio
    State University Press, 1966.
American-Asian Educational Exchange. New York, 1969–. [A series of pam-
    phlets of about 60 pages each.]
American University. *Internal Defense: An Annotated Bibliography.* Wash-
    ington, D.C.: American University Center for Research in Social
    Systems, 1968.
Andrzejewski, Stanislau. *Military Organization and Society.* London: Rout-
    ledge and Kegan Paul, 1955.
Angress, W. T. *The Stillborn Revolution: The Communist Bid for Power in
    Germany, 1921–1923.* Princeton: Princeton University Press, 1963.
Applegate, Colonel R. *Crowd and Riot Control.* Harrisburg, Pa.: Stackpole,
    1964. [Sixth and expanded version of *Kill or Get Killed.*]
"The Armies of Africa." *Africa Report* [special issue], January 1964.
Ashford, Douglas E. *National Development and Local Reform: Political
    Participation in Morocco, Tunisia and Pakistan.* Princeton: Princeton
    University Press, 1966.

Ayub Khan, Mohammad. *Friends Not Masters: A Political Autobiography.* New York: Oxford University Press, 1967.

Bajwa, Fauja Singh. *The Military System of the Sikhs.* Patna: Motilal Banarsidass, 1964.

Baker, Ross K. "Tropical Africa's Nascent Navies." *USNI Proceedings,* January 1969, 64–71.

Bankwitz, Philip Charles Farwell. *Maxime Weygand and Civil-Military Relations in Modern Europe.* Harvard Historical Studies, No. 81. Cambridge, Mass.: Harvard University Press, 1967.

Barnes, Leonard. *African Renaissance.* London: Gollancz, 1969. [Covers the decade since independence.]

Barnett, Frank R.; Mott, William C.; and Neff, John C. *Peace and War in the Modern Age: Premises, Myths and Realities.* New York: Doubleday, 1965.

Barnett, Raymond J. "The Problem of Lower Spectrum Violence." *Military Review,* February 1966, 90–93.

Barnett, Richard J. *Intervention and Revolution.* New York: World, 1968.

Barraclough, Geoffrey. *An Introduction to Contemporary History.* London: Pelican, 1967.

Barringer, Herbert R.; Blankstein, George L.; and Mack, Raymond W. *Social Change in Developing Areas: A Reinterpretation of Evolutionary Theory.* Cambridge, Mass.: Schenkman, 1965.

Ba Than, Colonel V. *The Roots of Revolution: A Brief History of the Defense Services of the Union of Burma and the Ideals for Which They Stand.* Rangoon: Guardian, 1962.

Beeby, C. E. *The Quality of Education in Developing Countries.* Cambridge, Mass.: Harvard University Press, 1966.

Bell, M. J. V. *Army and Nation in Sub-Saharan Africa.* London: Institute for Strategic Studies, 1965.

Bennett, Richard. *The Blacks and Tans.* London: E. Hulton, 1959.

Bienen, Henry. "Military Assistance and Political Development in Africa." (Mimeographed paper.) Chicago: Inter-University Seminar on Armed Forces and Society, 1967.

———, ed. *The Military Intervenes.* New York: Russell Sage Foundation, 1968.

Bjelajac, Slavko N. "Unconventional Warfare: American and Soviet Approaches." *Annals of the American Academy of Political and Social Science* 341 (May 1962).

Black, Cyril Edwin, and Thornton, T. *Communism and Revolution: The Strategic Uses of Political Violence.* Princeton: Princeton University Press, 1964.

Bloomfield, Lincoln P. *International Military Forces: The Question of Peacekeeping in an Armed and Disarmed World.* Boston: Little Brown, 1964.

Bohannan, Paul. *Africa and the Africans*. Garden City, N.Y.: Natural History Press, 1964.

Bopegamage, Albert. "Caste, Class and the Indian Military (A Study of the Social Origins of Indian Army Personnel)." Mimeographed pamphlet. Chicago: Inter-University Seminar on Armed Forces and Society, 1967.

Bramson, Leon, and Goethals, George W., eds. *War: Studies from Psychology, Sociology, Anthropology*. New York: Basic Books, 1964.

Bredin, A. E. C. *The Happy Warriors*. Gillingham, Dorset: Blackmore Press, 1961. [The Ghurka Brigade in Malaya.]

Brinton, Crane. *The Anatomy of Revolution*. Rev. ed. New York: Prentice-Hall, 1965.

Brock, William R., ed. *The U.S. Civil War*. New York: Harper and Row, 1969.

Broomfield, John. *Elite Conflict in a Rural Society: Twentieth Century Bengal*. Berkeley: University of California Press, 1968.

Buchan, Alistair. *War in Modern Society: An Introduction*. New York: Harper, 1968.

Burns, Lieutenant-General Eedson L. M. *Between Arab and Israeli*. New York: Obolensky, 1963 [London, 1962].

Callwell, Sir Charles E. *Small Wars*. London: H. M. Stationery Office, 1899.

Calvert, P. A. "Revolution: The Politics of Violence." *Political Studies* 15 (February 1967).

Calvocoressi, Peter. *World Order and New States*. London: Chatto and Windus, 1962.

Cameron, Joseph. *The Anatomy of Military Merit*. Philadelphia: Doran, 1960.

Canetti, Elias. *Crowds and Power*. London: Gollancz, 1962.

Challand, G. *Armed Struggle in Africa: With the Guerrillas in "Portuguese" Guinea*. London: Monthly Review Press, 1969.

Chandler, Alfred D. *Strategy and Structure: Chapters in the History of Industrial Enterprise*. New York: Doubleday Anchor, 1966.

Chase, John D. "South of Thirty." *USNI Proceedings* 470 (Apr. 1967): 30–39.

Chesswas, J. D. *Methodologies of Educational Planning for Developing Countries*. New York: UNESCO, International Institute for Educational Planning, 1969.

Claude, Inis L. *Swords into Ploughshares*. London: London University Press, 1965.

Condit, D. M., et al. *Challenge and Response in Internal Conflict*. Washington, D.C.: Center for Research in Social Systems, American University, 1968.

Coward, H. Roberts. *Military Technology in Developing Countries*. Cambridge, Mass.: Center for International Studies, M.I.T., 1964.

Craig, Gordon. *The Politics of the Prussian Army, 1640–1945*. Oxford: Clarendon Press, 1955.

Cruise O'Brien, Conor. "The Counterrevolutionary Reflex." *Columbia University Forum*, Spring 1966, 21–24.

Cunliffe, Marcus. *Soldiers and Civilians: The American Military Ethos, 1775–1865*. Boston: Little Brown, 1968.

Dahrendorf, Ralph. *Class and Class Conflict in Industrial Society*. Stanford, Cal.: Stanford University Press, 1959.

Dallin, Alexander. *German Rule in Russia, 1941–1945: A Study in Occupation Politics*. London: Macmillan, 1957.

Davidson, B. *The Liberation of Guinée: Aspects of an African Revolution*. Harmondsworth: Penguin, 1969.

Davie, M. R. *The Evolution of War: A Study of Its Role in Early Societies*. Port Washington, N.Y.: Kennikat Press, 1969. [Reprint of 1929 edition.]

Davies, J. "Toward a Theory of Revolution." *American Sociological Review* 27 (February 1962).

de la Gorce, Paul Marie. *The French Army: A Military–Political History*. New York: Braziller, 1963.

de Luna, Frederick A. *The French Government under Cavaignac, 1848*. Princeton: Princeton University Press, 1969.

Demeter, Karl. *The German Officer-Corps in Society and State, 1650–1945*. Translated by Angus Malcolm. London: Weidenfeld and Nicholson, 1965.

Denton, F. H., and Phillips, W. *Some Patterns in the History of Violence*. Paper 3609. Santa Monica, Cal.: Rand Corp., 1967.

Derthick, Martha. *The National Guard in Politics*. Cambridge, Mass.: Harvard University Press, 1965.

Dufty, N. F. *The Sociology of the Blue Collar Worker*. International Studies in Sociology and Social Anthropology, No. 9. Leiden: E. J. Brill, 1969.

Dunner, Joseph, ed. *Dictionary of Political Science*. London: Vision Press, 1966.

Eckstein, Harry. "Internal Wars: A Taxonomy." Mimeographed paper. Princeton: Center of International Affairs, 1960.

———. "On the Etiology of Internal Wars." *History and Theory* 4, No. 2 (1965).

———, ed. *Internal War: Problems and Approaches*. Glencoe, Ill.: Free Press, 1964.

Edwards, L. P. "Civil War." *International Encyclopedia of Social Sciences*, (New York: Macmillan, 1968), 3:523.

Elliott, Major J. C. *The Modern Army and Air National Guard*. Princeton: Van Nostrand, 1965.

Ellwood, C. "A Psychological Theory of Revolutions." *American Journal of Sociology* 11 (1905–06).

El Mahdi, Mandour. *A Short History of the Sudan*. New York: Oxford University Press, 1969.

Ely, Paul. *L'Armée dans la Nation.* Paris: A. Fayard, 1961.

Emmerson, Donald K. *Students and Politics in Developing Nations.* London: Pall Mall Press, 1969.

Engels, F. *The German Revolutions.* Chicago: University of Chicago Press, 1967.

Fage, J. D., ed. *Africa Discovers Her Past.* New York: Oxford University Press, 1969. [How African historiography has changed in the post-World War II period.]

Fanon, Franz. *The Wretched of the Earth.* New York: Grove Press, 1968. [Offences against the person in French colonies.]

Feldman, Herbert. *Revolution in Pakistan: A Study of the Martial Law Administration.* New York: Oxford University Press, 1967.

Finer, S. E. *The Man on Horseback.* London: Pall Mall Press, 1962.

Fisher, Sydney N., ed. *The Military in the Middle East: Problems in Society and Government.* Columbus: Ohio State University Press, 1963.

Foran, Major William Robert. *The Kenyan Police, 1887–1960.* London: R. Hale, 1962.

Fowler, A. W. *War and Civilization: Selected from a Study of History.* New York: Oxford University Press, 1950.

Friedrich, Carl J., ed. *Revolution: Yearbook.* New York: Atherton Press, 1966.

Garthoff, R. "Unconventional Warfare in Communist Strategy." *Foreign Affairs* 40 (July 1962).

Ghosh, Kalyan Kumar. *The Indian Army: Second Front of the Indian Independence Movement.* Meerut: Meenakshi Prakashan, 1969.

Giap, N. V. *People's War, People's Army.* Peking: Foreign Languages Publishing House, 1961.

Glick, E. B. *Peaceful Conflict: The Non-Military Uses of the Military.* Harrisburg, Pa.: Stackpole, 1967.

Goerlitz, Walter. *History of the German General Staff, 1657–1945.* New York: Praeger, 1954.

Goodspeed, Major Donald James. *The Conspirators: A Study of the Coup d'Etat.* London: Macmillan, 1962.

Graml, H., et al. *The German Resistance to Hitler.* Berkeley: University of California Press, 1970.

Gross, Feliks. *The Seizure of Political Power in a Century of Revolution.* New York: Philosophical Library, 1958.

Guevara, [Ernesto] Che. *Guerrilla Warfare.* New York: Monthly Review Press, 1961.

Gulick, Charles Adams. *Austria from Habsburg to Hitler.* Berkeley: University of California Press, 1948.

Gurr, Ted Robert. "Psychological Factors in Civil Violence." *World Politics* 20, No. 2 (1968).

———. *Why Men Rebel.* Princeton: Princeton University Press, 1969.

Gutkind, P. C. W., ed. *The Passing of Tribal Man in Africa.* International

Studies in Sociology and Social Anthropology, No. 10. Leiden: E. J. Brill, 1970.

Gutteridge, William. *Armed Forces in New States*. London: Institute of Race Relations, 1962.

——. *The Military in African Politics*. Studies in African History, No. 4. London: Methuen, 1969.

——. *Military Institutions and Power in New States*. New York: Praeger, 1965.

Halpern, Manfred. *The Politics of Social Change in the Middle East*. Princeton: Princeton University Press, 1963.

Harbottle, Brigadier Michael. *The Impartial Soldier*. London: Oxford University Press, 1970.

Hargreaves, Reginald. "The Evolution of Military Support for Civil Powers." *JRUSI* (December 1969), 77–80.

Hatch, John. *Africa Today and Tomorrow: An Outline of Basic Facts and Major Problems*. London: Dobson, 1962.

Hayden, Tom [Thomas]. *Rebellion in Newark: Official Violence and Ghetto Response*. New York: Vintage, 1967.

Henderson, Ian, and Goodhart, Philip. *The Hunt for Kimathi*. London: H. Hamilton, 1958.

Henissart, Paul. *Wolves in the City: The Death of French Algeria*. New York: Simon and Schuster, 1970.

Higgins, Rosalyn. "United Nations Peacekeeping: Political and Financial Problems." *This World Today*, 1965.

——. *United Nations Peacekeeping, 1946–1967: Documents and Commentary*. London: Oxford University Press, 1969.

Higham, Robin. *Armed Forces in Peacetime: Britain, 1918–1940*. London: Foulis, 1963.

——. *The Military Intellectuals in Britain, 1918–1939*. New Brunswick, N.J.: Rutgers University Press, 1966.

——, ed. *Bayonets in the Streets: The Use of Troops in Civil Disturbances*. Lawrence: University Press of Kansas, 1969.

Holsti, K. "Resolving International Conflicts: A Taxonomy of Behavior." *Journal of Conflict Resolution* 10, No. 3 (1966).

Hoover Institution. *United States and Canadian Publications* [and theses] *on Africa* [since 1961]. Stanford, Cal.: Stanford University Press, 1961–.

Howard, Michael, ed. *Soldiers and Governments*. Bloomington, Ind.: Indiana University Press, 1959.

Huck, Eugene R., and Moseley, Edward H., eds. *Militarists, Merchants and Missionaries: United States Expansion in Middle America*. University, Ala.: University of Alabama Press, 1970.

Hunter, Guy. *South-east Asia: Race, Culture and Nation*. New York: Oxford University Press, 1966.

Huntington, Samuel P., ed. *Changing Patterns of Military Politics*. New York: Free Press of Glencoe, 1962.

―――. *Political Order in Changing Societies*. New Haven: Yale University Press, 1969.

―――. *The Soldier and the State*. Cambridge, Mass.: Harvard University Press, 1957.

Iranian Embassy. *Military Civic Action Program in Iran*. Facts about Iran, No. 8. Washington, D.C.: Iranian Embassy, 1966.

Jacobs, Paul. *Prelude to Riot: A View of Urban America from the Bottom*. New York: Random House, 1968.

James, Alan. *The Politics of Peacekeeping: Studies in International Security*. New York: Praeger, 1969.

Janeway, Eliot. *The Economics of Crisis: War, Politics, and the Dollar*. New York: Weybright and Talley, 1968.

Janos, A. "Unconventional Warfare: A Framework and Analysis." *World Politics* 15 (July 1963).

Janowitz, Morris, ed. *Armed Forces and Society*. Sage Research Progress Series, No. 1. Beverly Hills, Cal.: Sage, 1971.

―――. *The Military in the Political Development of New Nations: An Essay in Comparative Analysis*. Chicago: University of Chicago Press, 1964.

―――. *The Professional Soldier*. Glencoe, Ill.: Free Press, 1960.

―――, ed. *The New Military: Changing Patterns of Organization*. New York: Russell Sage Foundation, 1964.

Johnson, C. *Revolution and the Social System*. Stanford, Cal.: Hoover Institution, 1964.

Johnson, John J., ed. *The Role of the Military in Underdeveloped Countries*. Princeton: Princeton University Press, 1962.

Johnstone, Major John Harold. *An Annotated Bibliography of the United States Marine Corps in Guerrilla, Anti-Guerrilla, and Small War Actions*. Washington, D.C.: USMC Historical Branch, 1961.

July, Robert W. *A History of the African People*. New York: Scribners, 1970.

Kahn, Herman A. *War Termination Issues and Concepts: Final Report*. Croton-on-Hudson, N.Y.: Hudson Institute, 1968.

Katenbrink, Irving G., Jr. "Military Service and Occupation Mobility." Working Paper No. 88. Chicago: Center for Social Organizational Studies, 1967.

Kemp, Vernon A. M. *Scarlet and Stetson: The Royal North-west Mounted Police on the Prairies*. Toronto: University of Toronto Press, 1964.

King, Jere Clemens. *Generals and Politicians*. Berkeley: University of California Press, 1951.

Kitchen, Martin. *The German Officer Corps, 1890–1914*. London: Oxford University Press, 1968.

Kling, M. "Cuba: A Case Study." *Annals of the American Academy of Political and Social Science* 341 (May 1962).

Klingon, C. "The Third Generation of Guerrilla Warfare." *Asian Survey* 8 (June 1968).

Knorr, Klaus. *Military Power and Potential*. Lexington, Mass.: D. C. Heath, 1970.

————. "Unconventional Warfare." *Annals of the American Academy of Political and Social Science* 341 (May 1962).

Koh, Sung Jae. *Stages of Industrial Development in Asia: A Comparative History of the Cotton Industry in Japan, India, China and Korea*. Philadelphia: University of Pennsylvania Press, 1966.

Korea, Republic of. *Military Revolution in Korea*. Seoul: Secretariat, Supreme Council for National Reconstruction, 1961.

Krüger, D. W. *The Age of the Generals: A Short Political History of the Union of South Africa, 1910–1948*. Johannesburg: Dagbreek Book Store, 1958.

Kühnrich, Heinz. *De Partisanen Krieg in Europe, 1939–1945*. Berlin: Dietz, 1965.

Lane, F. C. "Economic Consequences of Violence." *Journal of Economic History* 18 (December 1958): 401–17.

Lang, Kurt, "Sociology of the Military: A Selected and Annotated Bibliography." Mimeographed paper. Chicago: Inter-University Seminar on Armed Forces and Society, 1969.

Laqueur, W. "Revolution." *International Encyclopedia of Social Sciences* (New York: Macmillan, 1968), 13:501–07.

Lasswell, H. "A Sketch of Three Lines of Enquiry into Civil Disturbances." Paper to Princeton Conference on Internal War, 1961.

Lee, J. M. *African Armies and Civil Order*. Institute for Strategic Studies. Studies in International Security, No. 13. London: Chatto and Windus, 1969.

Legault, Albert. *Peace-Keeping Operations Bibliography*. Paris: International Information Center on Peace-Keeping Operations, 1967.

————. *Research on Peace-Keeping Operations: Current Status and Future Needs*. Monograph No. 5. Paris: International Information Center on Peace-Keeping Operations, 1967.

Leiden, C., and Schnitt, K., eds. *The Politics of Violence: Revolution in the Modern World*. Englewood Cliffs, N.J.: Prentice-Hall, 1968.

Leites, Nathan, and Wolfe, Charles, Jr. *Rebellion and Authority: An Analytic Essay on Insurgent Conflicts*. Chicago: Markham, 1970.

Levin, N. Gordon, Jr. *Woodrow Wilson and World Politics: America's Response to War and Revolution*. New York: Oxford University Press, 1968.

Levine, Isaac Don. *Intervention: The Causes and Consequences of the Czechoslovakian Invasion*. New York: McKay, 1970.

LeVine, Victor T. *Political Leadership in Africa*. Stanford, Cal.: Hoover Institution and Stanford University Press, 1969.

Little, Roger W. *Handbook of Military Institutions*. Beverly Hills, Cal.: Sage, 1970.

Lloyd, Frank Erie. *Rhodesian Patrol*. Ilfracombe: A. H. Stockwell, 1965. [British South African Police.]

Lovell, John P. "The Study of the Military in Developing Nations: Devising Meaningful and Manageable Research Strategies." Bloomington: Indiana University, Department of Government, and Carnegie Seminar on Political and Administrative Development, 1966.

Luttwak, Edward. *Coup d'Etat: A Practical Handbook*. London: Allen Lane, Penguin Press, 1968.

McCall, Daniel F. *Africa in Time Perspective: A Discussion of Historical Reconstruction from Unwritten Sources*. New York: Oxford University Press, 1969.

McGuire, Martin C. *Secrecy and the Arms Race: A Theory of the Accumulation of Strategic Weapons and How Secrecy Affects It*. Cambridge, Mass.: Harvard University Press, 1965.

MacMillan, W. M. *The Road to Self-Rule*. London: Faber, 1959.

McWilliams, Cary, ed. *Garrisons and Government: Politics and the Military in New States*. San Francisco: Chandler, 1967.

Mainland, Lieutenant-Commander Edward A. "Political Instability in Developing Areas." *Naval War College Review*, February 1969, 81–89.

Mair, Lucy. *New Nations*. Chicago: University of Chicago Press, 1963.

Malik, Charles H. *Developing Leadership in New Countries*. London: British Institute of Management, 1965.

Manera, E. "La estrategia revolucionaria." *Revista de Política Internacional* 59 (Jan.–Feb. 1962).

Mason, Herbert Molloy, Jr. *The Great Pursuit*. New York: Random House, 1970.

Masotti, L. H., and Bowen, D. R., eds. *Riots and Rebellion: Civil Violence in the Urban Community*. Beverly Hills, Cal.: Sage, 1968.

Marks, Shula. *Reluctant Rebellion: An Assessment of the 1906–08 Disturbances in Natal*. New York: Oxford University Press, 1970.

Marshall, C. B. "Unconventional Warfare as a Concern for American Foreign Policy." *Annals of the American Academy of Political and Social Science* 341 (May 1962).

Meisel, James H. *Counterrevolution: How Revolutions Die*. New York: Atherton Press, 1966.

Menard, Orville D. *The Army and the Fifth Republic*. Lincoln: University of Nebraska Press, 1967.

Menges, C. C. *Military Aspects of International Relations in the Developing Areas*. Paper 3580. Santa Monica, Cal.: Rand Corp., 1967.

Meyers, Samuel M., and Bradbury, William Chapman. *Mass Behavior in Battle and Captivity: The Communist Soldier in the Korean War*. Edited by Samuel Meyers and Albert D. Biderman. Chicago: University of Chicago Press, 1968.

Miller, J. D. B. *The Politics of the Third World*. London: Oxford University Press, 1966.

Mitchell, E. J. *Relating Rebellion to Environment: An Econometric Approach.* Rand Paper 3726. Santa Monica, Cal.: Rand Corp., 1967.

Mockler, Anthony. *The Mercenaries.* New York: Macmillan, 1970.

Momboisse, R. M. *Riots, Revolts and Insurrections.* Springfield, Ill.: C. C. Thomas, 1967.

Moore, Clark D., and Dunbar, Ann. *Africa Yesterday and Today.* New York: Praeger, 1969.

Mosca, Gaetano. *The Ruling Class.* Translated by Hannah D. Kahn. New York: McGraw-Hill, 1939.

Moskos, Charles C., Jr. *The American Enlisted Man: The Rank and File in Today's Military.* New York: Russell Sage Foundation, 1970.

Mountjoy, Alan B. *Industrialization and Underdeveloped Countries.* 2nd rev. ed. London: Hutchinson University Library, 1966.

Neumann, S. "The International Civil War." *World Politics* 1 (1948).

Ney, Virgil. "Bibliography on Guerrilla Warfare." *Military Affairs,* Fall 1960, 146–49.

Nye, Joseph S., Jr. *Pan-Africanism and East African Integration.* Cambridge, Mass.: Harvard University Press, 1965.

O'Ballance, Edgar. *The Algerian Insurrection, 1954–62.* London: Faber, 1967.

———. *The War in the Yemen* [1962–67]. Hamden, Conn.: Archon, 1971.

O'Neill, Robert J. *General Giap: Politician and Strategist.* New York: Praeger, 1970.

O'Zbudum, E. *The Role of the Military in Recent Turkish Politics.* Occasional Papers in International Affairs, No. 14. Cambridge, Mass.: Harvard University Center for International Affairs, 1966.

Paret, Peter. *French Revolutionary Warfare from Indo-China to Algeria: The Analysis of a Political and Military Doctrine.* New York: Praeger, and Center of International Studies, Princeton University, 1964.

———. *Internal War and Pacification: The Vendee, 1793–6.* Princeton: Princeton University Press, 1961.

Pauker, G. J. *The Role of the Military in Indonesia.* Santa Monica, Cal.: Rand Corp., 1960.

Paxton, Robert O. *Parades and Politics at Vichy: The French Officer Corps under Marshal Pétain.* Princeton: Princeton University Press, 1966.

Pelloux, R. "Remarques sur le mot et l'idée de revolution." *Revue Française de Science Politique* 2 (Jan.–Mar. 1952).

Pomeroy, William J., ed. *Guerrilla Warfare and Marxism.* London: Lawrence and Wishart, 1968.

Pruitt, Dean G., and Snyder, Richard C., eds. *Theory and Research on the Causes of War.* Englewood Cliffs, N.J.: Prentice-Hall, 1969.

Pye, Lucien W., ed. *Political Culture and Political Development.* Princeton: Princeton University Press, 1965.

———. *Politics, Personality and Nation Building: Burma's Search for Identity.* New Haven: Yale University Press, 1962.

Ralston, David B., ed. *Soldiers and States: Civil-Military Relations in Modern Europe.* Boston: D.C. Heath, 1966.

Rayner, William. *The Tribe and Its Successors: An Account of African Traditional Life and European Settlement in Southern Rhodesia.* London: Faber, 1962.

Rikhye, Major-General Indar Jit. "United Nations Peacekeeping Forces." *Journal of the United Service Institution of India* 94 (Oct./Dec. 1964): 349–57.

———. *United Nations Peace-keeping Operations: Higher Conduct.* Monograph No. 1. Paris: International Information Center on Peace-keeping Operations, 1967.

Robinson, E. A. G., ed. *Economic Consequences of the Size of Nations.* New York: St. Martin's Press, 1960.

Rosenau, J. *Internal Aspects of Civil Strife.* Princeton: Princeton University Press, 1964.

Rotberg, Robert I. *The Rise of Nationalism in Central Africa: The Making of Malawi and Zambia, 1873–1964.* Cambridge, Mass.: Harvard University Press, 1965.

Rothvelt, Hans. *The German Opposition to Hitler.* Hinsdale, Ill.: Regnery, 1948.

Royal Institute of International Affairs. *Ballot Box and Bayonets: People and Government in Emergent Asian Countries.* London: 1964.

Sanger, Richard H. *Summary of Major Political Violence, 1945–1966.* Fort Belvoir, Va.: Combat Research Command, 1967.

Schapera, I. *Government and Politics in Tribal Societies.* London: Watts, 1956.

Scott, Andrew McKay. *Informal Penetration: The Revolution in Statecraft.* New York: Random House, 1965.

———. *Insurgency.* Chapel Hill: University of North Carolina Press, 1971.

Singh, Baljit, and Ko-Wang Mei. "Guerrilla Warfare." *Indian Quarterly,* July–Sept. 1965, 285–310.

Singh, N. *The Theory of Force and Organization of Defence in Indian Constitutional History, from Earliest Times to 1947.* London: Asia Publishing House, 1969.

Singham, A. W. *The Hero and the Crowd in a Colonial Polity.* New Haven: Yale University Press, 1968.

Sithole, Ndabaningi. *African Nationalism.* 2nd ed. New York: Oxford University Press, 1968.

Skern, Lieutenant-Colonel L. M. K. *Military Staffing at UN Headquarters for Peace-Keeping Operations: A Proposal.* Monograph C. Paris: International Information Center on Peace-keeping Operations, 1967.

Slonaker, John. *The U. S. Army and Domestic Disturbances.* Special Bibliography No. 1. Carlisle Barracks, Pa.: U.S. Army Historical Research Collection, 1970.

Smith, Cecil N. "The Role of Agriculture in Developing Countries." *Naval War College Review*, February 1969, 90–112.

Smith, Donald E., ed. *South Asian Politics and Religion.* Princeton: Princeton University Press, 1966.

Solana, F. "Introduction á los cambios politicos." *Boletin Information del Seminario Derech Politico* 24 (March 1958).

Stanger, Roland J., ed. *Essays on Intervention.* Columbus: Ohio State University Press, 1964.

Stein, George H. *The Waffen SS.: Hitler's Elite Guard at War, 1939–1945.* Ithaca, N. Y.: Cornell University Press, 1966.

Stone, L. "Theories of Revolution." *World Politics* 18 (October 1965).

Tanter, R. "Dimensions of Conflict Behaviour within Nations, 1955–60: Turmoil and Internal War." *Peace Research Society Papers* 3 (1964).

————, and Midlansky, M. "A Theory of Revolution." *Journal of Conflict Resolution* 11, No. 3 (1967).

Thompson, Sir Robert. *Revolutionary War in World Strategy, 1945–1969.* New York: Taplinger, 1970.

Thomson, David. *Patterns of Peacemaking.* London: K. Paul, Trench, Trubner, 1945.

Tilly, C., and Rule, J. *Measuring Political Upheaval.* Research Monograph No. 19. Princeton: Center of International Studies, Princeton University, 1965.

Tinker, Hugh. *Experiment with Freedom: India and Pakistan, 1947.* New York: Oxford University Press, 1969.

Torrey, Gordon H. *Syrian Politics and the Military, 1945–1958.* Columbus: Ohio State University Press, [1964].

Tucker, Robert C. *The Marxian Revolutionary Idea: Essays on Marxist Thought and Its Impact on Radical Movements.* New York: W. W. Norton, 1969.

Tushnet, L. *To Die with Honor: The Uprising of the Jews in the Warsaw Ghetto.* New York: Citadel Press, 1965.

United States, Department of the Army. *Undergrounds in Insurgent, Revolutionary, and Resistance Warfare.* [Revised to *Human Factors Considerations of Undergrounds in Insurgencies.*] Pamphlet No. 550–104. 1966.

United States, Department of Defense, Industrial College of the Armed Forces. *The Military's Role in Cold War Education,* by Colonel Willis L. Helmantoler. Thesis 68. Washington, D.C.: ICAF, 1963.

United States, Department of State. *Foreign Relations of the United States.* Washington, D.C.: G.P.O., 1911–49.

————, Bureau of Research and Intelligence. *The Role of the Military in Less Developed Countries, January 1958–February 1964: A Selected Bibliography.* External Research Paper 147. Washington, D.C., 1964.

Vagts, Alfred. *A History of Militarism: Civilian and Military.* New York: W. W. Norton, 1937; rev. ed., 1959.

Van Doorn, J., ed. *Military Profession and Military Regimes: Commitments and Conflicts.* The Hague: Mouton, 1969.

Vatikiotis, P. J. *The Egyptian Army in Politics: Pattern for New Nations?* Bloomington: Indiana University Press, 1961.

———. *Politics and the Military in Jordan: A Study of the Arab Legion, 1921–1957.* New York: Praeger, 1967.

Waite, William. *The Vanguard of Nazism: The Free Corps Movement in Postwar Germany, 1918–1923.* New York: W. W. Norton, [c. 1952]; rev. ed., 1962.

Walker, Robert M. "The Military Mind." *Military Review,* August 1969, 55–62.

Walterhouse, H. F. *A Time to Rebuild: Military Civic Action—A Medium for Economic Development and Social Reform.* Columbia: University of South Carolina Press, 1964.

Waltz, Kenneth M. *Foreign Policy and Democratic Politics.* Boston: Little, Brown, 1967.

Weiner, Myron. *Party Building in a New Nation: The Indian National Congress.* Chicago: University of Chicago Press, 1967.

Wesler, Eugene Joseph. *The European Right: A Historical Profile.* Berkeley: University of California Press, 1965.

Wheeler-Bennett, John. *Nemesis of Power: The German Army in Politics, 1918–1945.* London: Macmillan, 1954.

White, W. *White's Political Dictionary.* New York: World Publishing Co., 1947.

Williams, Roger L. *The French Revolution of 1870–1871.* Scranton, Pa.: W. W. Norton, 1969.

Wilson, Godfrey, and Wilson, Monica. *The Analysis of Social Change Based on Observations in Central Africa.* London: Cambridge University Press, 1968.

Wolf, C. *Controlling Small Wars.* Paper 3994. Santa Monica, Cal.: Rand Corp., 1968.

Wolfe, J. N., and Erickson, John. *The Armed Forces and Society: Alienation, Management and Integration.* Edinburgh: Edinburgh University Press, 1970.

Wright, Quincy. *A Study of War.* Rev. ed. Chicago: University of Chicago Press, 1965; original multi-volume ed., 1942.

Yoder, D. "Current Definitions of Revolution." *American Journal of Sociology* 32 (1926).

Zawodny, J. "Internal Warfare." *International Encyclopedia of Social Sciences* (New York: Macmillan, 1968), vol. 7.

Zolberg, Aristide R. "Military Rule and Political Development in Tropical Africa." Mimeographed paper. Chicago: Inter-University Seminar on Armed Forces and Society, 1967.

Specialized Sources

AMERICAN REVOLUTION AND CIVIL WAR

Andreano, Ralph, ed. *The Economic Impact of the American Civil War.* Cambridge, Mass.: Schenkman, 1962.

Arendt, Hannah. *On Revolution.* New York: Viking Press, 1963.

Boorstin, Daniel J. *The Genius of American Politics.* Chicago: University of Chicago Press, 1953.

Britton, Wiley. *The Civil War on the Border.* 2 vols. New York: G. P. Putnam's Sons, 1890–99.

————. *Memoirs of Rebellion on the Border.* Chicago, 1882.

Coates, Charles H., and Pellegrin, Roland J. *Military Sociology: A Study of American Military Institutions and Military Life.* University Park, Md.: Social Science Press, 1965.

Connelly, William Elsey. *Life of Quantrill: Quantrill and the Border Wars.* Cedar Rapids, Iowa: Torch Press, 1910.

De Tocqueville, Alexis. *Democracy in America.* Translated by Henry Reeve; revised by Francis Bowen; edited by Phillips Bradley. New York: Knopf, 1945.

Donald, David, ed. *Why the North Won the Civil War.* New York: Collier, 1962.

Dunning, William A. *Reconstruction, Political and Economic.* New York: Harper and Brothers, 1907.

Franklin, John Hope. *The Militant South, 1800–1960.* Rev. ed. Cambridge, Mass.: Harvard University Press, 1969.

Horan, James D. *Confederate Agent: A Discovery in History.* New York: Crown Publishers, 1954.

Jensen, Merrill. "The American People and the American Revolution." *Journal of American History* 57 (June 1970): 5–35.

Johnson, Adam R. *The Partisan Rangers of the Confederate States Army.* Louisville, Ky.: G. G. Fetter Co., 1904.

Ketton-Cremer, R. W. *Norfolk in the Civil War: A Portrait of a Society in Conflict.* Hamden, Conn.: Archon, 1969.

Klement, Frank L. *The Limits of Dissent.* Lexington: University Press of Kentucky, 1970.

Lipset, Seymour Martin. *The First New Nation: The United States in Historical and Comparative Perspective.* New York: Basic Books, 1963; Doubleday Anchor, 1967.

McCague, James. *The Second Rebellion: The New York City Draft Riots of 1863.* New York: Dial, 1968.

Morison, Samuel Eliot; Merck, Frederick; and Freidel, Frank. *Dissent in Three American Wars.* Cambridge, Mass.: Harvard University Press, 1970.

Morris, Richard B. *The Emerging Nations and the American Revolution.* New York: Harper, 1970.

Nichols, Roy F. *American Leviathan*. New York: Harper and Row, 1966; reprint of *Blue Print for Leviathan: American Style* (New York: Atheneum, 1963).

Pike, James S. *The Prostrate State*. New York, 1874.

Randall, James Garfield, and Donald, David. *The Civil War and Reconstruction*. Lexington, Mass.: Heath, 1969

Rawlyk, G. A. *Revolution Rejected, 1775–76*. Scarborough, Ont.: Prentice-Hall of Canada, 1968.

Sefton, J. E. *The United States Army and Reconstruction, 1865–77*. Baton Rouge, La.: Louisiana State University Press, 1967.

Shugg, Roger W. *Origins of Class Struggle in Louisiana*. University, La.: Louisiana State University Press, 1939; rev. ed., 1970.

Steiner, P. E. *Disease in the Civil War: Natural Biological Warfare in 1861–1865*. Springfield, Ill.: C. C. Thomas, 1968.

United States Congress, House of Representatives. *Report of the Joint Committee to Inquire into the Condition of Affairs in the Late Insurrectionary States*. House Report 22, 42nd Congress, 2nd session, serial numbers 1529–1541. 13 vols. Washington, D.C., 1872.

United States, War Department. *The War of the Rebellion: A Compilation of the Official Records of the Union and Confederate Armies*. 70 vols. Washington, D.C.: G.P.O., 1880–1901.

Van Tyne, Claude H. *Causes of the War of Independence*. New York: 1922.

———. *War of Independence: American Phase*. New York, 1929.

Wilson, Edmund. *Patriotic Gore: Studies in the Literature of the American Civil War*. New York: Oxford University Press, 1969.

ARMS SALES

Be'eri, Eliezer. *Army Officers in Arab Politics and Society*. New York: Praeger, 1970.

Bell, M. J. V. *Military Assistance to Independent African States*. Adelphi Paper No. 15. London: Institute for Strategic Studies, 1964.

Englemann, B. *The Weapons Merchants: An Account of the Illegal Traffic in Arms by Individuals and Governments*. Translated from the German. London: Elek, 1968.

Frank, L. T. *The Arms Trade in International Relations*. New York: Praeger, 1969.

Great Britain, Parliament, House of Commons, Select Committee on Estimates. *Sale of Military Equipment Abroad*. Second Report. London: H.M.S.O., 1958.

Henderson, K. "The Sudan Today." *African Affairs* 64, No. 256 (July 1965).

Hovey, Harold A. *United States Military Assistance*. New York: Praeger, 1965.

Hurewitz, Jacob. *Middle East Politics: The Military Dimension*. London: Pall Mall, 1969.

Institute for Strategic Studies. *The Military Balance.* London, 1959.
Joshua, Wynfred, and Gilbert, Stephen P. *Arms for the Third World: Soviet Military Aid Diplomacy.* Baltimore: Johns Hopkins Press, 1969.
Kemp, G. "Arms Traffic and Third World Conflicts." *International Conciliation* 577 (March 1970).
Kyle, K. "The Southern Problem in the Sudan." *World Today,* December 1966.
McArdle, C. *The Role of Military Assistance in the Problem of Arms Control.* ACDA Report. Cambridge, Mass.: M.I.T. Press, 1964.
McKay, Vernon. *African Diplomacy.* London: Pall Mall, 1966.
Nagmani, I. T. "The Kurdish Drive for Self-Determination." *Middle East Journal,* Summer 1966.
Ra'anan, U. *The USSR Arms the Third World.* Cambridge, Mass.: M.I.T. Press, 1969.
Richardson, Lewis Fry. *Arms and Insecurity: A Mathematical Study of the Causes and Origins of War.* Pittsburgh: Boxwood Press, 1960.
————. *The Statistics of Deadly Quarrels.* Pittsburgh: Boxwood Press, 1960.
Russett, Bruce. *Trends in World Politics.* New York: Macmillan, 1968.
Stockholm International Peace Research Institute. *Yearbook of World Armaments and Disarmament, 1968–9.* London: Duckworth, 1970.
Sutton, G., and Kemp, G. *Arms to Developing Countries, 1945–65.* Adelphi Paper No. 28. London: Institute for Strategic Studies, 1966.
Thayer, George. *The War Business.* London: Wiedenfeld and Nicolson, 1966.
Tinker, H. *The Union of Burma.* London: Oxford University Press, 1961.
Trager, Frank N. *Burma.* London: Pall Mall, 1966.
United States Arms Control and Disarmament Agency. *The Control of Local Conflict.* ACDA/WEC-98. Washington, D.C.: G.P.O., 1967.
Wood, D. *The Armed Forces of African States.* Adelphi Paper No. 27. London: Institute for Strategic Studies, 1966.
————. *The Middle East and the Arab World.* Adelphi Paper No. 30. London: Institute for Strategic Studies, 1965.

CHINA

Boorman, Howard L. *Biographical Dictionary of Republican China.* 4 vols. New York: Columbia University Press, 1967–71.
Borg, Dorothy. *The United States and the Far Eastern Crisis of 1933–1938: From the Manchurian Incident through the Initial Stage of the Undeclared Sino-Japanese War.* Cambridge, Mass.: Harvard University Press, 1964.
Chang, Kia-ngau. *The Inflationary Spiral: The Experience in 1939–1950.* Cambridge, Mass.: Technology Press, 1958.
Chang, Kuo-t'ao. "O-te hui-i" [Memoir of Chang Kuo-t'ao]. *Ming-pao yueh-k'an* [Ming-pao Monthly.] Hong Kong: King-pao Yu-hsien Kung-szu, 1966–69.

Ch'en, Jerome. *Mao and the Chinese Revolution.* New York: Oxford University Press, 1965.

Chi, Hsi-hseng. *The Chinese Warlord System, 1916–1928.* Center for Research in Social Systems, American University; distributed by Clearinghouse for Federal Scientific and Technical Information, Springfield, Va., 1969.

Chiang, Siang-tseh. *The Nien Rebellion.* Seattle: University of Washington Press, 1954.

Ch'ien Tuan-sheng. *The Government and Politics of China.* Cambridge, Mass.: Harvard University Press, 1967.

Chow Tse-tsung. *The May Fourth Movement: Intellectual Revolution in Modern China.* Cambridge, Mass.: Harvard University Press, 1960.

Griffith, Samuel B. *The Chinese People's Liberation Army.* New York: McGraw-Hill, 1967.

Harrison, J. P. *The Communists and Chinese Peasant Rebellions: A Study in the Rewriting of Chinese History.* London: Gollancz, 1970.

Hsü, Immanuel C. Y. *The Rise of Modern China.* New York: Oxford University Press, 1970.

Hucker, Charles O. *China: A Critical Bibliography.* Tuscon: University of Arizona Press, 1962.

Hu Sheng. *Imperialism and Chinese Politics, 1840–1925.* Peking: Foreign Languages Press, 1955.

Iriye, Akira. *After Imperialism: The Search for a New Order in the Far East, 1921–1931.* Cambridge, Mass.: Harvard University Press, 1965.

Israel, John. *Student Nationalism in China, 1927–1937.* Stanford, Cal.: Stanford University Press, 1966.

Johnson, Chalmers W. *Peasant Nationalism and Communist Power.* Stanford, Cal.: Stanford University Press, 1962.

Koo, V. K. Wellington. *Memoranda Presented to the Lytton Commission.* 2 vols. New York: Chinese Cultural Society, 1932–33.

Liu, F. F. *A Military History of Modern China, 1924–1949.* Princeton: Princeton University Press, 1956.

Liu Ju-ming. *Liu Ju-ming hui-i lu* [Memoir of Liu Ju-ming]. Taipei: Chuan-Chi Wen-hsüeh Press, 1966.

Lo Chia-lun, comp. *Ko-Ming wen-hsien* [Documents on the Nationalist Revolution]. 40 vols. Taipei: Chung-kuo kuo-min-tang Chung-yang Wei-yüan-hui, Tang-shih Shih-liao Pien-chuan Wei-yüan-hui, 1958–67.

Maki, John M., ed. *Selected Documents: Far Eastern International Relations, 1689–1951.* Seattle: University of Washington Press, 1957.

Mao Tse-tung. *Selected Works of Mao Tse-tung.* 4 vols. Peking: Foreign Languages Press, 1965.

Muramatsu, Yuji. "Some Themes in Chinese Rebel Ideologies." In *The Confucian Persuasion,* ed. A. F. Wright (Stanford, Cal.: Stanford University Press, 1960), 241–67.

O'Ballance, Edgar. *The Red Army of China*. London: Faber, 1962.

Ogata, Sadako N. *Defiance in Manchuria: The Making of Japanese Foreign Policy, 1931–1932*. Berkeley: University of California Press, 1964.

Pye, Lucian W. *The Spirit of Chinese Politics: A Psychocultural Study of Authority Crises in Political Development*. Cambridge, Mass.: M.I.T. Press, 1968.

Schurmann, Franz. *Ideology and Organization in Communist China*. Berkeley: University of California Press, 1966.

Sheridan, James E. *Chinese Warlord: The Career of Feng Yü-hsiang*. Stanford, Cal.: Stanford University Press, 1966.

Shidehara, Kijūrō. *Gaikō gojunen* [Fifty Years of Diplomacy]. Tokyo: Yomiuri Shimbunsha, 1951.

Shigemitsu, Mamoru. *Shōwa no dōran* [The Shōwa Upheavals]. 2 vols. Tokyo: Chuō Kōronsha, 1952.

Tung Hsien-kuang. *Chiang Tsung-t'ung chuan* [A Biography of President Chiang Kai-shek]. Taipei: Chung-hua Wen-hua Ch'u-pan Shih-yeh Wei-yüan Hui, 1952.

United States, Department of State. *United States Relations with China, with Special Reference to the Period 1944–1949*. Washington, D.C.: G.P.O., 1966.

Waley, Arthur. *The Opium War through Chinese Eyes*. Stanford, Cal.: Stanford University Press, 1958.

Whiting, Allen S. *Soviet Russia in China, 1917–1924*. Stanford, Cal.: Stanford University Press, 1968.

Willoughby, Westel W. *China at the Conference*. Baltimore: Johns Hopkins Press, 1922.

———. *The Sino-Japanese Controversy and the League of Nations*. Baltimore: Johns Hopkins Press, 1935.

Young, Arthur N. *China and the Helping Hands, 1937–1945*. Cambridge, Mass.: Harvard University Press, 1963.

———. *China's Wartime Finance and Inflation, 1937–1945*. Cambridge, Mass.: Harvard University Press, 1965.

THE CONGO

Clarke, S. J. G. *The Congo Mercenary: A History and Analysis*. Johannesburg: South African Institute of International Affairs, 1968.

Cruise O'Brien, Conor. *To Katanga and Back*. New York: Simon and Schuster, 1962.

Gerard-Libois, Jules. *Katanga Secession*. Madison: University of Wisconsin Press, 1966.

Gordon, King. *The United Nations in the Congo: A Quest for Peace*. New York: Carnegie Endowment for International Peace, 1962.

Hoare, Mike. *Congo Mercenary*. London: Robert Hale, 1967.

Hoffman, Stanley. "Erewhon or Lilliput? A Critical View of the Problem." *International Organization* 17 (Spring 1963): 404–24.

Hoskyns, Catherine. *The Congo since Independence: January 1960–December 1961*. London: Chatham House, Oxford University Press, 1965.

Kitchen, Helen, ed. *Footnotes to the Congo Story*. New York: Walker and Co., 1967.

Lefever, Ernest W. *Crisis in the Congo: A U.N. Force in Action*. Washington, D.C.: Brookings Institution, 1965.

————. "The Limits of U.N. Intervention in the Third World." *Review of Politics* 30, No. 1 (January 1968): 3–18.

————. *Spear and Scepter: Army, Police, and Politics in Tropical Africa*. Washington, D.C.: Brookings Institution, 1970.

————. "The U.N. as a Foreign Policy Instrument: The Congo Crisis." In *Foreign Policy in the Sixties: The Issues and Instruments*, ed. Roger Hilsman and Robert C. Good (Baltimore: Johns Hopkins Press, 1965), 141–57.

————. *Uncertain Mandate: Politics of the U.N. Congo Operation*. Baltimore: Johns Hopkins Press, 1967.

Lemarchand, René. *Political Awakening in the Congo*. Berkeley: University of California Press, 1964.

Merriam, Alan P. *Congo: Background of Conflict*. Evanston, Ill.: Northwestern University Press, 1961.

Reed, David. *111 Days in Stanleyville*. New York: Harper and Row, 1965.

Russell, Ruth B. *United Nations Experience with Military Forces: Political and Legal Aspects*. Washington, D.C.: Brookings Institution, 1964.

Tondel, Lyman M., Jr., ed. *The Legal Aspects of the United Nations Action in the Congo*. Dobbs Ferry, N.Y.: Oceana Publications, 1963.

Young, Crawford. "Domestic Violence in Africa: The Congo." In Charles W. Anderson, Fred R. von der Mehden, and Crawford Young, *Issues of Political Development* (Englewood Cliffs, N.J.: Prentice-Hall, 1967), 120–42.

————. *Politics in the Congo: Decolonization and Independence*. Princeton: Princeton University Press, 1965.

GREECE

Chandler, Geoffrey. *The Divided Land: An Anglo-Greek Tragedy*. London: Macmillan, 1951.

Kousoulas, D. George. *Revolution and Defeat: The Story of the Greek Communist Party*. London: Oxford University Press, 1965.

O'Ballance, Edgar. *The Greek Civil War, 1944–1949*. New York: Praeger, 1966.

Woodhouse, C. M. *The Apple of Discord*. London: Hutchinson, 1951.

IRELAND

Bell, J. Bowyer. *The Secret Army: A History of the IRA, 1916–1970*. New York: Pantheon, 1970.

Caulfield, Max. *The Easter Rebellion*. New York: Holt, Rinehart, Winston, 1963.

Fitzgibbon, Constantine. *Out of the Lion's Paw: Ireland Wins Her Freedom*. London: Macdonald, 1969.

Hastings, Max. *Barricades in Belfast: The Fight for Civil Rights in Northern Ireland*. New York: Taplinger, 1970.

Holt, Edgar. *Protest in Arms*. London: Putnam, 1960.

King, C. *The Orange and the Green*. London: Macdonald, 1965.

Macardle, Dorothy. *The Irish Republic*. Dublin: Irish Press, 1951.

MacManus, Francis, ed. *Years of the Great Test, 1921–1939*. Cork: Mercier Press, 1967.

Neeson, Eoin. *The Civil War in Ireland, 1921–1923*. Cork: Mercier Press, 1967.

O'Donoghue, Florence. *No Other Law*. Dublin: Irish Press, 1954.

Younger, Carlton. *Ireland's Civil War*. New York: Taplinger, 1969.

LATIN AMERICA

Aaron, Harold R. "Guerrilla War in Cuba." *Military Review*, May 1965, 40–46.

Alexander, Robert J. *The Bolivian National Revolution*. New Brunswick, N.J.: Rutgers University Press, 1958.

————. *Prophets of the Revolution: Profiles of Latin American Leaders*. New York: Macmillan, 1962.

Andrelski, Stanislav. *Parasitism and Subversion: The Case of Latin America*. London: Weidenfeld and Nicolson, 1966.

Atkin, Ronald. *Revolution: Mexico, 1910–1920*. New York: John Day, 1970.

Bailey, Helen Miller, and Nasatir, Abraham P. *Latin-America: The Development of Its Civilization*. Englewood Cliffs, N.J.: Prentice-Hall, 1968.

Barber, Willard F., and Ronning, C. Neale. *Internal Security and Military Power: Counterinsurgency and Civic Action in Latin America*. Columbus: Ohio State University Press, 1966.

Blasier, Cole. "Studies of Social Revolution: Origins in Mexico, Bolivia, and Cuba." *Latin American Research Review*, Summer 1967, 28–64.

Brill, W. H. *Military Intervention in Bolivia*. Political Studies Series, No. 3. Washington, D.C.: Institute for the Comparative Study of Political Systems, 1967.

Calvert, Peter. *The Mexican Revolution, 1910–1914: The Diplomacy of Anglo-American Conflict*. Cambridge: Cambridge University Press, 1969.

Castro, Fidel. *History Will Absolve Me: The Moncada Trial Defence Speech, Santiago de Cuba, October 16, 1953.* London: Cape, 1969.

Cumberland, Charles. *The Mexican Revolution: Genesis under Madero.* Austin: University of Texas Press, 1952.

Davis, Harold E. *History of Latin America.* New York: Ronald Press, 1968.

Dix, Robert H. *Colombia: The Political Dimensions of Change.* New Haven: Yale University Press, 1967.

Draper, Theodore. *Castro's Revolution: Myths and Realities.* New York: Praeger, 1962.

Einaudi, Luigi R. *The Peruvian Military: A Summary Political Analysis.* Santa Monica, Cal.: Rand Corp., 1969.

————, and Goldhamer, Herbert. "An Annotated Bibliography of Latin American Military Journals." *Latin American Research Review*, Spring 1967, 95–122.

Fluharty, Vernon Lee. *Dance of the Millions: Military Rule and the Social Revolution in Colombia, 1930–1956.* Pittsburgh: University of Pittsburgh Press, 1957; reissued 1966.

Germani, Gino, and Silvert, Kalman. "Politics, Social Structure and Military Intervention in Latin America." *European Journal of Sociology* 2 (1961): 62–81.

Gilmore, Robert L. *Caudillism and Militarism in Venezuela, 1810–1910.* Athens, Ohio: Ohio University Press, 1964.

Goldwert, M. *The Constabulary in the Dominican Republic and Nicaragua: Progeny and Legacy of United States Intervention.* Gainesville: University of Florida Press, 1962.

Gonzalez Prada, Manuel. *Anarquia.* Santiago de Chile: Ediciones Ercilla, 1940. [A collection of earlier publications.]

Guevara, Ernesto Che. *Che Guevara on Guerrilla Warfare.* New York: Praeger, 1961.

Hahner, J. E. *Civil-Military Relations in Brazil, 1889–1898.* Columbia: University of South Carolina Press, 1969.

Helguera, J. Leon. "The Changing Role of the Military in Colombia." *Journal of Inter-American Studies*, July 1961, 351–58.

Herring, Hubert. *A History of Latin America from the Beginnings to the Present.* New York: Knopf, 1968.

Horowitz, Irving Louis. *Masses in Latin America.* New York: Oxford University Press, 1970.

Howard, Michael, ed. *Soldiers and Governments: Nine Studies in Civil-Military Relations.* (Chapter by R. A. Humphreys.) London: Eyre and Spottiswoode, 1957.

Humphreys, R. A. *Latin American History: A Guide to the Literature in English.* New York: Oxford University Press, 1958.

Johnson, John J. *Continuity and Change in Latin America.* Stanford, Cal.: Stanford University Press, 1964.

————. *The Military and Society in Latin America*. Stanford, Cal.: Stanford University Press, 1964.

————. *The Role of the Military in Underdeveloped Countries*. Princeton: Princeton University Press, 1962.

Lieuwen, Edwin. *Arms and Politics in Latin America*. New York: Praeger (published for the Council on Foreign Relations), 1960.

————. *Generals vs Presidents: Neomilitarism in Latin America*. New York: Praeger, 1964.

————. *Mexican Militarism: The Political Rise and Fall of the Revolutionary Army, 1910–1940*. Albuquerque: University of New Mexico Press, 1968.

————. "The Military: A Revolutionary Force." *Annals of the American Academy of Political and Social Science*, March 1961, 30–40.

————. "Neo-Militarism in Latin America: The Kennedy Administration's Inadequate Response." *Inter-American Economic Affairs*, Spring 1963, 11–19.

Loftus, J. E. *Latin-American Defense Expenditures, 1938–1965*. Santa Monica, Cal.: Rand Corp., 1968.

McAlister, L. N. "Civil-Military Relations in Latin America." *Journal of Inter-American Studies*, July 1961, 341–50.

————. *The "Fuero Militar" in New Spain*. Gainesville: University of Florida Press, 1957.

————. "Recent Research and Writings on the Role of the Military in Latin America." *Latin American Research Review*, Fall 1966, 5–36.

Madariaga, Salvador de. *The Fall of the Spanish American Empire*. New York: Crowell-Collier, 1963.

Mercier-Vega, Luis. *Guerrillas in Latin-America: The Technique of the Counter-State*. London: Pall Mall Press, 1969.

————. *Roads to Power in Latin America*. London: Pall Mall Press, 1969.

Meyer, Michael. *Mexican Rebel: Pascual Orozo and the Mexican Revolution, 1910–1915*. Lincoln: University of Nebraska Press, 1967.

Michael, Francis J. "Military Aid to Latin America in the U.S. Congress." *Journal of Inter-American Studies*, July 1964, 389–404.

Millett, A. R. *The Politics of Intervention: The Military Occupation of Cuba, 1906–1909*. Columbus: Ohio State University Press, 1968.

Needler, Martin C. "Political Development and Military Intervention in Latin America." *American Political Science Review*, September 1966, 616–26.

Payne, James L. *Patterns of Conflict in Colombia*. New Haven: Yale University Press, 1968.

Potash, Robert A. *The Army and Politics in Argentina, 1928–1945*. Stanford, Cal.: Stanford University Press, 1969.

Powell, John Duncan. "Military Assistance and Militarism in Latin America." *Western Political Quarterly*, June 1965, 382–93.

Quirk, Robert. *The Mexican Revolution, 1914–1915: The Convention of Aguascalientes.* Bloomington: Indiana University Press, 1960.

Schmitt, Karl M., and Burks, David D. "Revolution or Chaos." In *Dynamics of Latin American Government and Politics.* New York: Praeger, 1963.

Stokes, W. "Violence as a Power Factor in Latin American Politics." *Western Political Quarterly* 5 (1952).

Szulc, Tad. *Dominican Diary.* New York: Dell, 1965.

TePaske, John J., and Fisher, Sydney N., eds. *Explosive Forces in Latin America.* Columbus: Ohio State University Press, 1964.

Urbanski, Edmund Stephen. "Tres Revoluciones de Hispano-America: Mexico, Bolivia y Cuba." *Journal of Inter-American Studies,* July 1966, 419–36.

Veliz, Claudio, ed. *The Politics of Conformity in Latin America.* London: Royal Institute of International Affairs, 1967.

Villanueva, Victor. *El militarismo en el Peru.* Lima: Empresa Grafica T. Scheuch, 1962.

Wiarda, Howard J. "The Politics of Civil-Military Relations in the Dominican Republic." *Journal of Inter-American Studies,* October 1965, 465–84.

Womack, J. *Zapata and the Mexican Revolution.* New York: Knopf, 1969.

Wyckoff, Theodore. "The Role of the Military in Latin American Politics." *Western Political Quarterly,* September 1960, 745–63.

NIGERIA-BIAFRA

African studies being an emergent discipline, much of the material is still contained in periodicals such as:

Administration: The Quarterly Review of the Institute of Administration, University of Ife

Africa Report (Washington, D.C.)

Central Bank of Nigeria. *Annual Report and Statement of Accounts* (Lagos, 1965–1969)

Economist (London) and its Intelligence Unit Publications

Journal of Asian and African Studies

Journal of Modern African Studies

Nigeria, Office of Statistics. *Economic Indicators* (monthly, Lagos)

Nigerian Journal of Economic and Social Studies

Nigerian Opinion

Petroleum Press Service

Standard Bank (of Nigeria) *Review*

Venture

West Africa (London)

Adedeji, Adebayo. *Nigerian Federal Finance: Its Development, Problems and Prospects.* New York: Africana Publishing Corp., 1969.

Arikpo, Okoi. *The Development of Modern Nigeria.* Baltimore: Johns Hopkins Press, 1967.

Awolowo, Obafemi. *The Path to Nigerian Freedom.* London: Faber, 1966.

Basden, G. T. *Among the Ibos of Nigeria: An Account of the Curious and Interesting Habits, Customs and Beliefs of a Little Known African People by One Who Has for Many Years Lived amongst Them on Close and Intimate Terms.* London: Seely Service, 1921.

Bretton, Henry L. *Power and Stability in Nigeria: The Politics of Decolonization.* New York: Praeger, 1962.

Buchanan, K. M., and Pugh, J. C. *Land and People in Nigeria: The Human Geography of Nigeria and Its Environmental Background.* London: University of London Press, 1955.

Burns, Sir Alan Cuthbert. *History of Nigeria.* 7th ed. London: Allen and Unwin, 1969.

Coleman, James. *Nigeria: Background to Nationalism.* Berkeley: University of California Press, 1957.

Curtin, Philip D. *Africa Remembered: Narratives by West Africans.* Madison: University of Wisconsin Press, 1967.

Dudley, B. J. *Parties and Politics in Northern Nigeria.* London: Cass, 1968.

Eicher, Carl K., and Liedholm, Carl, eds. *Growth and Development of the Nigerian Economy.* Lansing: Michigan State University Press, 1970.

Forsyth, Frederick. *The Biafra Story.* Baltimore: Johns Hopkins Press, 1969.

Goodell, Charles E. "Biafra and the American Conscience." *Saturday Review,* April 12, 1969, 24–27.

Helleiner, Gerald K. *Peasant Agriculture, Government, and Economic Growth in Nigeria.* Homewood, Ill.: R. D. Irwin, 1966.

Hilton, Bruce. *Highly Irregular.* New York: Macmillan, 1969.

Johnson, Samuel. *The History of the Yorubas from the Earliest Times to the Beginning of the British Protectorate.* London: Routledge, 1921; reprinted, 1952.

Kilby, Peter. *Industrialization in an Open Economy: Nigeria, 1945–1966.* London: Cambridge University Press, 1969.

Langheld, Wilhelm. *Der Heidenkampf unserer Kolonien.* 3 vols. Berlin, n.d.

————. *Zwanzig Jahre in deutschen Kolonien.* Berlin, 1909.

Leonard, Arthur Glyn. *The Lower Niger and Its Tribes.* London: Cassells, 1968.

Lindsay, Kennedy. "How Biafra Pays for the War." *Venture* 21, No. 3 (March 1969): 26–28.

Moberly, Brigadier General F. J. *Military Operations: Togoland and the Cameroons, 1914–1916.* London: Macmillan, 1931.

Mok, Michael. *Biafra Journal.* New York: Time-Life, 1969.

Nafziger, E. Wayne. "Inter-regional Economic Relations in the Nigerian Footware Industry." *Journal of Modern African Studies* 6, No. 4 (1968): 531–42.

Niven, Rex. *The War of Nigerian Unity.* Ibadan, 1971

Ojukwu, General C. O. *Biafra.* 2 vols. New York: Harper and Row, 1969.

Okafor-Omali, Dilim. *A Nigerian Villager in Two Worlds.* London: Faber, 1965.

Okigbo, Pius N. C. *Nigerian National Accounts, 1950–57.* Enugu: Eastern Nigeria, Federal Ministry of Economic Development, 1962.

Okin, Theophilus Adelodum. *The Urbanized Nigerian: An Examination of the African and His New Environment.* New York: Exposition, 1969.

Oluwasanmi, H. A. *Agriculture and Nigerian Development.* London: Oxford University Press, 1966.

Proceedings of the Conference on National Reconstruction and Development in Nigeria. University of Ibadan, March 24–29, 1969.

Samuels, Michael A., ed. *The Nigeria-Biafra Conflict.* Washington, D.C.: Georgetown Center for Strategic and International Studies, 1969.

Schätzl, Ludwig. *Petroleum in Nigeria.* London: Oxford University Press, 1969.

Schwartz, Frederick A. O., Jr. *Nigeria: The Tribes, the Nation, or the Race: The Politics of Independence.* Cambridge, Mass.: Harvard University Press, 1965.

Sklar, Richard L. *Nigerian Political Parties: Power in an Emergent African Nation.* Princeton: Princeton University Press, 1963.

Stolper, Wolfgang F. *Planning without Facts: Lessons in Resource Allocation from Nigeria's Development.* Cambridge, Mass.: Harvard University Press, 1966.

Sullivan, John R. *Breadless Biafra.* Dayton, Ohio: Pflaum Press, 1969.

United States Air Force. *Africa.* Air University Bibliography No. 159, Supplement No. 9. 1969.

RUSSIA

Bradley, John. *Allied Intervention in Russia, 1917–1920.* London: Weidenfeld and Nicolson, 1968.

Brinkley, George A. *The Volunteer Army and the Allied Intervention in South Russia.* South Bend, Ind.: Notre Dame University Press, 1966.

Carr, E. H. *The Bolshevik Revolution, 1917–1923.* 3 vols. New York: Macmillan, 1950–53.

Chamberlin, William Henry. *The Russian Revolution.* Vol 2. New York: Macmillan, 1935; reprinted, 1965.

Erickson, John. *The Soviet High Command: A Military-Political History, 1918–1941.* New York: St. Martin's Press, 1962

Footman, David. *Civil War in Russia.* London: Faber, 1961.

Istoria grazhdanskoi voiny v SSSR [History of the Civil War in the USSR]. 5 vols. to date. Moscow: Gospolitizdat, 1935–.

Kenez, Peter. *Civil War in South Russia, 1918.* Berkeley: University of California Press, 1971.

Kennan, George F. *Soviet American Relations, 1917–1920*. 2 vols. Princeton: Princeton University Press, 1956–58.

Mayer, Arno J. *Politics and Diplomacy of Peacemaking*. London: Weidenfeld and Nicolson, 1968.

O'Ballance, Edgar. *The Red Army*. London: Faber, 1964.

Silverbright, John. *The Victors' Dilemma: Allied Intervention in the Russian Civil War*. New York: Weybright and Talley, 1970.

Stewart, George. *The White Armies of Russia*. New York: Macmillan, 1933; Russell and Russell, 1970.

Strakhovsky, Leonid I. *Intervention at Archangel*. Princeton: Princeton University Press, 1944.

Thompson, John M. *Russia, Bolshevism, and the Versailles Peace*. Princeton: Princeton University Press, 1968.

Ulam, Adam B. *The Bolsheviks*. New York: Macmillan, 1965.

Ullman, Richard H. *Anglo-Soviet Relations, 1917–1920*. 2 vols. Princeton: Princeton University Press, 1961–68.

White, John A. *The Siberian Intervention*. Princeton: Princeton University Press, 1950.

SPAIN

Balloten, Burnett. *The Grand Camouflage: The Spanish Civil War and Revolution*. New York: Praeger, 1968.

Blásquez, José Martín. *I Helped Build an Army*. London: Secker and Warburg, 1939.

Borkenau, Franz. *The Spanish Cockpit*. Ann Arbor: University of Michigan Press, 1963.

Brenan, Gerald. *The Spanish Labyrinth*. Cambridge: Cambridge University Press, 1940.

Broué, Pierre, and Témime, Émile. *La Révolution et la guerre d'Espagne*. Paris: Editions de Minuit, 1961. [English translation by the M.I.T. Press due in 1971.]

Carr, Raymond. *Spain, 1808–1939*. Oxford: Oxford University Press, 1966.

Catell, David T. *Communism and the Spanish Civil War*. Berkeley: University of California Press, 1955.

Chomsky, Noam. *American Power and the New Mandarins: Historical and Political Essays*, 72–158. New York: Vintage Books, 1969.

Christiansen, E. *The Origins of Military Power in Spain, 1800–1854*. New York: Oxford University Press, 1967.

Colodny, Robert G. *Spain: The Glory and the Tragedy*. New York: Humanities Press, 1970.

Hoar, V. *The Mackenzie-Papineau Battalion: Canadian Participation in the Spanish Civil War*. London, Ont.: Copp Clark, 1969.

Jackson, Gabriel. *The Spanish Republic and the Civil War, 1931–1939*. Princeton: Princeton University Press, 1965.

Morrow, Felix. *Revolution and Counter-revolution in Spain.* London: New Park Publications, 1963.

Orwell, George. *Homage to Catalonia.* London: Secker and Warburg, 1938.

Payne, Robert, ed. *The Civil War in Spain.* New York: Fawcett World, 1962.

Payne, Stanley G. *Falange: A History of Spanish Fascism.* Stanford, Cal.: Stanford University Press, 1961.

————. *Politics and the Military in Modern Spain.* Stanford, Cal.: Stanford University Press, 1967.

————. *The Spanish Revolution: A Study in Social and Political Tensions that Culminated in the Civil War in Spain.* New York: W. W. Norton, 1970.

Puzzo, D. A. *The Spanish Civil War.* London: Van Nostrand, 1969.

Thomas, Hugh. *The Spanish Civil War.* New York: Harper and Row, 1961.

Traina, Richard P. *American Diplomacy and the Spanish Civil War.* Bloomington: Indiana University Press, 1968.

VIETNAM

Barnet, Richard J. *Intervention and Revolution.* New York: World Publishing Co., 1968.

Bator, Victor. *Vietnam: A Diplomatic Tragedy.* Dobbs Ferry, N.Y.: Oceana Publications, 1965.

Brandon, Henry. *Anatomy of Error: The Inside Story of the Asian War on the Potomac, 1954–1969.* Boston: Gambit, 1970.

Browne, Malcolm W. *The New Face of War.* Indianapolis: Bobbs-Merrill, 1965.

Draper, Theodore. *Abuse of Power.* New York: Viking Press, 1967.

Duncanson, Dennis J. *Government and Revolution in Vietnam.* New York: Oxford University Press, 1968.

Fall, Bernard. *The Two Vietnams.* 2nd rev. ed. New York: Praeger, 1967.

————. *Vietnam Witness, 1953–66.* New York: Praeger, 1966.

Gurtov, Melvin. *The First Vietnam Crisis.* New York: Columbia University Press, 1967.

Halberstam, David. *The Making of a Quagmire.* New York: Random House, 1965.

Hoopes, Townsend W. *The Limits of Intervention.* New York: D. McKay Co., 1969.

Kahin, George McTurnan, and Lewis, John W. *The United States in Vietnam.* New York: Dial Press, 1967.

Lacouture, Jean. *Vietnam between Two Truces.* Translated by Konrad Kellen and Joel Carmichael. New York: Random House, 1966.

Lyon, Peter. *War and Peace in South-East Asia.* New York: Oxford University Press, 1969.

McCarthy, Eugene J. *The Year of the People.* Garden City, N.Y.: Doubleday, 1969.

McCarthy, Mary. *Hanoi.* New York: Harcourt, Brace and World, 1968.

O'Ballance, Edgar. *The Indo-China War, 1945–1954: A Study in Guerrilla Warfare.* London: Faber, 1964.

———. *Korea, 1950–1953.* London: Faber, 1969.

———. *Malaya: The Communist Insurgent War, 1948–1960.* London: Faber, 1966.

Pfeffer, Richard M., ed, *No More Vietnams?* New York: Harper and Row (published for the Adlai Stevenson Institue of International Affairs), 1968.

Pike, Douglas. *War, Peace and the Viet Cong.* Cambridge, Mass.: M.I.T. Press, 1969.

Randle, Robert. *Geneva 1954: The Settlement of the Indochinese War.* Princeton: Princeton University Press, 1969.

Schlesinger, Arthur M., Jr. *The Bitter Heritage.* Boston: Houghton Mifflin, 1966.

Schoenbrun, David. *Vietnam: How We Got In, How to Get Out.* New York: Atheneum, 1968.

Shaplen, Robert. *The Lost Revolution: The United States and Vietnam, 1945–1966.* New York: Harper and Row, 1965.

Trager, Frank N. *Why Vietnam?* New York: Praeger, 1966.

J. BOWYER BELL, of the School of Public Administration at Harvard University, is the author of a number of books, including *The Secret Army: A History of the IRA since 1916* (1970).

JAMES C. CAREY, professor of history at Kansas State University, has written *Peru and the United States, 1900–1962* (1964).

PAO-CHIN CHU was born and brought up in China during the civil war; he is now an assistant professor of history at San Diego State College.

CLARENCE C. CLENDENEN, military curator emeritus at the Hoover Institution on War, Revolution, and Peace, has written on areas ranging from the Mexican frontier to West Africa.

MARTIN EDMONDS, lecturer in Strategic Studies at the University of Lancaster, is coeditor of the forthcoming *Warfare in the Seventies* (1972).

NORMAN A. GRAEBNER is the Edward R. Stettinius Professor of Modern American History at the University of Virginia and the author of innumerable works in American diplomatic history.

ROBIN HIGHAM, professor of history at Kansas State University and editor of *Military Affairs* and *Aerospace Historian*, has written extensively on British military history.

JIM DAN HILL, former president (1931–64) of the University of Wisconsin at Superior, is the author of *The Minuteman in Peace and War* (1964).

ERNEST W. LEFEVER, a senior fellow on the Foreign Policy Studies staff of the Brookings Institution, is the author of a number of books, including *Uncertain Mandate: The Politics of the UN Congo Operation* (1967).

EDWARD E. MALEFAKIS, professor of history at the University of Michigan, has recently published *Agrarian Reform and Peasant Revolution in Spain: Origins of the Civil War* (1970).

E. WAYNE NAFZIGER, a Kansas State University economist, publishes in the fields of Nigerian and Indian entrepreneurship and interregional economic relations.

ROBERT D. WARTH, professor of history at the University of Kentucky, is the author of *Joseph Stalin* (1969).

CIVIL WARS are a continuing problem in the twentieth century, but so far little attention has been devoted to them by historians and political scientists. This book brings together the thinking of twelve scholars in history, political science, and economics. By examining the major civil wars of this century, they suggest characteristics common to such conflicts and point to the difficulties of preventing civil wars and of dealing with the belligerents.

Each author examines one facet of the civil war he knows best. The conflicts analyzed are the Russian, Chinese, Spanish, Irish, Nigerian, and Vietnamese civil wars. Other chapters examine the American legacy of civil conflict, the background for civil warfare in Latin America, the consequences of interference by peacekeeping forces, and the role of armed forces in civil warfare. Also included is an extensive bibliography.

The Editor

ROBIN HIGHAM, the book's editor, is professor of history at Kansas State University. He has previously edited *Bayonets in the Streets* and is the author of *Armed Forces in Peacetime* and *The Military Intellectuals*. Mr. Higham also edits two periodicals, *Military Affairs* and *Aerospace Historian*.